D0219818

Toward a Literacy of Promise

"From discussions of ways literacy has been withheld from, foisted upon, but rarely reveled in for African American students, to the rich discussions of critical literacy in classrooms, *Toward a Literacy of Promise* has it all—theory, research, history, personal stories, and visions for teaching."

Carole Edelsky, Arizona State University

"*Toward a Literacy of Promise* gives us strategies for bringing life back to school; it allows us to think creatively about connecting instruction to the lives of children who have not been well-served; it helps us learn to value the gifts with words our children of color bring; and it gives us hope for educating a generation that can change the status quo, that will build the America we have yet to see . . . the one that made that as-yet-unfulfilled promise of 'liberty and justice for all.'"

Lisa Delpit, from the Foreword

Toward a Literacy of Promise examines popular assumptions about literacy and challenges readers to question how it has been used historically both to empower and to oppress. The authors offer an alternative view of literacy—a "literacy of promise"—that charts an emancipatory agenda for literacy instructional practices in schools. Weaving together critical perspectives on pedagogy, language, literature, and popular texts, each chapter provides an in-depth discussion that illuminates how a literacy of promise can be realized in schools and classrooms.

Although the major focus is on African American middle and secondary students as a population that has experienced the consequences of inequality, the chapters demonstrate general and specific applications to other populations.

Linda A. Spears-Bunton is Associate Professor of English Education and an affiliated faculty member in African New World Studies at Florida International University, Miami, Florida.

Rebecca Powell currently serves as Dean of Education at Georgetown College in Georgetown, Kentucky, where she has taught since 1993. She holds the Marjorie Bauer Stafford Endowed Professorship and was awarded the Cawthorne Excellence in Teaching Award in 2003.

Language, Culture, and Teaching
Sonia Nieto, Series Editor

Toward a Literacy of Promise
Joining the African American Struggle

Edited by
Linda A. Spears-Bunton and
Rebecca Powell

Routledge
Taylor & Francis Group

NEW YORK AND LONDON

First published 2009
by Routledge
270 Madison Ave, New York, NY 10016

Simultaneously published in the UK
by Routledge
2 Park Square, Milton Park, Abingdon, Oxon OX14 4RN

Routledge is an imprint of the Taylor & Francis Group, an informa business

© 2009 Taylor & Francis

Typeset in Minion by
Swales & Willis Ltd, Exeter, Devon
Printed and bound in the United States of America on acid-free paper by
Edwards Brothers, Inc.

All rights reserved. No part of this book may be reprinted or
reproduced or utilised in any form or by any electronic, mechanical, or
other means, now known or hereafter invented, including
photocopying and recording, or in any information storage or retrieval
system, without permission in writing from the publishers.

Trademark Notice: Product or corporate names may be trademarks or
registered trademarks, and are used only for identification and
explanation without intent to infringe.

Library of Congress Cataloging in Publication Data
Toward a literacy of promise: joining the African American
struggle/edited by Linda A. Spears-Bunton, and Rebecca Powell.
    p. cm. – (Language, culture, and teaching)
    Includes bibliographical references and index.
    ISBN 978–0-8058–4536–5 (pbk.: alk. paper)   1. Literacy—Social
aspects—United States.   2. African American students—Education.
3. Critical pedagogy—United States.   I. Spears-Bunton, Linda A.
II. Powell, Rebecca.
    LC151.T69 2008
    302.2'244—dc22   2008017323

ISBN10: 0–8058–4536–4 (pbk)
ISBN10: 0–415–99518–3 (hbk)

ISBN13: 978–0-8058–4536–5 (pbk)
ISBN13: 978–0-415–99518–4 (hbk)

Dedication

*We dedicate this book
to all the teachers who have the courage
to teach about things that really matter.*

Contents

Foreword

What is it about us? About Black folks? African Americans? People of color? This love affair with words? We are so enthralled with words that every few years we even tire of our own appellation and seek new names to describe ourselves. I believe there must be a spiritual connection between us and the sounds we use to connect ourselves to the universe. The ancient Hebrews had a word—*dabar*—"sound," which also meant "power." We change the world through the power of sound, through the potency of words.

Our love of words is primal. In Africa, battles were fought with words. Warriors squared off, one across from the other, not to cast spears, but to hurl words. The winner? He, designated by the audience, to have out-spoken the other. During our enslavement the words of spirituals kept us going psychically as well as physically. They changed the world by empowering not only our spirits, but our bodies as their coded messages led toward freedom. From our preachers to our hustlers to our rappers, the "man (or woman) of words" reigns supreme. From the grandfather who tells the white world of his pain with the incisive comment, "Don't piss on me and call it rain," to the four-year-old who watches the shadows in her room at night and calls me to see the "night mirrors." We love words. And we pull them from our souls, feed them in our hearts, taste their sweetness on our tongues, and release them with the gentleness of a breeze or the force of a raging tempest to bring the power of our warm vibrant selves to a cold hard world.

And there are those who say we cannot become literate? We, the masters of words, who have coded meanings into spirituals, jazz, metaphors, poems, arguments, etc., etc., are incapable of coding them into little black squiggles? Impossible!

So what is the problem? Could it be that those institutions responsible for "teaching" literacy, the schools, are responsible? Can it be that they manage to suck the life out of words, steal the meaning from print, deaden the vitality of the written phrases? So many stories come to mind. I remember the Alaska Native child who, when asked to complete yet another worksheet to "check for understanding" said with an exasperated sigh, "I just like to read, I don't like to *understand!*"

When my own daughter was in first grade, her teacher asked her to write four sentences for homework. Excited that my little one was about to officially enter the literate world, I sat down to chat with her about what she could write. I reminded her of her recent visit from her grandmother that she had enjoyed so much. We talked about the new bicycle she had just received. When the telephone rang I suggested that she go ahead and write while I was on the phone. When I returned I was delighted that she wanted to read her sentences to me. She held her paper up with a great flourish and read, "*The boy can run. The cat can sit. The dog is brown. The man is talking.*" Hmm . . . I tried to think fast about how to support these initial efforts.

"Maya, that's wonderful, but what happened to talking about your grandmother or your bike?"

"Mom, I'm supposed to write *sentences*."

"Hmm." I tried to figure out what she meant.

"Well, what are sentences, honey?"

"Oh, you know, mom. Stuff you write, but you never would say."

Well, the problem became obvious. Here was a child who had learned the hidden curriculum of first grade: Reading and writing belong to the artificial world of school and have nothing to do with real life! Unfortunately, that curriculum does not change much throughout most children's school lives. It only becomes less hidden and the failure to adopt its peculiar mores more consequential.

Some children are immersed in "school literacy" from their earliest memories. These are the children whose home lives are so similar to what happens in school that they scarcely miss a beat when they enter the school door. They have been answering "recall" and "comprehension" questions for years— "What color is that bunny's fur?" "Why did that little piggy build his house of brick?" They are familiar with "test questions"—adults asking questions that they already know the answers to. And they feel the stories in books are culturally familiar reflections of their family and community interactions at home.

But other children come from different lives. Their lives, equally as full, sometimes more difficult, are not those reflected in school texts. Their time with their parents is not spent answering "known" questions. They spend much of their time with people instead of with books. They learn "critical thinking skills" in the context of real problems they face in their everyday lives. These children find schools particularly off-putting and artificial.

Furthermore, the school's attitudes often subtly suggest that there is something wrong with them, with their families, with their communities. The language of their mothers, their "mother-tongue" is defined as "incorrect English," while at the same time the language that they are asked to learn is often riddled with deeply rooted aspersions. Robert Moore wrote in an article entitled "Racism in the English Language," which presents with some humor the racially loaded words we so unconsciously use in everyday life:

Some may blackly (angrily) accuse him of trying to blacken (defame) the English language, to give it a black eye (a mark of shame) by writing such black words (hostile). They may denigrate (to cast aspersions; to darken) him by accusing him of being blackhearted (malevolent), of having a black

outlook (pessimistic, dismal) on life, of being a blackguard (scoundrel)—
which would certainly be a black mark (detrimental fact) against him.
Some may blackbrow (scowl at) him and hope that a black cat crosses in
front of him because of this black deed. He may become a black sheep
(one who causes shame or embarrassment because of deviation from the
accepted standards), who will be blackballed (ostracized) by being placed
on a blacklist (list of undesirables) in an attempt to blackmail (to force
or coerce into a particular action) him to retract his words.

(Moore, 1995, p. 377)

If we are to truly educate all of our children, we must look carefully at how
we attend to literacy. Examining the results of schooling for poor children and
children of color, there can be no doubt that we have to rethink our past actions.
What might "work" for some children, may be toxic for others. (Although I have
become convinced that much of the instruction in schools does little to "teach"
literacy skills, it primarily gives those children whose home cultures are most
like that of the schools a chance to display what they came to school already
knowing!) We cannot afford to continue poisoning our young. This book
presents antidotes. It gives us strategies for bringing life back to school; it allows
us to think creatively about connecting instruction to the lives of children who
have not been well-served; it helps us learn to value the gifts with words our
children of color bring; and it gives us hope for educating a generation that can
change the *status quo*, that will build the America we have yet to see. You know
the one, the one that made that as-yet-unfulfilled promise of "liberty and justice
for all."

Lisa Delpit

Reference

Moore, R.B. (1995). Racism in the English language. In P.S. Rothenberg (Ed.) *Race, class and gender in the United States* (3rd ed.), pp. 376–386. New York: St. Martin's.

Preface

The purposes of this book are to examine the historical and theoretical contexts of a "literacy of promise" for African Americans, and to provide pedagogical insights for secondary teachers who wish to implement a more critical literacy in their classrooms. The authors in this volume raise fundamental questions concerning our notions about literacy, traditional teaching practices, and the academic underachievement of African American students. Readers are encouraged to analyze critically the current rhetoric on literacy and the historical role of literacy in our society, and to envision a more transformative, emancipatory agenda.

In this volume, a "literacy of promise" refers to a literacy that potentially empowers students and teachers and that gives them a voice. A literacy of promise requires students to negotiate meaning and to be actively engaged in discerning relationships of power and repression in society. It assumes that no text is neutral, and that all forms of communication can become objects of critique. Further, a literacy of promise legitimates students' ideas and experiences and celebrates diverse ways of interpreting and constructing texts.

A literacy of promise can be contrasted with "schooled literacy," which obscures or denies the non-neutrality of texts and the reality of social and economic inequities in society. Schooled literacy endorses the language forms and cultural knowledge of those with privilege, thereby fulfilling a gatekeeping function that perpetuates hierarchical relations of power.

Given the realities of power and privilege in our society, a literacy of promise has often remained an elusive ideal for those who have been enslaved, oppressed, disenfranchised, and marginalized. In this book, we explore the quest for literacy from a variety of perspectives, from the ways in which literacy has been used historically to maintain oppression, through the false promises of schooled literacy and the transformative goal of critical pedagogy.

How This Book Is Organized

Chapter 1, the Introduction, outlines the characteristics of "schooled literacy" and a "literacy of promise," and introduces the ideas presented in Chapters 2 to 10. The book is structured in three sections. Part I, "Problems and Promises" (Chapters 2 to 4), provides a theoretical and historical framework for the concept of literacy promoted throughout this text. Chapter 2 illustrates a literacy of promise through examining various students' responses to written texts. Chapter 3 explores the transformative ideology of Paulo Freire, and compares a "banking" curriculum model with Freire's notions of a humanizing pedagogy.

Chapter 4 looks at the ways literacy has been used historically to promote the legal disenfranchisement of persons of color, thereby denying the promise of literacy for liberation.

Part II, "Realizing a Literacy of Promise through Literary Texts" (Chapters 5 and 6), explores how teachers might realize a literacy of promise through using multicultural literary texts. Chapter 5 examines how African American male students responded to a critically framed unit of study based on the novel *A Lesson Before Dying*, and in Chapter 6, the author analyzes the literary responses of two female European American students to African American literature.

In Part III, "Realizing a Literacy of Promise Through Oral and Popular Texts" (Chapters 7 to 10), three chapters explore the ways in which oral language has been used for both transformative and oppressive ends and one looks at popular texts as sites for critique and possibility. Chapter 7 links language and culture and presents a theoretical overview of the linguistic issues and debates that have emerged within a hegemonic society. Chapter 8 looks at oracy—the verbal form of literacy—and shares ways that educators can promote oracy in their classrooms. Chapter 9 focuses on antiracist social justice theater and the various ways that the arts can be used to address social issues in schools and society. Chapter 10 examines the use of critical media literacy for creating a counterhegemonic discourse.

The Questions for Discussion and Extension Activities at the end of each chapter are not intended to lead to definitive answers, but rather are designed to extend the author's ideas, to promote further investigation, and to facilitate critical inquiry and reflection. References at the end of each chapter encourage additional reading.

Intended Uses of this Book

This book is primarily intended for graduate courses in literacy theory and practice. It will be particularly useful for addressing issues relating to teaching literacy in a diverse society. It is our intent that this book will help teachers and other readers to integrate knowledge about language, literature, law, and literacy research with literacy theory and practices. While a major focus of the text is on persons of African descent, it nevertheless represents a history of colonization, the results of which have both general and specific applications to other populations.

We also hope that this book will be used to promote scholarly inquiry so that teachers and other stakeholders might begin to envision education in general— and literacy instruction in particular—differently. This book provides insights into questions that relate directly to the educational underachievement of students of color: How has literacy been used historically both to empower and to oppress? How has literacy been conceptualized in schools, and how have our notions about literacy affected African American and other marginalized student populations? How have the ways in which we have conceptualized and taught literacy actually *produced* failure? How might we reconceptualize literacy so that it becomes a literacy of promise? These issues take readers beyond the traditional rhetoric about literacy, encouraging them to engage in a broader discourse about the role of literacy and schooling in a diverse society.

Acknowledgments

We are indebted to many individuals who have led us along our own paths toward social justice teaching. Our mentors at the University of Kentucky—most notably, Christine Pappas, Connie Bridge, Beth Goldstein, and Linda Levstik—all helped to shape our conceptions about literacy and language. These remarkable women not only served as role models to us as their students, but also inspired us to think differently about teaching and learning.

We are especially grateful to the various scholars who contributed to this volume. We are humbled by their eagerness to share their knowledge and to devote their time and talent to helping make this book a reality. We particularly wish to thank Lisa Delpit for her willingness to write the Foreword. We also wish to acknowledge our students, who undoubtedly have taught us more than we have taught them, and whose ideas and voices resonate throughout this text.

We wish to thank Naomi Silverman, Senior Editor at Routledge, for helping us to conceptualize this book. Her insights as an editor and a scholar were invaluable as we began to shape our intentions into a final product. We also wish to thank Sonia Nieto and two anonymous reviewers, whose thoughtful comments and suggestions were extremely helpful as we began to revise the manuscript.

1

Introduction

REBECCA POWELL

The smell of bacon filled the stairway as I knelt down at the top of the landing, straining to identify the strange voice down in the kitchen with Daddy and Mama. "Libby could get hurt if she attends school today," he pleaded. "I came by to warn you 'cause I don't want to see nobody get hurt."

"That voice belonged to Sarah Beth's father," I thought.

Mama's voice was shaking, "My child will be there if I have to personally patrol the hallways of Check Elementary School. It's 1964, Mr. Vest! These schools have finally been integrated and you have to learn how to deal with it whether you like it or not!"

Before Mama could say another word, Daddy shouted, "I don't understand you John! Why aren't you convincing *them* to stay home. For once in my life the law is on my side, so you need to get out of my home before I throw you out." As the door slammed shut, cold chills raced through my body and silence filled the kitchen.

I tiptoed down the hallway and climbed back into my warm, safe bed. I couldn't figure out why Daddy and Mr. Vest were yelling and swearing at each other. "They didn't sound very neighborly," I thought.

As I pulled the covers up around me, I thought about how much I had looked forward to the day when I could go to the big, brick school with my best friend Sarah Beth. Her farm was across the creek from ours, and her birthday was three days before mine.

We had been inseparable since we were little babies except when we went to school last year. I attended first grade at a little, cinderblock building forty miles across the county, while Sarah Beth went to the big brick school about a mile from our farm. Last year, Daddy told us that in this county, it was against the law for White children and Negro children to go to school together, so every evening, after we did our chores, Sarah Beth and I would go to the "milkin' barn" and teach each other everything we had learned that day. We were hoping that since that silly law had been changed, we could be in the same classroom this year.

Trembling, I tried to remember all the neat things Sarah Beth had told me about her smiling teacher, Mrs. Prillaman, and all the reading books about Jack, Sally and Spot. A queasy feeling came up from my stomach warning me that this day might not be the adventure that my best friend had promised.

As the sunlight started to fill the room, my new yellow jumper trimmed with white lace caught my eye. Mama had hung it on the curtain rod so that I could see it as I went to sleep. It was the most beautiful dress that I had ever owned. Last week, when Mama and I rode the Trailways bus into the city to shop for underwear and shoes, we saw it in the store window. I promised to give up my allowance for a whole year if she would buy me that "store bought" dress like Sarah Beth had.

The sound of Mama's footsteps coming up the stairs caused my stomach to churn again. I closed my eyes just a little, and pretended to be asleep. When the door opened, Mama stood there, with her smiling mouth and red puffy eyes. She was holding a lacy, white butterfly bow for my hair. "Wake up 'sleepyhead'," she teased. "This might be a difficult day for you." Her voice was shaking again and her eyes were glued to the yellow dress that hung beside me.

"Mama, second grade won't be too difficult for *me*," I bragged. "I can already read *every* word in the Bible, and Daddy said I could write as good as him. Don't worry! According to Sarah Beth, there were a bunch of idiots in her class last year."

She turned to me with a smile that made her eyes water, "It's the idiots that I'm worried about," she whispered. "Get up and let me look at that head of yours," Mama said, wiping her face with the skirt of her dress.

I jumped out of bed and kissed both of her bloated eyelids. She pulled me close to her and held me so tight that I could feel her big heart beating like a giant drum against my chest.

After she braided my hair, she carefully placed the lacy white bow in the back of my head. While she cut the tags from the yellow dress, I put on my white patent leather shoes that pinched my big toe. When I finished dressing, Mama watched as I danced around every mirror in the house. I practised greeting my new teacher, laughing with my classmates, and saying "thank you" every time someone admired my beautiful dress. When my stomach started growling, I made my way to the kitchen for breakfast.

The breakfast table was unusually quiet. Mama stared out the window of the front door as she sipped her coffee, and Daddy's eyes cut right through me as he picked some lint from my dress. "How do you like my new dress?" I was fishing for some kind of response from him. "Sarah Beth said that I would be the only one in our class with a dress like this. Did you see the new bow Mama made for me?" He patted me on the head as if I were his favorite coon dog and slowly got up from the table to put on his shoes.

"Go and get your lunch and your book bag, or you'll be late the first day of school. I'll go warm up the truck. Hurry up now," he said hoarsely.

"Why can't I ride the bus with Sarah Beth?" I tried to muster up a few tears. That usually worked with Daddy. "I told her I would meet her at the 'big tree' and we would walk to the bus stop together. P-l-e-a-s-e, Daddy," I begged. By this time the tears were really flowing.

Daddy looked down at me, and as he gritted his teeth a huge wrinkle fell down and landed on his brow. I knew what that meant! I slid into the truck between him and Mama and held my hands between my knees. As we turned down the road to the school, Mama wet her handkerchief with her tongue and wiped the dried oatmeal from my cheek.

While I sat there daydreaming, I heard a "thump" hit the hood of the truck. Daddy cursed. Mama grabbed my hand as the truck started to rock. I peeked over the dashboard and saw hundreds of people yelling and screaming at us. Some of them were hanging onto the truck. "What's happening, and why are they doing this?" I screamed.

Mama looked out the window and then over at Daddy. "They think they are better than us because they were born with white skin. They are trying to scare us off because they don't want Negroes and Whites to go to school together."

"That's dumb!" I thought.

I got up on Mama's lap so I could see what was going on. Many of the screaming faces were very familiar to me. They were neighbors who had bought country hams from us every Christmas and Easter. All of a sudden, the policemen and army men were pushing them away from the truck and Mama finally released my hand from her powerful grip.

As Daddy parked the truck, three officers came over. They told Daddy that they would walk us into the building *if* we wanted to stay. Mama nodded her head and we got out of the truck. Daddy was talking to me as we moved through the crowd toward the school, but the only thing I could hear was their anger.

As the policemen opened the front door, the smell of yeast and fresh paint hovered over the crowd in the hallway. Sweat was dripping from Daddy's face onto my bare arm, so he let go of my hand for a moment to wipe his brow.

Someone behind me was yelling, "Go back home; we don't want you here!" As I turned to identify that voice, a hurling wad of chewing tobacco and spit exploded on my forehead, oozed down my face, and dripped all over the front of my new yellow dress. The juice from the tobacco burned my eyes as I stared blankly at the screaming man and then at my stained yellow dress.

As Daddy tackled him, a warm, wetness bathed my legs, and formed small yellow puddles on the newly waxed floor. Silent screams and tobacco juice choked me as the angry faces spinned around and around in my head. My heavy head was reeling as I gasped for air: light. . . , then darkness. . . , light. . . , then darkness. . . , light. Mama kept calling me back as she held my limp body, feverishly wiping the brown venom from my face with her damp handkerchief. Moments later the screaming voices disappeared and darkness rescued me. . . from my neighbors.

Mama and Daddy took me home and put me to bed, but the "screaming man" would not let me sleep.

That evening, Sarah Beth's mother brought her over to visit me. We talked for over an hour. I told her about the new "boogie man" that had found its way into my life, lurking under my bed, in the closet and on the stairway, whenever I closed my eyes. We made a pact that evening to *never* judge anyone by the color of their skin.

Two weeks later, another yellow dress with white lace was left in Daddy's truck one night.

The Yellow Dress: A Portrait of School Integration by Irma Johnson[1]

The Elusive Promise of Literacy

This story, like so many stories of the African American people, is one of shattered promises, subverted by a system of racism and subjugation that has denigrated and even dehumanized persons of color in this nation. Those in power knew that educating the Black race would be acknowledging their humanness. Folks who were in bondage did not need to be educated—did not need the voice that literacy would afford them. Perry, Steele, and Hilliard (2003) write that, for African American people, "You pursued learning because this is how you asserted yourself as a free person, how you claimed your humanity" (p. 11). Literate folks could not be enslaved, nor could they be regarded as inferior; the very act of being literate was evidence of one's worth. Many who endured the institution of slavery showed indomitable courage in their quest to become literate, despite legislation to keep them ignorant. Hence, when the opportunity for acquiring literacy legally finally became a reality, the ability to read and write was seen by African Americans as a means "for the racial uplift, for the liberation of your people" (p. 11).

The quest for literacy by persons of color has been a relentless struggle—a struggle which has been met by resistance by those who wish to retain a system of White privilege. Although gains have been made, the fact remains that the education of students of color and the integration of our public schools has done little to eradicate racism and classism in our society. Thus for many, literacy has not fulfilled its promise. Despite becoming literate, many persons of color and other disenfranchised groups remain underemployed and impoverished, the products of a system of privilege that continues to perpetuate an underclass that is dependent less upon the acquisition of basic reading ability and more upon corporate interests (Besser, 1993; Cary, 1997; Shannon, 1998). With the schooling of generations of African Americans and other under-represented groups, for many the promise of literacy for upward mobility remains a facade; persons of color continue to earn substantially less than Whites of the same age and ability levels, despite ever-increasing levels of literacy (Carter & Wilson, 1996; Pincus & Ehrlich, 1999; Shannon, 1998). Given the social and economic realities associated with racism, classism, and other oppressive forces in our society, many have lost faith in the American Dream. Schooled literacy—the form of literacy traditionally endorsed in schools—has done little to eradicate this sense of hopelessness and to revitalize abandoned dreams. Indeed, as the authors suggest in Chapter 4, the literacy of schools and society has actually been used historically to disenfranchise and to further oppress persons of color.

Yet state legislators and many literacy scholars continue to engage in a game of trivial pursuit, ignoring questions of race, ethnicity, and power in an effort to find the "best" way to teach reading and writing to our children. We have become enmeshed in debates about "phonics" versus "whole language," "basals" versus "literature-based programs," standardized tests versus portfolios, while thousands of children in our educational institutions still fail to become fully literate. What seems to be missing in our quest for "best practice" is the notion that for many students, a failure to learn *may be intentional.* That is, it is a resistance to a literacy that is based upon a racist ideology of White privilege. It is a resistance to a literacy that for them holds no meaning or promise, that historically has failed them in their quest to overcome the hegemonic forces of power in our society. And it is a resistance to a literacy that they find essentially irrelevant, that denigrates their cultural knowledge, that denies their voice (Delpit, 1988; Fox, 1994; Kohl, 1995; MacLeod, 1995; Ogbu, 1987).

Thus, perhaps the questions we need to be asking should not only involve how we ought to teach literacy, but also how we perceive literacy and what we conceptualize as "literate behavior." That is, are there certain ways of speaking, writing, and taking from texts that are seen as "more literate," and hence, more worthy of society's rewards, than other ways of using oral and written language? Whose literacy is being endorsed, and what are the standards for one to be considered "literate"? Finally, we might also ask: In what ways do our perceptions of literacy alienate or marginalize those whose cultural knowledge differs from White, middle/upper-class norms? In other words, in what ways might we be *creating failure* not only through the ways in which literacy is taught, but also through the ways that it is being perceived?

This book is about language, literacy, and the continuous struggle for civil rights for persons of African descent. Through the various chapters of this text, we take the reader along a journey in the quest for freedom, from the repressive practices of Jim Crow, to potentially liberatory literacy practices in schools. Throughout this nation's history, literacy has been both a means for liberation, and a means for control. With the increasing popularity of critical literacy theory, our definitions of literacy have expanded to include reading both "the word and the world" (Freire & Macedo, 1987). Thus, those who embrace a critical literacy—or what we refer to in this book as a "literacy of promise"— acknowledge the ways in which reading, writing, and language can be used to promote a more just, equitable, and compassionate society. Taken collectively, the chapters in this book reveal how literacy has been used both to reinforce and to resist oppression, and provide examples for how a literacy of promise might be realized in secondary schools and classrooms.

In this introductory chapter, we define a "literacy of promise" and examine the theoretical perspectives that frame the remaining chapters in the book. We begin by providing an overview of traditional literacy practices in schools and the ways in which these practices have tended to perpetuate the status quo, thereby undermining the quest for social and economic parity by persons of color. Next, we discuss the characteristics of a literacy of promise and examine how such a literacy might be used to help realize a social justice agenda.

Schooled Literacy and the Discourses of Power

At the outset, it is important to point out that literacy is both a cultural and a social expression. That is, as Ira Blake argues in Chapter 7, the ways in which we use spoken and written language are culturally determined, and our identity is integrally related to the particular discourse(s) that we use. Of course, the "discourse of power" in our society is the standard discourse, which serves as a gatekeeper in determining who is eligible for certain rewards (Delpit, 1998; Gee, 1990; Purcell-Gates, 2002).

Schools are cultural institutions, and hence they sanction certain norms for appropriate language use. These norms include not only the use of the standard vernacular ("Standard English") in producing oral and written texts, but also particular "styles" of speaking and writing. In other words, some linguistic forms are deemed "more literate" than other discourses and hence, more desirable. In addition, all other discourses are judged against the dominant, standard discourse. Thus, while all discourses have been found to be complex linguistic systems, only the dominant discourse—or what high school English teacher Linda Christensen (1999, 2000) calls the "cash language"—is endorsed in our educational institutions.[2]

Beyond actual language use, however, schools have also endorsed a particular "style" of speaking, writing, and behaving. According to sociolinguist James Paul Gee (1989, 1990), discourses include both the form that the language takes as well as certain associated non-verbal cues which serve to distinguish one discourse from another. In fact, for Gee, discourses are ideological in that they

> involve a set of values and viewpoints about the relationships between people and the distribution of social goods . . . One must speak and act, and at least appear to think and feel, in terms of these values and viewpoints while being in the Discourse, otherwise one doesn't count as being in it.
>
> (1990, p. 144)

Hence, Gee differentiates between "discourse"—a particular linguistic form—and "Discourse"—a way of speaking, behaving, and valuing that signals membership in a particular community. For example, teachers have a particular Discourse that not only includes a distinct vocabulary, but also involves certain ways of believing, behaving, talking, dressing, and "acting like" a teacher. Would-be teachers who fail to conform to the expected Discourse of "teacher" often find that they are denied entrance into the profession. Indeed, every social group has a distinct Discourse (for example, we might point to the Discourses of "bartender," "church-goer," "librarian," "professional athlete").

As cultural institutions, schools also have prescriptive norms and values for linguistic behavior. Students, therefore, are expected to conform to the Discourse of "student," which entails speaking, writing, behaving, and valuing in certain predefined ways. As Jessica Bryant points out in Chapter 8, if students fail to conform to these expectations for appropriate linguistic behavior, cultural mismatches can occur. Some students—particularly those from educated (and generally Anglo, middle/upper-class) homes—can readily adapt to the school's Discourse. These students come with a primary (home) Discourse that is consistent with the Discourse of the school; that is, their primary discourse and the school's discourse are relatively compatible, and they tend not to question the ideology of the educational institution. Other students, however, have a primary Discourse that is essentially incompatible with the school's Discourse, and therefore may have differing expectations from the normative behaviors typically associated with school-based linguistic forms (Ballenger, 1999; Heath, 1983; Michaels, 1981; Redd & Webb, 2005). They may also have differing viewpoints on the functions of literacy and schooling. In addition, their primary language—despite its complexity and its usefulness within certain social settings—is generally viewed as less valuable than upper-class, so-called "educated" discourses, e.g. the language of television anchors, politicians, and so forth. It is these students, whose norms for linguistic behavior contradict the school's norms, who often struggle in their attempts to master the "academic prose" of the educational institution (Fox, 1994; Rose, 1989). Similarly, it is these students who may resist or even reject altogether the "Discourse" of the school.

It is important to point out that the Discourses that we use are integrally related to our social identity. According to Gee, we all have a primary Discourse and several secondary Discourses, and these Discourses essentially serve as our "identity kits." Because the language we use is a part of how we define ourselves, students who come to school with a primary Discourse that is viewed as inferior by the educational institution are torn between adopting the "Discourse of power"—the language and associated behaviors and values of those whose societal status enables them to determine whose Discourses becomes "standard," and whose are denigrated—and the Discourse of their home community. That is, adopting the "Discourse of power" requires that students of color embrace the language and behaviors of those who historically have devalued the students' own primary Discourses—i.e., their community's ways of speaking, behaving, valuing. These issues are further addressed in Chapter 7 (Blake).

Given these dynamics, it is critical that we acknowledge that a failure to learn the standard vernacular (and other knowledge associated with schooling) is not always a problem with our teaching methodologies or with students' inability to learn, but is often an act of resistance to a system that forces students to choose between the language and values (the Discourses) of the home, and the White, upper/middle-class language and values of the school. Viewing educational failure as resistance to schooled literacy and the dominant Discourses it embraces, rather than as a problem with methodology or with the learners themselves, is a radical departure from popular rhetoric about literacy instruction. Such notions call for a different conceptualization of literacy—one that is grounded in the lives of students and that values their language and cultural knowledge.

Schooled Literacy and Traditional Forms of Literacy Instruction

Beyond expectations for language use, there are certain forms and structures of literacy that have been identified in the professional literature that are uniquely associated with the language of schooling. These forms emerge from textbooks, standardized reading materials, and literacy kits that carry with them particular ways of using language and responding to text. Often these materials promote an "input/output" ideology, whereby students are required to master "basic skills" and "comprehension" of text through successful completion of various exercises versus meaningful and authentic uses of print (Edelsky, 1991; Irvine & Larson, 2007). Hence, literacy instruction is viewed as "objective" in that the ideological perspective of the texts themselves—as well as the underlying assumptions of such "scientifically" managed programs—are ignored. One of the primary aims of such instructional programs is to teach students how to conform to the materials so that their responses will be "accurate," rather than to teach them the relevance of literacy for their lives (Shannon, 1990).

In the stages of early literacy, for instance, students learn how to complete the worksheets and workbook pages that often accompany literacy instructional programs. As a second grade teacher, Richard Meyer (1996) found that the teacher's guides accompanying the basal reading series were so scripted that many of his students could easily teach the lessons. He writes:

> The basal, by its very nature, sets up a classroom process with specific structures of participation that ignore, deny, or even undermine success in reading. Basals can also disempower teachers and children who believe, as I did, that basals teach reading.
>
> (p. 42)

Learning to adapt to schooled literacy forms, however, is not limited to elementary classrooms. Instruction in "traditional grammar" often merely consists of learning the surface features of language, as opposed to immersing students in meaningful uses of print. Generally students are provided with exercises in "mechanics" and "correctness"—often through worksheets or English grammar texts—and are denied opportunities to learn the conventions of written language through writing for real audiences about things that really matter to them (Street, Lefstein, & Pahl, 2007). Hence, rather than revealing the potential of written language for critique and the significance of literacy for their lives, students learn that writing is essentially mastering a series of rules that have little personal meaning. That is, the function of written language is ignored in favor of acquiring its superficial properties—properties that Gee suggests are "the most impervious to overt instruction" and are emphasized "[p]recisely because [they] are the best test as to whether one was apprenticed in the 'right' place, at the 'right' time, with the 'right' people" (1989, p. 11).

Textbooks and pre-packaged literacy programs often promote ritualized, mechanical responses that have little to do with students' lived experiences. Indeed, as research by Bloome (1987) and Tharp and Gallimore (1991) indicate, such curricula often promote a particular language for talking about texts. Bloome, for instance, examines a form of text reproduction that he refers to as "procedural display," i.e., a typical interactional pattern that is designed to reconstruct—rather than question or challenge—the essential information found in a text. Tharp and Gallimore refer to such discourse patterns as "recitation" which emphasizes "rote learning and student passivity, facts and low-level questions, and low-level cognitive functions" (p. 1). Absent is any meaningful dialogue that might lead to reflection and critique; rather, the primary aim becomes one of mastering the objectives and "getting through the lesson." Responding to text becomes a matter of arriving at the "correct" answer versus exploring divergent perspectives and possibilities. Indeed, often knowledge is reduced to a limited set of interpretive options—options that have been predetermined and hence can be used for purposes of accountability (Luke, 1988).

Certainly, recent trends in literacy instruction (e.g., cooperative learning groups, "literacy circles," etc.) provide an important response to such text-driven programs. Generally, the intent of such discussion groups is to promote divergent interpretations of text, and as will be examined in Letitia Fickel's chapter (Chapter 3) and revisited throughout this book, dialogue is essential for promoting a counter-hegemonic pedagogy. It is important to recognize, however, that genuine discussion in classrooms is not easily attained, in that differential relationships of power and varying cultural expectations for linguistic behavior often make collaborative inquiry and negotiation challenging for teachers who seek to implement a more critical and participatory pedagogy. These cultural differences in linguistic norms are explored in Chapters 7 and 8 (Blake and Bryant).

Such skills-driven, teach-and-test models "illustrate how power relations are embedded in the material forms of schooling. By denying the importance of legitimate human enquiry, such programs obscure the social, cultural, and political dimension of literacy and learning" (Powell, 1999, p. 31). That is, as Fickel argues in Chapter 3, both teachers and students are denied the opportunity to construct knowledge; rather, *what* and *whose* knowledge is to be legitimated is determined by those outside the instructional setting.

In this book, we provide options to such reductionist models of literacy. In Chapter 5, Julia Johnson Connor and Arlette Ingram Willis describe the multiplicity of responses that can occur in a critically framed secondary literature classroom. In Chapter 6, Linda Spears-Bunton shows the intensity and complexity of the responses of White female students as they are challenged to reevaluate their taken-for-granted assumptions through a critical reading of multicultural texts. Drama can serve as an important avenue for giving students a voice in creating the curriculum, and in Chapter 9, Karen McLean Donaldson discusses the power of theater for engaging students in a social justice agenda. Contrary to traditional literacy instruction, all of these literacy practices encourage students and teachers to respond to texts in both personal and critical ways. In so doing, they invite students and teachers to be co-participants in negotiating and creating knowledge, rather than merely receiving it.

Schooled Literacy and Official School Knowledge

It might be argued that schooled literacy marginalizes students' cultural knowledge by forcing them to learn the "official knowledge" of the school (Apple, 1993b, 2003). Edelsky (1991) has argued that the literacy promoted in schools often positions the student as "object" rather than "subject." Students generally have little control over schooled literacy events in terms of what they read or write, where the event takes place, how long they have to complete the event, how it is assessed, etc. Edelsky further suggests that many literacy events that students experience in school are "exercises" rather than authentic opportunities for communication. That is, students often perceive schooled literacy events as being solely for the purposes of instruction or evaluation. In contrast, genuine literacy is purposeful and intentional; it is used to reflect, to express ideas, to entertain, to persuade. We would argue, therefore, that the literacy students generally experience in schools is problematic, in that they often do not see its relevance for their lives. In other words, students have few opportunities for actually *constructing* knowledge through reading, writing, and dialogue—to promote freedom of thought, to provide alternative perspectives, to communicate their ideas to others, to share their lives. Essentially, the "hidden curriculum" of schooled literacy is to encourage students to *receive* knowledge and hence, to accept the status quo.

Textbooks, too, position students as "objects" in that they have little voice as to what information they are to learn, and how they are to learn it. For students from historically underrepresented populations, the problem is particularly acute, for they rarely have the opportunity to "see themselves" in the texts that they read. Generally, textbooks promote the "official knowledge" of the educational institution; when non-mainstream knowledge is incorporated, it is primarily through a phenomenon that Michael Apple refers to as "mentioning":

> As disenfranchised groups have fought to have their knowledge take center stage in the debates over cultural legitimacy, one trend has dominated in text production. In essence, little is usually dropped from textbooks. Major ideological frameworks do not get markedly changed. Textbook publishers are under considerable and constant pressure to include *more* in their books. Progressive items are perhaps mentioned, then, but not developed in depth.
>
> (1993a, p. 206)

In fact, publishing companies intentionally avoid controversial topics such as racism in an attempt to appear "neutral," yet the illusion of neutrality ultimately results in perpetuating current systems of power and privilege (Peterson, 1998). In other words, by taking a "colorblind" stance, the content of most textbooks serves merely to advance a Eurocentric, upper/middle-class perspective and to marginalize the perspectives and cultural experiences of historically under-represented populations.

One of the underlying assumptions of schooled literacy is that it can be taught as a series of neutral "skills." Hence, the belief is that language learning can be removed from its sociopolitical context. Yet, it is important to recognize that a belief in the neutrality of texts is an ideological assumption that denies the fact that written and oral language are both *social* and *cultural* expressions. As Letitia Fickel argues in Chapter 3, the notion that certain skills and knowledge can be "transmitted" to students is essentially disempowering in that students are required merely to learn the "official knowledge" of the school (Apple, 1993b) rather than to engage actively in dialogue and critique. Paulo Freire

(1970/1993) refers to the transmission form of instruction as "banking education," whereby information is "deposited" in students' minds which they are later required to withdraw for a test. With its emphasis upon the acquisition of particular "skills" and "facts," schooled literacy is an example of how the banking concept is applied in our literacy instructional practices. Knowledge is seen as static and predefined—determined by the so-called "experts"—rather than as dynamic and culturally determined. Hence, students rarely read and write about things that really matter to them; their own ideas and perspectives are seen as irrelevant to the entire educational enterprise.

Even when students' stories are legitimated in the classroom, students of color are at a particular disadvantage in that their cultural knowledge is generally viewed as less significant, both in our educational institutions and in society at large. For instance, elsewhere Arlette Willis writes of her third grade son, who came to dislike writing because he felt that the personal experiences he wrote about would be misinterpreted by his peers (Willis, 1995). The promotion of primarily Anglo, middle/upper-class perspectives effectively silenced him; rather than feeling that he was an integral part of a "community of writers," he felt excluded and marginalized. Thus, even when students are given choices in terms of what and when to write, they nevertheless can be silenced by the sociopolitical climate of the school or classroom.

The literary canon, too, has traditionally excluded the voices of persons of color. As Connor and Willis (Chapter 5) and Spears-Bunton (Chapter 6) argue in this volume, such exclusion not only denies students of color the opportunity to "see themselves" in the literary texts that they read, but it also denies *all* students the opportunity to learn about the depth and richness of the whole human experience. We would also argue that practices that limit the voices of a vast number of our citizens are inconsistent with a multicultural democracy, which espouses an ideology of justice, fairness, and inclusion.

The Results of Schooled Literacy

Thus far we have argued that schooled literacy endorses certain standards of appropriate literate behavior, promotes conformity to particular forms and structures of written and oral language, and denies the cultural knowledge of historically underrepresented groups. Thus, we would suggest that rather than being "neutral," schooled literacy is decidedly political in that it reflects a culturally racist ideology—an ideology that endorses White (upper/middle-class) cultural norms, values, and traditions over those of other groups (Helms, 1993; Jones, 2006; Powell, 2001). That is, the linguistic standards, forms, and cultural knowledge of schooled literacy traditionally have been those that are consistent with White, middle/upper-class norms. Those students who come to school with a primary discourse that differs from the standard discourse and with cultural knowledge that differs from the "official" knowledge of the school are placed at a disadvantage. Indeed, research by Heath (1983) also shows that White, middle-class children may even be better prepared to adapt to the characteristic forms and structures of schooled literacy in that the "book talk" that occurs in the home tends to parrot the "comprehension" questions often asked in classroom literacy lessons (see Chapter 8).

Given all of this, it perhaps should not be surprising that students of color tend to achieve at lower levels than their White counterparts. It also should not be surprising that many find school to be irrelevant and hence tend to drop out in greater numbers.[3] Thus, instead of being a means for enablement—a source of promise and possibility—the literacy provided by our educational institutions is often a source of frustration and alienation. In fact, many theorists have argued that, because schooled literacy endorses White norms and tends to denigrate the language and experiences of other populations, students of color often view the acceptance of schooled literacy as "joining the opposing camp" (Davidson, 1996; Fordham, 1988; MacLeod, 1995; Ogbu, 1987, 2003). To reiterate a point made earlier in this discussion, it is important to acknowledge that students' failure to learn may be intentional, as Herb Kohl connotes through his book title "*I Won't Learn From You—And Other Thoughts on Creative Maladjustment*" (1995).

Schooled literacy, however, affects all students and not just students of color. By invoking conformity rather than divergent thought, students rarely have the opportunity to experience the power of literacy for their lives. Instead of inviting students to seek knowledge and to challenge the information found in texts, they are encouraged to remain passive, to learn the "right" facts, to give the "right" answers to questions. That is, students are taught that their role is to receive someone else's knowledge, rather than to construct knowledge through creative and critical thought. Hence, schooled literacy is essentially disempowering for all students in that it becomes a language of control versus a language of critique.

Finally, it is important to note that the ultimate result of schooled literacy is to maintain the status quo. In this sense, then, schooled literacy is inherently anti-democratic in that diverse perspectives are silenced. The literacy of democracy is one of liberation, where all voices are encouraged and legitimated. It must be acknowledged that for every text there are multiple interpretations, and the richness of a text's meaning emerges from participatory dialogue. Indeed, one might argue that the essence of democracy is dialogue, where ideas are debated and multiple opinions sought (Pradle, 1996). In contrast, schooled literacy promotes acquiescence and passivity, thereby denying students the social and linguistic competence required for democratic participation. As Powell (1999) has written elsewhere, "treating students as 'clients' or 'objects' to be manipulated and controlled, and denying the 'appetites and passions' [Greene, 1978, p. 113] of young learners, reflects an underlying ideology that counteracts our professed democratic ideals" (p. 50).

Toward a Literacy of Promise

Schooled literacy can be contrasted with a literacy of promise, a literacy that encourages teachers and students to question social and economic inequities and to work for justice. Literacy, in this sense, requires that we read the word and the world critically so that we might examine our taken-for-granted assumptions—assumptions that are embedded in a society plagued by racism, classism, sexism, homophobia. Henry Giroux (1993) writes that:

> Literacy cannot be viewed as merely an epistemological or procedural issue but must be defined primarily in political and ethical terms. It is political in that how we read the world is always implicated in relations of power. Literacy is ethical in that people "read" the world differently depending, for instance, on circumstances of class, gender, race, and politics . . . If a politics of difference is to be fashioned in emancipatory rather than oppressive practices, literacy must be rewritten in terms that articulate difference with the principles of equality, justice, and freedom rather than with those interests supportive of hierarchies, oppression, and exploitation.
>
> (p. 368)

A literacy of promise acknowledges the inequities in society and the ways in which literacy has been used historically to exploit and to silence rather than to liberate and transform. Unlike schooled literacy, which assumes a neutral stance through reducing knowledge to "skills" and "information," a critical literacy is intentionally political and non-neutral. Readers are challenged to examine the inherent race, class, and gender biases in texts, and are encouraged to consider how these messages affect both the ways in which we view the world, and our personal and collective identities as individuals and as a society. As we explore in the next chapter, a literacy of promise exploits the social and cultural nature of literacy in that readers are led to reconceptualize the ways in which they "read" the word and the world.

A literacy of promise also expands our notions of what constitutes legitimate texts for study. With a literacy that is critical, "texts" are not confined to books and other print resources typically found in schools and classrooms; rather, the whole world becomes a "text," as students are challenged to examine the messages portrayed in the media, on billboards, in daily conversations, and so on. Wendy Morgan (1997) writes:

> By "texts" is understood whatever in our social environment can be read as a text: whatever constructs a meaning through shared codes and conventions, signs and icons. Indeed, critical literacy inevitably entails a cultural studies approach to texts in refusing to confine its examination to words-on-the-page.
>
> (p. 29)

Thus, readers are encouraged to examine the cultural assumptions implicit in all forms of communication. For example, critical teachers have used children's cartoons for exploring inequitable power relations (Christensen, 2000), and have asked students to keep personal journals to record the racist, classist, sexist, and homophobic messages they find in the popular media (Cortés, 2000). Ways for using popular media to explore racism and racial identity are examined in greater detail in Chapter 10. Such explorations can provide substance for essays, articles, and poems, as well as for classroom discussions and debates.

Finally, a literacy of promise provides students with a voice—a voice for creating, celebrating, critiquing, and constructing meaning. Literacy becomes personally relevant in that students' cultural knowledge and experiences are validated. African American students read texts that speak to them personally, and discover themselves in the words and worlds of Maya Angelou, Alice Walker, Gwendolyn Brooks, and Langston Hughes. They celebrate their rich linguistic heritage by examining the extensive repertoire of African American discourse as revealed in novels, poetry, speeches, and sermons—from the powerful words of Martin Luther King, Jr. in *I Have a Dream*, to the words of Celie in Alice Walker's *The Color Purple* (Jordan, 1988). Further, like Irma Johnson, author of "The Yellow Dress," they are given time and space to write about the experiences that define their lives, and to share, discuss, and critique those experiences with others.

Conclusion

Taken collectively, the authors of this volume argue for a literacy that is enabling rather than controlling, empowering rather than repressive. They argue for a literacy that helps both teachers and students to illuminate reality, that challenges systems of privilege, and that encourages us to work for change. We are calling this literacy a "literacy of promise"—a literacy that has the potential of giving voice to the voiceless and renewed hope to those who have historically been marginalized. A literacy of promise has often remained elusive for those who have been enslaved, dehumanized, and disenfranchised.

A literacy of promise can be contrasted with schooled literacy, which promotes passivity and acquiescence and obscures the reality of racism, classism, and other forms of oppression. The literacy envisioned in this book encourages students and teachers to imagine a different reality for themselves and for society, one that is grounded in equity and that embraces the democratic ideals of justice, equality, and freedom for all. If this volume helps readers to conceptualize such a literacy, then it will have fulfilled its aim.

Questions for Discussion

1. When have you felt that you were positioned as "object" in school? When have you felt that you were positioned as "subject" in school?
2. Give examples of the social uses of literacy. In what ways is literacy "social"? In what ways is literacy "cultural"?
3. Is literacy instruction ever really "neutral"? Why or why not?
4. How would you characterize a literacy that is empowering? disempowering?
5. Does the way literacy is taught matter in a democracy? Why or why not?

Extension Activities

1. Consider your own "Discourse." Write down words and phrases that you use when communicating in various social situations. Brainstorm the beliefs and values that you are expected to possess to be considered a part of various groups and to participate in the "Discourse."
2. Interview students about the various discourses that they use in different social situations. With which discourses are they the most comfortable? Which do they find more difficult? What "secondary discourses" (i.e., those outside their immediate community) do they use, and how did they acquire them?
3. Analyze the content of current textbooks for their inclusion or exclusion of controversial topics such as racism.
4. Interview students on their experiences with "schooled literacy."

Notes

1. Ms. Irma Johnson is a former student of ours who currently directs the Service Learning Program at Kentucky State University. We are grateful to her for allowing us to include her story, "The Yellow Dress," which is a true account of her experiences with school desegregation.
2. We do not wish to imply that we are opposed to teaching "Standard English" in schools. Certainly, learning the standard discourse is essential for negotiating within the current power structure. Rather, we are suggesting that we ought to consider the "context of situation" in which language is being used, and to acknowledge that (1) all discourses are complex, and (2) there are legitimate social contexts for using non-standard discourse forms.
3. While the number of students of color earning a high school diploma or equivalency degree has increased in recent years, they still fall behind their White counterparts. Data from a 2007 report published by the U.S. Department of Education reveal that 10.4 percent of African American youth and 22.4 percent of Hispanic youth aged 16–24 were high-school dropouts, compared with 6.0 percent of White youth in the same age group (U.S. Department of Education).

References

Apple, M. W. (1993a). Between moral regulation and democracy: The cultural contradictions of the text. In C. Lankshear & P. L. McLaren (Eds.), *Critical literacy: Politics, praxis, and the postmodern* (pp. 193–216). Albany: SUNY Press.

Apple, M. W. (1993b). *Official knowledge: Democratic education in a conservative age.* New York: Routledge.

Apple, M. W. (2003). *The state and the politics of knowledge.* New York: RoutledgeFalmer.

Ballenger, C. (1999). *Teaching other people's children: Literacy and learning in a bilingual classroom.* New York: Teachers College.

Besser, H. (1993). Education as marketplace. In R. Muffoletto & N. N. Knupfer (Eds.), *Computers in education: Social, political, and historical perspectives* (pp. 37–69). Cresskill, NJ: Hampton Press.

Bloome, D. (1987). Reading as a social process in a middle school classroom. In D. Bloome (Ed.), *Literacy and schooling* (pp. 123–149). Norwood, NJ: Ables.

Carter, D. J., & Wilson, R. (1996). *Minorities in higher education: 1995–96 fourteenth annual status report.* Washington, DC: American Council on Education.

Cary, R. (1997). IQ as commodity: The 'new' economics of intelligence. In J. L. Kincheloe, S. R. Steinberg, & A. D. Gresson, III (Eds.), *Measured lies: The bell curve examined* (pp. 137–160). New York: St. Martin's Press.

Christensen, L. M. (1999). Critical literacy: Teaching reading, writing, and outrage. In C. Edelsky (Ed.), *Making justice our project* (pp. 209–225). Urbana, IL: NCTE.

Christensen, L. M. (2000). *Reading, writing, and rising up: Teaching about social justice and the power of the written word.* Milwaukee: Rethinking Schools.

Cortés, C. (2000). *The children are watching: How the media teach about diversity.* New York: Teachers College Press.

Davidson, A. L. (1996). *Making and molding identity in schools: Student narratives on race, gender, and academic engagement.* Albany: SUNY Press.

Delpit, L. D. (1988). The silenced dialogue: Power and pedagogy in educating other people's children. *Harvard Educational Review, 58*(3), 280–298.

Delpit, L. (1998). What should teachers do? Ebonics and culturally responsive instruction. In T. Perry & L. Delpit (Eds.), *The real Ebonics debate* (pp. 17–26). Boston: Beacon Press.

Edelsky, C. (1991). *With literacy and justice for all: Rethinking the social in language education.* Bristol, PA: The Falmer Press, Taylor & Francis.

Fordham, S. (1988). Racelessness as a factor in Black students' school success: Pragmatic strategy or pyrrhic victory? *Harvard Educational Review, 58*, 54–84.

Fox, H. (1994). *Listening to the world: Cultural issues in academic writing.* Urbana, IL: NCTE.

Freire, P. (1970/1993). *Pedagogy of the oppressed.* New York: Continuum.

Freire, P., & Macedo, D. (1987). *Literacy: Reading the word and the world.* South Hadley, MA: Bergin & Garvey.

Gee, J. P. (1989). Literacy, discourse, and linguistics: Introduction [Special issue]. *Journal of Education, 171,* 5–17.

Gee, J. P. (1990). *Social linguistics and literacies: Ideology in discourses.* Bristol, PA: The Falmer Press, Taylor & Francis.

Giroux, H. A. (1993). Literacy and the politics of difference. In C. Lankshear & P. L. McLaren (Eds.), *Critical literacy: Politics, praxis, and the postmodern* (pp. 367–377). Albany: SUNY Press.

Greene, M. (1978). *Landscapes of learning.* New York: Teachers College Press.

Heath, S. B. (1983). *Ways with words: Language, life, and work in communities and classrooms.* Cambridge: Cambridge University Press.

Helms, J. E. (Ed.) (1993). *Black and White racial identity.* New York: Praeger.

Irvine, P. D., & Larson, J. (2007). Literacy packages in practice: Constructing academic disadvantage. In J. Larson (Ed.), *Literacy as snake oil: Beyond the quick fix* (pp. 49–72). New York: Peter Lang.

Jones, S. (2006). *Girls, social class, and literacy: What teachers can do to make a difference.* Portsmouth, NH: Heinemann.

Jordan, J. (1988). Nobody mean more to me than you and the future life of Willie Jordan. *Harvard Educational Review, 58,* 363–374.

Kohl, H. R. (1995). *"I won't learn from you": And other thoughts on creative maladjustment.* New York: The New Press.

Luke, A. (1988). *Literacy, textbooks and ideology: Postwar literacy instruction and the mythology of Dick and Jane.* Philadelphia, PA: The Falmer Press.

MacLeod, J. (1995). *Ain't no makin' it: Aspirations and attainment in a low-income neighborhood.* Boulder, CO: Westview Press.

Meyer, R. J. (1996). *Stories from the heart: Teachers and students researching their literacy lives.* Mahwah, NJ: Lawrence Erlbaum.

Michaels, S. (1981). "Sharing time": Children's narrative styles and differential access to literacy. *Language in Society, 10,* 423–442.

Morgan, W. (1997). *Critical literacy in the classroom: The art of the possible.* New York: Routledge.

Ogbu, J. U. (1987). Variability in minority school performance: A problem in search of an explanation. In E. Jacob & C. Jordan (Eds.), Explaining the school performance of minority students [Theme Issue]. *Anthropology and Education Quarterly, 18,* 312–334.

Ogbu, J. U. (2003). *Black Americans in an affluent suburb: A student of academic disengagement.* Mahwah, NJ: Lawrence Erlbaum.

Perry, T., Steele, C. & Hilliard III, A. (2003). *Young, gifted, and Black: Promoting high achievement among African-American students.* Boston, MA: Beacon Press.

Peterson, B. (1998). Where's the r-word? Speaking out on textbook silences. *Rethinking schools, 12*(4), 20.

Pincus, F. L., & Ehrlich, H. J. (Eds.) (1999). *Race and ethnic conflict: Contending views on prejudice, discrimination, and ethnoviolence* (2nd ed.). Boulder, CO: Westview.

Powell, R. (1999). *Literacy as a moral imperative: Facing the challenges of a pluralistic society.* Lanham, MD: Rowman and Littlefield.

Powell, R. (2001). *Straight talk: Growing as multicultural educators.* New York: Peter Lang.

Pradl, G. M. (1996). *Literature for democracy: Reading as a social act.* Portsmouth, NH: Boynton/ Cook.

Purcell-Gates, V. (2002). ". . . As soon as she opened her mouth!": Issues of language, literacy, and power. In L. Delpit (Ed.), *The skin that we speak: Thoughts on language and culture in the classroom.* New York: The New Press.

Redd, T. M., & Webb, K. S. (2005). *A teacher's introduction to African American English: What a writing teacher should know.* Urbana, IL: NCTE.

Rose, M. (1989). *Lives on the boundary.* New York: Penguin.

Shannon, P. (1990). *The struggle to continue: Progressive reading instruction in the United States.* Portsmouth, NH: Heinemann.

Shannon, P. (1998). *Reading poverty.* Portsmouth, NH: Heinemann.

Street, B., Lefstein, A., & Pahl, K. (2007). The national literacy strategy in England: Contradictions of control and creativity. In J. Larson (Ed.), *Literacy as snake oil: Beyond the quick fix* (pp. 123–154). New York: Peter Lang.

Tharp, R. G., & Gallimore, R. (1991). *The instructional conversation: Teaching and learning in social activity* (Research Report 2). Santa Cruz, CA: University of California, The National Center for Research on Cultural Diversity and Second Language Learning.

U.S. Department of Education, National Center for Education Statistics (2007). *The condition of education 2007* (NCES 2007–064, Indicator 23). Retrieved December 3, 2007 from http://nces.ed.gov/fastfacts/

Willis, A. I. (1995). Reading the world of school literacy: Contextualizing the experience of a young African American male. *Harvard Educational Review, 65,* 30–49.

I
Problems and Promises

2

Along the Road to Social Justice
A Literacy of Promise
LINDA A. SPEARS-BUNTON AND REBECCA POWELL

Traditionally, literacy has been a part of the "cultural capital" of the privileged—the capital of those who have the power to own knowledge and to present that knowledge as significant, as "that which is important to know." Power grants certain groups the privilege to write the rules, to change them, and to apply them in ways that perpetuate their status. Thus, historically, becoming "literate" meant that one had to acquire that capital, i.e., the knowledge, the perspectives, the cultural and linguistic forms, the literary traditions of privileged groups. For some, the acquisition of literacy offered exclusive access to citizenry and the bestowal of power, reward and recognition. A "literacy of promise," as we are defining it here, gives ownership to the oppressed, validating their linguistic and literary heritage, giving them a voice. A literacy of promise is inclusive and advocates for collective ownership rather than elite proprietary rights. This kind of literacy invites marginalized groups to affirm their past, to critique the present, and to re-envision their future. A literacy of promise intentionally presents a challenge to the status quo.

In this chapter, we explore the ways in which literacy has been used to perpetuate a system of marginalization. We then conceptualize a "literacy of promise," a literacy that affirms diverse voices, that promotes critique, that inspires transformation. We begin this journey with Linda's story.

The Struggle for Literacy: A Personal Odyssey

The genesis for this chapter was in my encounter with a university professor in Oakland, California several months before the assassination of Dr. King. The college is nestled snugly in the hills among ancient redwoods overlooking the flatlands of Oakland and its largely Black population. A freeway and poor public transportation separated Black West Oakland from us. There was only one student from West Oakland living on campus; all of the maids and cooks were Black. Even so, the voices of change and of hope were so powerful at the time that they could be heard nearly everywhere except in our curriculum.

There were no courses in Black history, literature, psychology, sociology or philosophy. The only way to study Black artistic or intellectual thought was independently—without a teacher or course credit. Yet an opportunity to choose a research topic, although subject to the professor's approval, prompted me to try. I carefully prepared my request with a good deal of unassigned reading and practiced aloud—using Black and White dorm mates as an audience.

When the big day came to discuss my ideas with the class, I sat in the back of the classroom, listening to my peers. Resisting the temptation to raise my hand to ask or to answer questions, I waited in vain to be called on. After class I followed the professor, lugging a big bag of books and notes, trying politely to get her attention. She was in the bright, open indoor courtyard—the nexus of student activity—when she finally stopped and turned toward me.

"Professor, I would like to do my research project on Black literature . . ." The sentence hung incomplete in mid-air as she declared loudly enough for the students exiting Literary Criticism and Aesthetics and all passersby to hear, "There is no such thing as Black literature. There are only a few sociological writings, like *Manchild in a Promised Land* and *The Autobiography of Malcolm X*." She made this proclamation with the authority of the Chair of the English Department; there was no opportunity to rejoin with Alain Locke, W.E.B. Du Bois, Ralph Ellison, Langston Hughes or the Harlem Renaissance or any other work I had summarized in preparation.

"Well," I replied, "if you do not know the difference between novels, poems, dramas, short stories and sociology, how can you presume to be the Chair of anybody's English department, anywhere?" A snappy two-heeled pirouette presented me with her back, sent her nun's habit billowing in the air and cut off any further possibility for dialogue. There was only one Black English major; there were a dozen Black students in the college and there were no full-time Black faculty. She taught four challenging required courses, seemed fond of members of the Young Republican party working on George Wallace's presidential campaign and waxed poetic about her hometown in Alabama throughout the late sixties.

With a wave of her hand, she had the power to dismiss an entire people and their contributions to civilization and to render universal ideas as non-existent. I did not know at the time that the African American literary canon was four hundred years old. Growing up in walking distance of the Schomburg Center for Research in Harlem, I did know there were more than two books, and that there were poets, novelists, essayists and playwrights who were quite famous. Yet, she had the power to maintain the status quo, to enforce her view of the world, to silence challenge and to give grades. Sister Claire did not have to exercise the depth of reading to provide evidence to support her hypothesis or to argue her point in an academic way, as we were required to do. She exercised the right of might awarded to a middle-aged, White professor whose garb symbolized her commitment to God.

I remember leaving her presence that day fighting back tears, expecting a call from the dean of students about my insouciant talk to my superior and dreading the intensified close reading to which my papers would be subjected. The threat of expulsion or flunking out was a real possibility. I wrote in my diary, "it's not fair; college is supposed to be fair." This injustice was not just to an individual student, but to all students, because it denies their access to alternative ideas and to opportunities to explore the ways in which diverse people see the world. Such injustice denies access to the whole human experience.

Why I did not transfer or change majors I do not know. Three years passed and although I read voraciously in order to present alternative views in class and in my papers, Sister Claire never called on me and always found something wrong, albeit often vague, with my verbal expression. The fact that she did not flunk me out may be related to the public nature of our points of departure. In our small community everyone knew what was going on. Additionally, change followed Dr. King's death. A new multi-racial students' union lobbied for a Black History course and a part-time Black faculty person was hired to teach; several Black men from a nearby Catholic men's college sat in on the classes. By senior year, a record number of fifty Black women were admitted into the college with full scholarships.

Sister Claire remained unflappable. In red ink, she simply wrote "B—verbal expression;" in conference, she simply said, "You have not learned to articulate ideas properly." Still, reading nearly every Sister Claire book twice and reading Black literature with related themes or time periods, and slipping Black authors into my references, provided some private solace. Sitting in the front of the room waving my hand vigorously and speaking out of turn became public entertainment and comic relief. These behaviors, marginally acceptable in a college setting, would not likely be tolerated from a high school student. I wonder:

- In what ways does such silencing affect the educational progress of our secondary students?
- What do you think the consequences of Linda's behavior might be in your school?
- What label(s) might be applied to this student and her behavior?

Years later, an African American high school junior in an inner city, honors English class wrote the following in place of the school newspaper article she was assigned by her White teacher:

Why is it that a high school junior with a love of reading and very good grades can not write an article on this topic [Black History Month]? The answer is simple; I cannot write it because I am ignorant. I am ignorant because I have not been taught. By teaching only the history and literature of White Americans, this school is perpetuating racism and ignorance . . . I'm tired of not knowing anything about Black History except about Dr. Martin Luther King. He was good and all, but we've been hearing about him since 3rd grade—every year—the same thing. Besides, I didn't want to write about a person, I wanted to write about Black History month, what it is, how it began—you know. I wanted to write about Black history but I don't know anything except these few books we've been reading in here. I want more than that, I need more than that.

(Dana, 1992)

Debunking the Neutrality Myth

Sister Claire reminds us that both the canon and the role of the literature teacher are partially reflective of American educational history and the pedagogical presumptions about the purposes of education generally, and literacy in particular. Why we teach literature, what literature we teach, and how literature is taught is underscored by the political, social, and educational history of a society complexly founded upon the ideology of human equality and democracy, yet grounded in conflicting perceptions of race, culture, class and gender.

The canon—the officially sanctioned set of literary texts judged to be standard and universal—is neither colorblind nor neutral. Rather, it is a persuasive agent of hegemony because it presents a view of the world based upon the dominant rationality (Anyon, 1983; Apple, 1982). Hegemony references the system of domination in society that delimits acceptable standards for social and cultural behavior. "Hegemony is the ubiquitous and taken-for-granted status of dominant culture within a culturally plural and class stratified society such as the United States" (Erickson, 1987, p. 352). This rationality so permeates social agencies, such as schools, that although English has been the only high school subject required for each of the four years for over two hundred years, it is possible to complete thirteen years or more of formal schooling and never read a book written by a Black author, or obtain a Ph.D. and yet boast about being ignorant of non-traditional texts (Morrison, 1992). A similar portrait of literary and cultural exclusion exists for all non-mainstream groups. The canon maintains its status as the dominant voice through human agency in many ways, including practicing aliteracy, an irresponsible exercise of power, acritical approaches to teaching and learning, disrespect, and sometimes dishonesty.

To be literate means, among other things, to be knowledgeable. In these vignettes of personal experience, it is possible to see that a curriculum based upon an ideology that reflects the perspectives of those who conquered and rule limits opportunities for examining the equation that constitutes the human experience, and may create a false sense of racial and cultural superiority or inferiority. Importantly, opportunities to formulate critical judgments of texts, contexts and events are delimited. A by-product of a mono-cultural curriculum may also be disengagement, rejection of schooling, limited participation and school failure (Delpit, 1995; Kohl, 1995).

Moving Toward Higher Ground: Conceptualizing a Literacy of Promise

Inner-city public education
How did I end up the Caucasian
In front of the Haitian
Bahamian African Jamaican?
Cultural domination?

I teach with hesitation
Racism, poverty, segregation.
I shy away from Langston Hughes
A dream deferred *ain't my blues*

Me, the Caucasian,
In front of the Haitian
Bahamian African Jamaican
Ideological management
Advancing development?

Teach them the white *way*
To write a poem
Don't let them use
Their native tongue

Something needs to change
Ideas curriculum rearrange
Standard written English
Cultural voices diminish

Am I appeasing
Too pleasing
Making it too easy?
I want to inspire
Not tire
Find their fire

And the veteran educator yells,
"No,
our students deserve an equal chance!"

chance
thus the dance
the balance
administrative giants
vs. student silence

and me, the Caucasian
in front of the Haitian

Bahamian African Jamaican
In America
In the public schools

And so I embrace spoken word
Draw the map
Between poetry and rap
Tupac Sylvia Plath
Busta Rhymes Kerouac
Slip slam
And then snap

Me, the Caucasian
Trying to teach the Haitian
Bahamian African Jamaican
Not the perfect combination
Inner-city public education

(Klein, 2000)

As we noted in Chapter one, schooled literacy emerges from White cultural norms that legitimate certain texts, discourses, and cultural knowledge. By denying alternate interpretations and reinforcing the "official" knowledge of the school, schooled literacy tends to promote passivity and acquiescence among both teachers and students. A literacy of promise, in contrast, taps into students' passions; it gives them a voice; it validates their experiences. Like this poem written by a young White teacher, distressed by the racist system in which she finds herself, it compels us to read, write, and speak about things that really matter. Importantly, Kristina examines her role as a teacher and a member of the elite group. Her use of African Diasporic, urban references combined with the poetic cadences of the popular music/talk genre, evidences a fundamental respect for the students she teaches and the cultures they represent. Moreover, her poem presents a direct challenge to the status quo in her school community.

In this section, we explore several characteristics of a literacy of promise. First, we suggest that a literacy of promise begins with the self. It engenders personal and critical interpretations of text, and makes connections among the reader, the text, and a particularized socio-cultural context. Second, a literacy of promise celebrates learning and encourages shared experiences and collaborative inquiry among a community of learners. Third, a literacy of promise is potentially transformative; it urges a social consciousness that transcends the boundaries of class, race, gender, and ignorance.

A Literacy of Promise Engenders Personal and Critical Interpretations of Text

Reader-response theory provides a viable way of looking at the interaction of the reader with the text by giving us a theory-driven conceptualization of the reader as a human actor who evokes and recreates the text. An understanding of the nature of the interrelationship between the culture of the reader and response to literature can shed light upon critical elements of reader-response that influence the interaction between the meaning readers bring to and construct from literary texts. These elements include: (1) prior experiences and literary conventions that the reader uses in order to construct meaning from a text; (2) the affective dimensions of response, specifically the reader's volition and motivation to engage in the world of the text, e.g., the reader's feelings about the text and character identification; and (3) the posture the reader takes towards the text (Rosenblatt, 1996) which determines whether the text is read for factual information to be used in other contexts (an efferent posture), or for the experience of living through the text (an aesthetic posture).

Rosenblatt has demonstrated that in order to understand the process of reading and responding to literature, indeed to most forms of text, we must recognize that it is readers' lived experiences—their native understanding and feelings about the text and character identification—and the posture that readers take towards the text, which determines whether the text is read for factual information (efferent posture) or to experience the text (aesthetic posture). Thus, the reader interacts with the author's message in personal and often unique ways.

A literacy of promise, as we are conceptualizing it here, moves beyond traditional reader response theory in that it also includes readers' critical responses to text. That is, readers are encouraged to react to texts in both personal and critical ways. To illustrate, we share an example from a university student who is responding to a personal and critical reading of *Zlata's Diary: A Child's Life in Sarajevo* (Filipovic, 1994):

> One of my own misconceptions of Sarajevo was that I thought that the people in Yugoslavia were much more ethnically distinct. Thus, it would have been easy to figure out who was Muslim, Serb or Croatian based on where people lived, how they looked and who they associated with. I also was surprised at Zlata's familiarity with American culture and the widespread influence of American television programs such as *The Fresh Prince of Bel Air*, and movies such as *The Witches of Eastwick*, as well as American music. Of course, I should not have been surprised at this when I think of my own husband's familiarity with American music, film, and television, and he grew up in Spain. I guess what happens is since I think the action of war is so barbaric, "uncivilized" and "foreign," I forget that it can happen in places such as Sarajevo and now Kosovo where people are familiar with American culture. And I forget that it could happen here

too. There is a certain degree of complacency in thinking that war would never happen in "America" or American allied countries since we have already "been there, done that."

What's frightening to realize is how most citizens of most countries in the world can be made victims of the political instability of the country they are living in. It's like, to quote an old cliché, "being in the wrong place, at the wrong time." I get angry when I think of a child like Zlata and her family, and others who are at the whims of a government who has gained power and has decided to wield it, in the lower evolutionary way, of using might. Of course, I think it too easy to say, one side is right or one side is wrong. No side necessarily has a sniper fire to make amends. I remember hearing one of my coworkers say, when the United States had decided to bomb Belgrade, that it was the best thing to do. After all, the Serbs were at fault and were committing the same atrocities that Hitler had done to the Jews. Flinching at this comment, I thought to myself, all Serbs? What about the ones who didn't agree with what the government was doing, but didn't necessarily have the freedom to choose? I just don't like to justify another seeming mistake of lumping people together by ethnicity and labeling them all bad.

In this excerpt, the student first responds to the text by comparing Zlata's experiences with her own life: "I should not have been surprised at this when I think of my own husband's familiarity with American music, film, and television . . ." Yet she quickly moves into a more critical rendering of the ideas in the text: "There is a certain degree of complacency in thinking that war would never happen in 'America' or American allied countries . . . Flinching at this comment, I thought to myself, all Serbs?" Throughout the text, her personal experiences and reactions become intertwined with a critique of justifications for war and the role of government in waging conflict:

This student's response to *Zlata* reminds us of the political critiques of historian Howard Zinn, whose work provides alternative perspectives to the "official knowledge" generally found in U.S. history texts (e.g., Zinn, 1995). In his recent book *Passionate Declarations: Essays on War and Justice* (2003), Zinn argues that no war could ever be "just." Throughout this book, he recounts the atrocities committed by western forces in World War II—a war in which he personally participated. In discussing America's decision to drop atomic bombs on Japan, he writes:

The American public, already conditioned to massive bombing, accepted the atomic bombings with equanimity, indeed with joy. I remember my own reaction. When the war ended in Europe, my crew flew our plane back to the United States. We were given a thirty-day furlough and then had to report for duty to be sent to Japan to continue bombing. My wife and I decided to spend that time in the countryside. Waiting for the bus to take us, I picked up the morning newspaper, August 7, 1945. The headline was "Atomic Bomb Dropped on Hiroshima." My immediate reaction was elation: "The war will end. I won't have to go to the Pacific."

I had no idea what the explosion of the atomic bomb had done to the men, women, and children of Hiroshima. It was abstract and distant, as were the deaths of the people from the bombs I had dropped in Europe from a height of six miles; I was unable to see anything below, there was no visible blood, and there were no audible screams. And I knew nothing of the imminence of a Japanese surrender. It was only later when I read John Hersey's *Hiroshima*, when I read the testimony of Japanese survivors, and when I studied the history of the decision to drop the bomb that I was outraged by what had been done.

It seems that once an initial judgment has been made that a war is just, there is a tendency to stop thinking, to assume then that everything done on behalf of victory is morally acceptable. I had myself participated in the bombing of cities, without even considering whether there was any relationship between what I was doing and the elimination of fascism in the world. One of my bombing missions had been on the city of Pilsen (now Plzen) in Czechoslovakia. The inhabitants were Czechs—the very people who had been among the first victims of Nazi expansion—yet we were dropping bombs on them. I don't remember being conscious of that irony, or questioning our mission.

(p. 96)

A literacy of promise is a literacy of critique—one that requires readers, writers and listeners to respond both personally and critically to the messages they receive (both oral and written). Zinn's initial response to the written word was personal; it was one of "elation." Only later, after reading further about the events at Hiroshima, did Zinn begin to question the U.S. government's decision to use atomic force. That is, acquiring information that originally had been concealed allowed Zinn to reread the original newspaper text through a different lens, causing him to react critically to an event that had previously appeared justified.

Like Zinn, the student commentary above shows both a personal and a critical response to a written text. Through personalizing the experiences of Zlata, the reader examines the inhumanity of national and international conflict and takes an "aesthetic" stance, that is, she "lives through" the text. Yet, she also provides social and political critique, questioning the justification for war and the racial and ethnic divides that often perpetrate it. A literacy of promise encourages such critique, and thereby moves beyond an individualistic response toward examining the economic, social and political contexts that frame the human experience.

A Literacy of Promise Celebrates Learning and Encourages Shared Experiences and Collaborative Inquiry

One of the central tenets of a literacy of promise is dialogue. Contrary to many discourse patterns found in schools, where the intent is to transmit information or to test students' knowledge (Powell, 1999), dialogue involves the free exchange of ideas within a collaborative community of learners. Thus, dialogue is undermined when individuals within that community (such as the teacher) seek to control knowledge. Paulo Freire (1970/1993) writes:

> Dialogue is the encounter between men [*sic.*], mediated by the world, in order to name the world. Hence, dialogue cannot occur between those who want to name the world and those who do not wish this naming— between those who deny others the right to speak their word and those whose right to speak has been denied them.
>
> (p. 69)

In classrooms where there is shared dialogue, students' questions become central. In our own teaching, for example, students keep "TP" journals ("talk back and pose questions"), similar to those used by high school English teacher Linda Christensen (2000), in which students interact with the text as they read. At the start of each class, students are asked to share ideas from their journals, and their comments and questions serve as points of discussion. In other classes, students keep "RAP" cards—Respond, Apply, Pose a Question—and their questions become starting points for dialogue.

Further, student assignments are shared in a variety of ways. For example, in some of our classes, students' journal entries are e-mailed both to the professor and to the class. In this way, we all participate in an ongoing discourse about the issues, and we share our insights and perceptions as individuals and as a community. Other journals are read by students in class. Tears, laughter, questions and debate emerge as a natural part of the learning/teaching enterprise. Critical to the process is the way in which it helps to personalize and critique texts, people and response.

What follows is an excerpt from a teacher's journal, whose students have read and responded to the book *Krik? Krak!* (Danticat, 1995). In this entry, we see the power of reader response and collaborative inquiry in classrooms.

> "Okay, so everyone loves this book, why is that?" This is the second year in a row that many of my students' interest has been piqued by this book and they have asked to devour its pages greedily. Is it the cover that first attracts them—the colors, its sheen, an attractive young woman that looks culturally familiar to them? And then, as they read they become captivated, especially by the first story, as if they are involved in a mystery and all the secrets do not become easily divulged. Before we embark on

the adventure of reading *Krik Krak*, I always prompt a discussion on what they know of Haiti. Much of what they know is marred by negative stereotypes and ignorance like, "they eat cats over there, don't they," and there are ripples of laughter. However, since I do have some Haitian students the conversation becomes lively as they share their own cultural background. Then I split them up into book clubs and have them do their own analyses. Afterwards, we come together as a class and share their questions and insights.

Why are high school children so afraid to speak up? For example, I had them all write one question to the story "A Wall of Fire Rising," and you should have seen some of the questions! "What does the balloon symbolize?" "Why do Lili and Guy no longer have sexual relations?" "Why does Lili rub lemon juice on her skin?" "How does little Guy react to his father's death?" Of course getting them to ask these questions out loud in class is like trying to pull off gum from the bottom of shoes. I will have to remember that my students have wonderful (wonder filled) questions even if the room remains silent when provoked. I really wish I had enough time to ask all of their questions, to let all of them speak. Once they speak, they are a child who has just made the tottering walk without the help of mother's outstretched hands . . . I admit it. I do not develop a lesson plan with specific questions that the students have to cover. Instead I am more spontaneous in the classroom. For example, instead of deciding for the class, "today we are going to analyze the color red in *Krik Krak* as opposed to the European concept of red," I let them initiate a discussion, and then I play off their questions. For example, if we are talking about *1937*, and a student mentions how the mother flew in 1937 when she escaped from the river, I would ask them why the mother glowed red when she came out of the river. Do you know I didn't even have to ask them or worse, tell them right off, what 1937 meant in Haitian history. That was one of my student's questions and she eagerly answered it, while three other hands swept up to answer it. I love my kids! I am afraid I am rambling . . . I love my kids and the learning process.

As this commentary reveals, a literacy of promise "gives voice to the voiceless" (McElroy-Johnson, 1993). The primary purpose of dialogue is the presentation of diverse perspectives; thus, genuine discussion requires that all members of the learning community have a voice. Yet, contrary to promoting a literacy that encourages shared inquiry, research shows that most classrooms generally silence students. This silence is often triggered by a perceived need for control (McNeil, 1988). That is, teachers may feel a need to "cover" certain content and/or are fearful that welcoming students' ideas might lead to anarchy. Yet, as the excerpt above illustrates, when genuine discussion is sought and encouraged, teachers often find that they develop more positive and productive relationships with their students—relationships that are based upon equity and trust rather than upon a desire to maintain power.

A Literacy of Promise is Potentially Transformative

As history shows, literacy itself does not transform, nor does it necessarily lead to upward mobility (Graff, 1987). In fact, we would argue that a literacy that denies critique and that conceives of reading and writing as neutral "skills" can actually become a tool for advancing the status quo. Powell (1999) writes that

> In the United States, as in England and elsewhere, literacy has played a major role in transmitting the national ideology and socializing students into the mainstream culture, and the responsibility for teaching literacy (and hence, for inculcating dominant values through legitimating the dominant discourse) has largely become the province of schools . . .
>
> Functional literacy, in fact, plays a critical role as we move from an industrial to an information age. Consistent with a skills model of written language development, a functionalist model conceptualizes reading and writing as essentially neutral decoding/encoding processes. The possession of reading and writing skills facilitates the transmission of information, yet does not demand critical reflection. The functionalist perspective, therefore, allows individuals to learn the so-called facts of U.S. history without examining the various social and economic struggles that have shaped current policies. It permits the dissection of literary texts (e.g., symbolism, characterization, plot development, etc.) without a critical inquiry into the sociopolitical context that influences the construction and interpretation of those texts. It encourages a cursory reading of popular publications such as newspapers and magazines, without a deeper understanding of the historical developments that have led to contemporary problems.
>
> (pp. 16–17)

In contrast to "schooled literacy," a literacy of promise invites students to engage in social and political critique in which they deconstruct the cultural assumptions that support and perpetuate a hegemonic system of power and privilege. Thus, a literacy of promise challenges students and teachers to grapple with the "hard questions"—those that lead to a critical analysis of racism, classism, and other forms of oppression in society. The following excerpt from a teacher's journal is illustrative:

> I just did an exercise with my students on race after having given them a quote that said, "After all, there is but one race, the human race" . . . In addition, we read two articles about teens in the United States who considered themselves "multiracial" and what they were doing about this.

And in class we discussed a tidbit of English/Irish history. We had previously done some Irish literature at the beginning of the year so it connected nicely. This was in continuation of a theme of race, diversity, and oppression in the world and the triumph of the human spirit that I have pretty much targeted all year.

I asked my students to think about how they felt about race and to convince me to accept their viewpoint on whether or not they should have to categorize themselves racially speaking. What is interesting to note here is the classroom dynamics that occur when we begin a discussion on race or ethnic discrimination. Some of my students who physically represent the dominant group begin to get uncomfortable. Consequently, what I like to do is ask, for example, that just because the English government and many English citizens oppressed the Irish, does that mean that if you are English you should feel guilty? Naturally, the answer depends on what they have chosen to do as individuals . . .

As this excerpt suggests, a literacy of promise does not avoid the hard questions. Rather, it acknowledges that such questions are essential to overcoming ignorance.

One of the lingering results of cultural racism has been *internalized oppression*—the belief in and acceptance of one's inferior status. That is, a system of White privilege has resulted in a pervasive ideology where White ways of "being in the world" are viewed as "normal" and therefore superior to the cultural knowledge of others (Goodman, 2000; hooks, 1995). Because this worldview is embedded in the material forms and structures of society, many persons of color have internalized this ideology, leading to caste systems within marginalized communities themselves. As Diane Goodman (2000) writes, this negative internalization has been psychologically damaging, often leading to submissiveness and acquiescence in the face of domination:

> The control of the dominant belief system and major institutions results in psychological domination as well. People from both privileged and marginalized groups often begin to accept the messages from the dominant culture about dominant-group superiority and subordinate-group inferiority. For people from oppressed groups, this *internalized oppression*—the belief in their own inferiority—undermines their self-esteem, sense of empowerment, and intra-group solidarity. It encourages unhealthy, dysfunctional behavior. In addition, people from oppressed groups are encouraged to develop personal and psychological characteristics that are pleasing to the privileged group . . . As long as people believe that they are inferior or deserve their plight, consider their treatment fair or for their own benefit, or are constrained in their development, they will not effectively challenge the current system.
>
> (pp. 15–16)

For those from dominant groups, a system of privilege has perpetuated *internalized supremacy*—a sense of superiority and entitlement that results in a genuine belief that one has legitimately earned one's privileges (Goodman, 2000). Such psychological repercussions have encouraged members of privileged groups to remain oblivious to the pervasiveness of racism, thereby inhibiting their ability to form productive alliances with those from diverse groups and to work for change. A literacy of promise helps to expose the ways in which racism, classism, and other oppressive forces have damaged both the oppressor and the oppressed (Douglas, 1999). By encouraging readers, writers and listeners to engage in analysis and critique, a literacy of promise helps us to unlock the ways in which cultural hegemony is perpetuated through the cultural assumptions found in oral and written texts.

A potentially transformative literacy is one that truly educates. Acquiring information does not lead to power; *knowledge* does. A literacy of promise empowers both teachers and students, by illuminating the 'reality' of others and helping them to understand how certain cultural knowledge (the "cultural capital" of the elite) contributes to a system of inequity. A literacy of promise has as its primary aim the ability to use oral and written language for liberatory ends. Such transformation can occur at an individual level, by promoting academic involvement and enablement and thereby allowing historically marginalized students to have access to higher levels of social, academic and economic achievement. Transformation at a societal level is supported, by encouraging all students to work for social justice.

We would argue that students of color who are denied access to the literary traditions of historically oppressed groups struggle mightily to experience personal transformation. Research shows that literary texts written by authors of color often allow students to make meaningful connections to the text, and thus inspire active engagement and participation (Spears-Bunton, 1996). For instance, the video *Freedom Writers: Fighting Hatred with Language Arts* recounts the story of an inner city classroom in Long Beach, California, located in one of the toughest neighborhoods in the city. When students read *The Diary of Anne Frank* (Frank, 1999) and *Zlata's Diary: A Child's Life in Sarajevo* (Filipovic, 1994), they were able to make personal connections by comparing the lives of these young women to the violence they experienced in their own neighborhoods. These texts inspired them to write about their own experiences and to fight against oppression. Calling themselves the Freedom Writers (after the Freedom Riders of the Civil Rights era), their narratives have subsequently been published (Gruwell and The Freedom Writers, 1999).

We would further argue that a literacy of promise is essential for a participatory democracy. A strong democratic system requires vigilance on the part of its citizenry, whereby the decisions of those in power are continuously questioned and challenged. It also requires action beyond the voting booth. When students engage in dialogue about issues that really matter, when they critique the messages and assumptions found in texts, when they use literacy beyond the classroom to solve real problems, then they are learning how to use literacy for transformative ends. It is this kind of literacy that inspired fourth graders in Kentucky to save the highest mountain in their state from the destruction of strip mining (Powell, Cantrell, & Adams, 2001). It is this kind of literacy that led elementary students in San Francisco to confront a racist store owner and demand a public apology at a school assembly (Garcìa-Gonzàlez, Mejìa, & Porter, 1999). And it is this kind of literacy that inspired students in Portland, Oregon to take action against global sweatshops (Bigelow, 1998).

A literacy of promise does not just inspire individual transformation and upward mobility, but also encourages social transformation. That is, a literacy of promise invites social critique which becomes part of the discourse about what it means to be human and to act humanely; thus, it engenders and sustains the movement towards genuine social justice. A literacy of promise seeks wisdom and truth; it gives rise to social consciousness and transcends the boundaries of class, race, gender, ignorance, hopelessness and learned helplessness. In essence, a literacy of promise is one that can truly make a difference in students' lives.

Teaching and learning along the road toward social justice are lifetime occupations and must include "all" the people. More than reading and more than books, social justice presents a lofty yet realistic goal for our educational and political endeavors. As the world becomes smaller and our lives increasingly interconnected, it is imperative that we come to know and have opportunities to understand one another. Contrary to much of what we hear in academic and political discourses, it is not the bottom line that is most important, but the higher ground of human efficacy, knowledge and compassion which will allow us to construct humane and humanizing societies and institutions. It is difficult to treat those we have come to know as others with respect and sometimes even compassion when we have little knowledge of who people are as human beings and as members of distinct cultural, ethnic, class and gendered groups. We have argued that a literacy of promise is a main artery of the road to social justice. Travel along this road requires that learners, including teachers, act with the agency of determined minds and hearts moving toward the higher ground with a vision of what can be when many hands pick up the yoke.

Questions for Discussion

1. Think about your experiences with various texts. What texts have you read that elicited a more personal, aesthetic response? Why, and in what ways, were you able to connect with the text?

2. Think of your own experiences with schooling, and in particular your experiences with literacy instruction. In what ways did these experiences promote passivity? In what ways did these experiences challenge the status quo?

3. Consider the various characteristics of a "literacy of promise" outlined in this chapter. Share some instances when you think you have experienced a "literacy of promise."

4. What types of texts are necessary for promoting a "literacy of promise"?

5. In what ways is a "literacy of promise" necessary not only for the poor and disenfranchised in society, but also for those who are privileged?

Extension Activities

1. Find several texts on a related theme (e.g., poems, narratives, films, essays, articles, etc.). Design questions and learning activities that would reflect the characteristics of a "literacy of promise."

2. Examine films, literary texts, etc. for their underlying assumptions relating to race, class, and gender privilege. Discuss how racism, classism, sexism, and other forms of oppression can become embedded in the text as part of our "taken-for-granted assumptions" about the world.

3. Choose a common text that deals with a social justice issue. Ask students to free-write about a personal experience related to the theme. (Examples might include: Write about a time when you experienced violence; write about a time when you experienced discrimination.) Read and share students' texts orally. Read the common text and relate the theme to students' own experiences.

References

Anyon, J. (1983). Workers, labor and economic history and textbook content. In M. W. Apple and L. Weis (Eds.), *Ideology and practice in schooling* (pp. 37–59). Philadelphia, PA: Temple University Press.

Apple, M. W. (1982). The other side of the hidden curriculum: Culture as lived I & II. In M. W. Apple, *Education and Power* (pp. 66–134). Boston, MA: Routledge & Kegan Paul.

Bigelow, B. (1998). The human lives behind the labels: The global sweatshop, Nike, and the race to the bottom. In W. Ayers, J. A. Hunt, & T. Quinn (Eds.), *Teaching for social justice* (pp. 21–38). New York: The New Press and Teachers College Press.

Christensen, L. (2000). *Reading, writing, and rising up: Teaching about social justice and the power of the written word.* Milwaukee, WI: Rethinking Schools.

Dana (1992). This is a pseudonym. Personal journal response entry.

Danticat, E. (1995). *Krik? Krak!* New York: Soho.

Delpit, L. (1995). *Other people's children: Cultural conflict in the classroom.* New York: The New Press.

Douglas, F. (1999). *Narrative of the life of Frederick Douglas: An American slave.* Oxford: Oxford University Press.

Erickson, F. (1987). Transformation and school success: The politics and culture of educational achievement. *Anthropology & Education Quarterly, 18*, 335–336.

Filipovic, Z. (1994). *Zlata's diary: A child's life in Sarajevo.* New York: Penguin.

Frank, A. (1999). *Diary of a young girl.* New York: Scholastic.

Freedom writers: Fighting hatred with language arts (2000). Princeton, NJ: Films for the Humanities and Sciences.

Freire, P. (1970, 1993). *Pedagogy of the oppressed.* New York: Continuum.

Garcìa-Gonzàlez, R., Mejìa, P., & Porter, W. J. (1999). ¡Si Se Puede! Teaching for transformation. In C. Edelsky (Ed.), *Making justice our project: Teachers working toward critical whole language practice* (pp. 77–95). Urbana, IL: NCTE.

Goodman, D. J. (2000). *Promoting diversity and social justice: Educating people from privileged groups,* vol. 2. Thousand Oaks, CA: Sage Publications.

Graff, H.J. (1987). *The labyrinths of literacy: Reflections on literacy past and present.* New York: Falmer Press.

Gruwell, E. and The Freedom Writers (1999). *The Freedom Writers diary: How a group of teens used the power of the pen to wage a war against intolerance.* New York: Broadway Books.

hooks, b. (1995). *Killing rage: Ending racism.* New York: Henry Holt.

Klein, K. (2000) *Reflections from a New Inner-City High School English Teacher.* Unpublished poem from a personal journal. Printed with written consent.

Kohl, H. R. (1995). *"I won't learn from you": And other thoughts on creative maladjustment.* New York: The New Press.

McElroy-Johnson, B. (1993). Giving voice to the voiceless. *Harvard Educational Review, 63* (1), 85–104.

McNeil, L. (1988). *Contradictions of control: School structure and school knowledge.* New York: Routledge.

Morrison, T. (1992). *Playing in the dark: Whiteness and the literary imagination.* New York: Vintage.

Powell, R. (1999). *Literacy as a moral imperative: Facing the challenges of a pluralistic society.* Lanham, MD: Rowman & Littlefield.

Powell, R., Cantrell, S. C., & Adams, S. (2001). Saving Black Mountain: The promise of critical literacy in a multicultural democracy. *The Reading Teacher, 54* (8), 772–781.

Rosenblatt, L. (1996). *Literature as exploration,* 5th ed. New York: Modern Language Association.

Spears-Bunton, L. A. (1996). Welcome to my house: African American and European American students' responses to Virginia Hamilton's *House of Dies Drear.* In E. R. Hollins (Ed.), *Transforming curriculum for a culturally diverse society* (pp. 227–239). Mahwah, NJ: Lawrence Erlbaum.

Zinn, H. (1995). *A people's history of the United States, 1492–present.* New York: HarperCollins Publishers.

Zinn, H. (2003). *Passionate declarations: Essays on war and justice.* New York: HarperCollins Publishers.

3

"Unbanking" Education

Exploring Constructs of Knowledge, Teaching, Learning

LETITIA HOCHSTRASSER FICKEL

In the United States, education is often held up as a primary mechanism for achieving a more just and equitable society by expanding both the individual's and society's opportunities and possibilities. Moreover, literacy, broadly defined as the ability to decode, comprehend, interpret, and create written texts, is understood by most people to be the keystone of this educational process. However, far too many of our young people, particularly African Americans, are ill served by the current educational process. For them, schooling is a dehumanizing process that serves to limit, not expand, their life choices and opportunities. Of particular concern to those committed to an empowering education for African American youth are the literacy practices, experiences and opportunities to learn that schools and teachers provide. In his seminal work *Pedagogy of the Oppressed*, Freire (2000) presents a passionately articulated philosophy for a humanizing education, one that, through critical literacy, offers the potential for education to serve as a liberating and transformative force in society.

Though developed through his work in Brazil, Freire's philosophy transcends this context, offering insights and critiques relevant to current educational and literacy practices. His explicit focus on an interconnection between literacy, power, and oppression are particularly salient to the lived experiences of African Americans past and present. The central argument of Freire's philosophy is his assertion of the constitutive and generative nature of language; that is, that our reality is created by the language we choose to describe it. In the United States the cultural, social, educational, and legal languages used by the dominant, White majority have given shape to a vast array of oppressive and dehumanizing images, policies, institutions, and practices for African Americans.

Yet, paradoxically, literacy and the ability to own, shape, and wield knowledge and language, has historically been the cornerstone of the African American struggle to overcome oppression, thus liberating one's self and subsequent generations. A wide array of African Americans, from Frederick Douglas, Dr. Martin Luther King, Jr., and Marian Wright Edelman, to Langston Hughes, Maya Angelou, and John Hope Franklin, have used the power of literacy and language to provide critiques of and counter-narratives to the existing social structures and cultural viewpoint. In this way they have been instrumental in moving the

United States toward more fully living out its promise. As its own counter-narrative and critique of traditional educational and literacy practices, Friere's philosophy similarly holds enormous potential for creating an empowering and liberatory education that supports African American youth in fulfilling their life's promise.

Undoubtedly, Freire's call for a more humanizing education has inspired many teachers and has found root and blossomed within some classrooms. Nevertheless, for many teachers, fulfilling Freire's call to "unbank" education and unleash its transformational power and engender social justice has been a less than successful proposition. I believe this is because too often his educational and pedagogical arguments are distilled into a singular focus on the dialogic approach. Thus, the notion of liberatory education for many has become a simple methodological problem: we only need to change how we teach. However, separating pedagogical actions from the philosophical and epistemological roots that ground them renders them powerless as means to a liberatory educational end for students.

When we as teachers narrow our focus to only methodological issues it appears to allow us to sidestep the value-laden philosophical questions of "What knowledge is of most worth for students to learn? Why? And, for what purposes or to what ends should learning occur?" If we then go even deeper into these questions and begin to ask them with specific reference to our African American students, "What is of most worth for them to learn? Why? To what end goal?," the issue becomes even more complex. We must then confront our tacit, and sometimes uncomfortable and invalid assumptions, regarding our students' race, class, culture, ability, possibility, and the academic expectations we hold for them. Clearly, a purely methodological approach does not require us to examine and question these beliefs and assumptions about our students, or the nature of knowledge, teaching, and learning. Nor does it challenge our beliefs specifically about literacy learning and teaching.

However, in truth we can never escape these questions because our actions are our manifest answers. We either act based on explicit and thoughtful examination of our beliefs or act "thoughtlessly" from our unexamined and tacit beliefs. Either way, our beliefs and assumptions about knowledge, teaching, and learning matter greatly, as they give rise to our actions. This is why I believe that a teacher who wants to embark on the journey that can ultimately lead to a humanizing pedagogical practice for African Americans must begin with a critical examination of both his or her own epistemological beliefs and assumptions and those of Freire. What follows is a first leg in this journey. It is an exploration of Freire's philosophical framework and the expanding body of cognitive-constructivist research about learning, that illuminates the epistemological links between the two regarding the nature of knowledge, teaching, and learning, particularly as they relate to issues of literacy.

"Banking" Education

Freire (2000) refers to the traditional model of teaching as "banking education." He describes this practice as one where teachers make deposits of official knowledge in the minds of students who passively receive it, like one might deposit money in a bank. In this model of education, the teacher is conceived of as an expert whose role is to transmit a specified curriculum so as to "fill" the students with this predetermined content. The students, on the other hand, are understood to be empty vessels, devoid of ideas or knowledge until such time as the content is transmitted, or deposited, by the teacher. In this model, education is treated as a "gift bestowed by those who consider themselves knowledgeable upon those whom they consider to know nothing" (Freire, 2000, p. 58). This conception of teaching as transmission results in a definition of a "good teacher" as one who most faithfully and fully "fills" her students with the appropriate knowledge, and a "good student" as one who easily and compliantly receives and reflects back such knowledge. Furthermore, when teachers perceive themselves as the sole bearers of knowledge, they tend to view students as ignorant, and as bringing nothing of intrinsic value to the learning process. Such a characterization of students and teachers, Freire (2000) argues, reflects the attitudes and practices of an oppressive society.

The traditional "banking" model of education is founded on the epistemological belief that reality exists externally to humans, in the "outside world." Reality and knowledge in this "outside world" are assumed to be fixed, predictable, compartmentalized, and to exist independently from human experience, action, or thought. In turn, people are spectators in this world, who wait passively with empty "minds" for deposits from the external world, and in doing so, come to understand and to gain knowledge. This presumption by traditional education of a dichotomy between man and the world led Freire (2000) to believe it to be an inherently dehumanizing process; dehumanizing because it fails to recognize people as the primary actors in the construction of reality and the world. When students are treated as passive receivers of knowledge, their long-term experiences in this role result in a passive acceptance of the reality that is presented to them. They no longer see themselves as actors and creators in the world, forces that shape reality. In accepting both the fixed and transmitted view of reality and their passive role, they begin to focus their efforts on adapting to this unquestioned "reality" of the world. In fact, in the banking model, "the educated man is the adapted man" (Freire, 2000, p. 63). For Freire, this passive acceptance and adaptation is the essence of dehumanization.

Traditional assumptions of reality and knowledge also have implications for the content and structure of the curriculum. The typical banking curriculum tends to focus narrowly on content as a collection of isolated ideas, events, or skills, which are removed from the very context that gives them their significance. Such a curriculum inevitably consists, Freire (2000) argues, mainly of topics that are alien to the existential experiences of students. This type of fragmentation of skills and bodies of knowledge "creates the inability to make linkages" that would allow for the development of a "coherent comprehension of the world" (Macedo, 2006, p. 17). Moreover, such a curriculum mythologizes reality in ways that conceal certain facts or events that could help explain the way humans exist in the world. It fails to recognize humans as historical beings by portraying the status quo as the "natural" order of the world. In this way, it serves to reinforce a fatalistic perception of both the individual's situation and the human condition. In sum, both the process and the content of banking education "serve to obviate thinking" (Freire, 2000, p. 63) in ways that dehumanize the learner and perpetuate social inequality and oppression.

The "banking" model of education is a current reality in our schools and is all too frequently that to which African American youth are relegated. Many teachers still perceive students as "blank slates" who come to school with no knowledge. Of even greater concern are those who assume that their African American students come from a "culture of poverty" and therefore arrive with "deficits" that need to be "fixed" before learning can even take place. They are overly focused on gaining student, and parent, compliance and unquestioning adherence to school rules and protocols. The curriculum that African American students confront presents the worldview and perspectives of the dominant White middle-class culture as a given, what is "normal" and"right." Rarely are they offered more than a mere mention of the historical or contemporary lives and experiences of African Americans.

"Banking" Education's Roots in Behaviorist Learning Theory

This traditional transmission model that Freire describes as "banking" reflects the application of behaviorist theories of knowledge to teaching and learning. Such ideas and beliefs about knowledge have long been with us. However, formal behaviorist theories, firmly rooted in the positivist and modernist theoretical frameworks, serve to codify and give "scientific" validity to these beliefs. The epistemological assumptions of these theories hold that reality and knowledge exist independently of, and externally to, humans. Knowledge of reality is, therefore, received either through the senses, or transmitted to the learner by someone who already has attained this knowledge.

Behaviorist theorists such as Skinner (1954) argue that knowledge is acquired when the bond between a stimulus and response is strengthened by use of a reinforcer. In this way, learning can be understood as the accumulation of these bits of knowledge that must be presented in a tightly sequenced and hierarchical manner (see Shepard, 2000). Thus, in the behaviorist learning paradigm the teacher's role is to present reality to students by disseminating prescribed information in a sequenced and hierarchical fashion. The teacher is also to demonstrate necessary procedures, and then to reinforce and reward student behaviors that reflect the reality as presented by the teacher and texts. The student's role is to listen, rehearse and recite the transmitted information (Scheurman, 1998). The goal of the behaviorist model of education echoes that which was described by Freire as "banking" in that it strives to ensure that students replicate with fidelity the reality transmitted by the teacher. Since the knowledge presented for students to replicate is typically that valued by the dominant classes, or elites of the culture, such learning and the tandem teaching practices engendered by this perspective, generally serve to reinforce and reproduce the current, unequal, and oppressive social structure (see Anyon, 1988; Giroux, 1983; Oakes, 2005).

We can see this epistemological orientation to knowledge manifested in traditional literacy practices and curricula. Within the behaviorist paradigm we see two trends in literacy curriculum: the "functional literacy" model and the "cultural literacy" model (Cadiero-Kaplan, 2002). In a "functional literacy" model, teaching and learning focuses on the sequenced accretion of specific reading skills, as well as phonics, phonemic awareness and spelling. The learning in classrooms using this functional approach focuses on decoding words and responding to predetermined comprehension questions. The curriculum materials in a functional literacy model are further restrictive in that they typically include highly specific scripts for teachers to follow as a means to facilitate direct instruction of the skills and include specified assessments to monitor skills acquisition. As Cadiero-Kaplan (2002) notes, the emphasis in this type of literacy curriculum is on " 'learning to read' not 'reading to learn,' and thus ... does little to engage texts and stories critically or to engage the historical and lived contexts of student lives" (p. 374). This functional approach to literacy limits students' abilities to engage creatively with text by proscribing the types of ideas, images, and language forms they encounter in the curriculum.

The "cultural literacy" model reflects other aspects of the behaviorist paradigm. While it overtly recognizes the importance of the content, images, and ideas found in the curriculum, it limits and proscribes what that content should be. This type of curriculum embodies a "national image of cultural and social harmony" where "everything works out for the good of our citizenry" (Cadiero-Kaplan, 2002, p. 376). In treating knowledge as static and generated externally to human lived experience, this type of literacy curriculum seeks to "normalize" and "make natural" the existing social structures and the values, morals and cultural understandings of the dominant culture group. In this way it serves to maintain the status quo and cannot be an avenue for transformative learning. Rather, it is an adaptive model of learning in that students learn to "fit" in a world created by others. As previously noted, for Freire, this notion of learning as adapting to the "reality" of the world is the very process of dehumanization. It is dehumanizing because it actively negates the lived experiences of students who are not members of the dominant culture or social group. In doing so it fails to help them make sense of the world and their experiences in the world.

Freire's Humanizing Educational Philosophy

For Freire, liberation is the process of becoming human, which for him means living fully *with* the world and others, not simply *in* the world. He recognizes that achieving liberation is difficult, because the existing "oppressive reality absorbs those within it and thereby acts to submerge men's consciousness" (p. 36). Nevertheless, he asserts that liberation can be achieved through an educational process of conscientization that engages students in developing a more accurate conception of reality through the development of a critical consciousness of the world. In turn, this critical consciousness allows them to take action in their world and potentially transform reality.

Unlike the traditionalist or behaviorist view of knowledge as static and external to human consciousness, Freire (2000) argues that knowledge emerges "through invention and re-invention, through the restless, impatient, continuing hopeful inquiry men [sic] pursue in the world, with the world, and with each other" (p. 58). In other words, he views knowledge as the engagement of the human consciousness in the process of inquiry within the world. He does not believe humans to be separate from their world nor passive receptacles of knowledge from the world outside. Rather, they are actors in and creators of their world. As he writes,

> It is as transforming and creative beings that men [sic], in their permanent relations with reality, produce not only material goods—tangible objects—but also social institutions, ideas, and concepts. Through their continuing praxis, men [sic] simultaneously create history and become historical-social beings.
>
> (Freire, 2000, p. 91)

Freire's view of knowledge has implications for how he envisions the relationship between teacher and student, and their perceived roles in the learning process. If knowledge is taken to be internal to the human consciousness, then a teacher cannot presume that students are empty and devoid of ideas or knowledge. Therefore, unlike in the traditional model, the teacher cannot presume to be the sole bearer of knowledge or interpreter of texts, nor to be alone able to wield the power of knowledge in the classroom. She cannot think for her students, nor impose her thinking on them. Rather, both students and teachers must recognize that they are educated by and learn from each other. In this respect they are both "simultaneously teachers and students" (Freire, 2000, p. 59) and "become jointly responsible for a process in which all grow" (p. 67). Thus, teachers and students collaboratively engage in the process of becoming human.

Based on these epistemological assumptions about knowledge, Freire not only recasts the relationship between teachers and students, he reframes the content and pedagogical practice of education. To achieve his liberatory goals, he suggests that educational practice should focus on the "posing of problems of men [sic] in their relationship with the world" (Freire, 2000, p. 66). He argues that problem-posing education by its very nature breaks the vertical pattern of banking education by requiring students and teachers to jointly engage in critically thinking about and questioning reality and the human condition. As Freire (2000) explains, rather than attempting to submerge reality, "problem-posing education involves a constant unveiling of reality," and "strives for the emergence of consciousness and critical intervention in reality" (p. 68). In this sense, it is liberating because it demythologizes reality and emphasizes praxis, i.e., reflection upon the world and action in the world in order to transform it.

Since depositing externally derived knowledge is no longer the focus of learning in a problem-posing education, teachers and students must engage with learning in new ways. What Freire advocates is a dialogic method in which students become "critical co-investigators in dialogue with their teacher" (Freire, 2000, p. 68). He views dialogue as engagement in critical thinking, which he defines as thinking that perceives reality as process and as transformation. Dialogue is "the encounter between men [sic], mediated by the world, in order to name the world" (p. 77). For Freire, dialogue is the foundation of a humanizing education because it is the primary avenue for unveiling reality and developing a critical consciousness of the world. In dialogue, teachers and students engage in a curriculum that critically examines the human condition, and questions the "why" and "how" of that reality.

Unlike the traditional model, a problem-posing education necessarily takes humanity's historicity as a starting point (Freire, 2000). The curriculum of a problem-posing education begins with the "here and now," the reality of the situation in which the teacher and student currently exist. The content of such a curriculum is not developed decontextualized from the lives, ideas, interests, and experiences of the students. Rather, it is "constituted and organized by the students' view of the world, where their own generative themes are found" (p. 101). As learners identify problems, questions, and concerns, they generate themes for guiding their learning. Once themes are identified, the task of the dialogic teacher becomes one of "'re-present[ing]' that universe to the people from whom he first received it—and "re-present" it not as a lecture, but as a problem" (p. 101). In this way, the humanizing curriculum is a jointly decided upon and collaboratively crafted body of content that engages the teachers and students in inquiry about these significant themes and problems in life.

This does not negate the connection of such a curriculum to the structured subject-matter knowledge, represented by the systematic inquiry and ways of knowing in the various social and natural science disciplines, and the arts and humanities. Nor does it mean that teachers' academic expertise has no role in the classroom. Teachers should participate in generating themes not previously suggested that could help expand or deepen the inquiry, or help link the students' ideas and views to disciplinary knowledge. "Formal bodies of knowledge, standard usage, and the teacher's academic background all belong in the critical classroom" (Shor, 1992, p. 35). Rather, this type of dialogic curriculum development is better understood as a "synthesis between the educator's maximally systemized knowing and the learner's minimally systemized knowing" (Freire, 1984, pp. 54–55). Moreover, Freire (2000) argues that such a synthesis should be interdisciplinary in nature. For the learner, this can provide a fuller vision of the context of the problem, so that he or she might subsequently "separate and isolate its constituent elements and by means of this analysis achieve a clearer perception of the whole" (p. 95). Nevertheless, student knowledge, thinking, and perspectives remain a respected and central part of the curriculum, and formal bodies of knowledge are not "presented as facts and doctrines to be absorbed without question," but are "critiqued and balanced from a multicultural perspective" (Shor, 1992, p. 35).

A humanizing and liberatory educational practice for African American youth recognizes non-elite groups and individuals as active participants in the knowledge generating process. It does not accept the mythologizing of the traditional curriculum. Rather, the learning is rooted in the history, lives, struggles, and accomplishments of African American youth, their families, and their communities. Such a curriculum draws equally from the diverse knowledge embodied within the disciplines and the "funds of knowledge," the cultural artifacts and bodies of knowledge that are the inherent cultural resources found in communities (Moll, 2000).

Freire and Constructivist Learning Theory

For Freire a "liberatory" or "humanizing" educational model places human consciousness and knowledge at the center of the work, and sets as the educational aim critical consciousness for understanding and transforming human reality. Given this epistemological framework, Freire's ideas are clearly consistent with constructivist theories of knowledge (Finlay & Smith, 1994). Unlike behaviorists, constructivists do not make the epistemological assumption that reality and knowledge exist independently of the knower. Rather, they view knowledge as a human construction that is "intersubjectively constructed rather than being a reflection of reality in the mind of the knower"(Finlay & Smith, 1994, p. 75). The constructivist paradigm is grounded in the following theoretical principles (Shepard, 2000):

- Intellectual abilities are socially and culturally developed.
- Learners construct knowledge and understandings within a social context.
- New learning is shaped by prior knowledge and cultural perspectives.
- Intelligent thought involves "metacognition" or self-monitoring of learning and thinking.
- Deep understanding is principled and supports transfer.
- Cognitive performance depends on disposition and personal identity.

In the last two decades, cognitive researchers and constructivist theorists have challenged the behaviorist model of the mind and helped us come to understand learning as an active process of mental construction and sense-making. Research in this area has also illuminated how a learner's culturally rooted knowledge, the existing schema a person uses to engage in sense making, serves not only as a filter, but can actually modify the way an activity is experienced (Reynolds, Sinatra & Jetton, 1996, as cited in Scheurman, 1998). Moreover, the research has demonstrated that "expertise" in an area, that is "knowing," is more than a simple accumulation of facts and information. It is a principled, systematic way of thinking and representing problems. The complexity of thought and action embodied by this notion of "expertise" negates the behaviorist assertion that knowledge is merely transmitted from one person to another.

Furthermore, constructivists have helped us recognize that learning is a social rather than an individual process. The most influential of these theorists, Lev Vygotsky (1978), argues that learning is a socially and culturally mediated activity in which people work jointly to make collective sense of their world. Knowledge, therefore, is better understood as being co-constructed and distributed among individuals as they "interact with one another and with cultural artifacts, such as pictures, texts, discourse, and gestures" (Vygotsky, 1978, p. 90). This interaction results not in a personal form of sense making, but rather, a shared, public understanding of the object, problem, or event.

A central tenet of constructivism, and one that clearly resides at the heart of Freire's philosophical framework, is that language is the primary force in human learning and knowledge construction. The scholarship and research in constructivist theory has helped us better understand the constitutive nature of language as the cultural medium through which we humans create and stipulate our realities (Bruner, 1987). We humans use language, and other symbolic tools, to help structure our understandings and make sense of our world (Vygotsky, 1978). These symbolic tools—language in all its forms and uses—help people solve intellectual problems. Thus, language embodies the collective historio-cultural knowledge of a society, yet is also always in the process of changing, expanding, and transforming as humans use it to solve problems and engage in and with their world. From this epistemological perspective, knowledge, including language, cannot be assumed to be value-free or neutral, because it is, by its nature, shaped and influenced by the social activities that have given rise to it, and the ends to which these activities are directed. As Bruner (1987) explains, "language . . . can never be neutral, it imposes a point of view, not only about the world to which it refers, but toward the use of mind in respect of this world" (p. 121). Even though language and knowledge are recognized as value-laden, they are also understood to be dynamic and everchanging as people engage with and make sense of their world.

Learning generally, and literacy learning specifically, then is best understood as a collective process where people within the social or cultural group come to use, understand, co-construct, and transform sociocultural knowledge. Learning occurs for members through participation in joint activities, and language is the mediating structure for interpersonal meaning making during such joint activity. Yet language also becomes the internalized, mental constructions of memory and knowledge for the learner. Through the discourse that occurs within the context of the social activity, the learner constructs for herself the necessary mental functions and procedures for using the tool of language as a resource for subsequent individual mental activity. "Every function of the child's cultural development," Vygotsky (1978) argues, "appears twice: on the social level, and later on the individual level; first, between people (interpsychological), and then inside the child (intrapsychological) . . . all the higher functions originate as actual relationships between human beings" (p. 63).

As with behaviorism, the epistemological assumptions of constructivism provide a framework for understanding the role of both teacher and learner. However, these roles look far different from those suggested by the behaviorist "banking" model, and far more like those Freire suggests will lead to a humanizing education. In the constructivist framework the teacher is seen as a more knowledgeable other, who brings to the joint activity more expertise in the use of the cultural tools, such as language, and understandings of the world. This does not mean, however, that students are void of knowledge, understandings, or facility with cultural tools, including language. Learners clearly bring with them existing knowledge structures and ways of understanding their reality that will shape how they individually, and the group as a collective, go about their joint activity or problem solving. This theoretical framework recognizes the student as a knowledge bearer with existing and valuable knowledge, understandings, and language and literacy skills in ways that value his or her ability to serve as a knowledgeable other within the learning group.

We see this epistemological assumption reflected in Freire's (2000) assertion that participants in the learning process are teacher-students and student-teachers who each simultaneously teach and learn within the context of the shared activity. The teacher's role, then, will change throughout the learning activity, and she will serve variously as guide, mentor, collaborator, and co-learner as she challenges and leads the joint activity toward developing a shared understanding of reality that reflects all members' contributions. The role of the students is to develop both a culturally shared understanding of knowledge and language, and to experiment with and question the uses of language and knowledge. The ultimate goal of such learning is the development and identification of new understandings, needs, or problems in their world, not to accept and assimilate a predetermined understanding and worldview. Such a framework for learning, Wells (1994) argues, focuses simultaneously on learning the existing culturally valued understandings and knowledge of the learners' community and on providing for the continuous transformation, elaboration, and renewal of that cultural knowledge.

In this dynamic process of drawing on current cultural knowledge to create new knowledge, we can see reflections of Freire's notions of the dialogic process of shared problem-posing and problem-solving through engagement both with student-generated ideas, interests, and perspectives, and with more formalized bodies of knowledge. However, because of the constitutive nature of language (Bruner, 1987) we must look beyond the operative learning theory to consider carefully the content of the curriculum. For, if language is the primary "tool" for learning, and the process of learning is the construction of one's mind, then the texts one reads, the ideas one engages with, and the ways in which one engages with and uses language seem to be the key to a humanizing education.

As Wells (1994) explains, "What we learn depends crucially on the company we keep, on what activities we engage in together, and on how we do and talk about these activities" (p. 8). When applied to a literacy curriculum, the company that we keep are the texts we engage with and the way we engage with them. The ways we talk about the ideas found in the texts will have a profound influence on our literacy development, our personal investment in schooling, and our likely educational progress. So, while a curriculum that "affirms and legitimize[s] the cultural universe, knowledge, and language practices that students bring into the classroom"(McLaren, 1988, as cited in Cadiero-Kaplan, 2002, p. 376) is necessary, it alone is not sufficient for creating a humanizing education. What must accompany it is the commitment to the inclusion of a political and cultural context for questioning ideas, knowledge, perspectives, and texts. Thus, both the process of learning and the content of the literacy curriculum matter equally if we want education to be transformative.

Toward a Humanizing Educational Practice

While the constructivist learning paradigm informs our understanding of knowledge as socially constructed, and can inform us about how to teach, it does not and cannot inform us about what to teach if we wish to support a humanizing and liberatory education for our African American students. These theories do not illuminate the philosophical and epistemological issues regarding the questions, ideas, images, and perspectives that encompass a liberatory and humanizing curriculum. What resides at the heart of Freire's philosophy of humanizing and liberatory education is the development of conscientization; the ability to critically examine and critique the subjective reality of one's world. Conscientization requires that we unveil those forces in society that serve to privilege and oppress. To achieve this educational aim, teachers and students must engage in a dialogic process in which they collaboratively critique their cultural knowledge. They must question it so that they might ultimately act to transform it. Thus, the content of a humanizing literacy curriculum must include a rich variety of texts, ideas, and perspectives and these texts, ideas, and perspectives must be contextualized and embedded in the world of the students, they must emerge from their reality in order to allow for a critique of that reality.

What does it mean to engage in a dialogic process that contextualizes and embeds literacy learning in the world of our students? First, it means recognizing that we live in a world of texts. They are embedded in our lives in ways that we too often take for granted. We are surrounded on a daily basis by television, magazines, billboards, advertisements, movies, newspapers, and a myriad of other texts. These texts embody and convey important ideas and values that reflect cultural and social perspectives. Yet, we seldom ground our literacy instruction in an engagement with such ordinary, everyday texts, even though they contain powerful messages about reality for our students. To contextualize education for our students, we must draw from these sources and then engage with them in a critical examination of these texts. The purpose of this critical examination is to help students come to understand the texts as social, political, and ideological statements that reflect conceptions of "right," "good," "truth," and other beliefs about "the way the world does and should work." Such a critical examination helps the students unpack the texts to illuminate the hegemonic images they reflect so that the students can see how this hegemony operates in society. In helping our students understand these texts as statements of hegemony, we are supporting our students in the process of conscientization.

As teachers, in order for us to engage in humanizing and liberatory education with our students, we must ensure that we remain simultaneously focused on contextualization and critique. Take, for example, a literacy lesson focused on reading a newspaper article. Newspapers are common texts drawn from our students' daily lives, and a teacher who has her students read articles and engage with ideas found in the newspaper might rightly argue that she is contextualizing education for her students. But, how she has her students engage with the newspaper articles is critical. If she has the students read "for the facts" alone and questions them only on those facts, then the discourse pattern implies to the students that there is a single "truth" and "reality" that the text possesses, and one can understand it by knowing those facts. Thus, while she has drawn a text from the context of students' lives, she has used the text as a tool for "banking" education.

On the other hand, she could have them read the articles "for the facts," but then ask questions about how those facts affect their lives. The discourse pattern of this lesson at least recognizes the possibility of multiple realities and "truths" because it asks students to make connections or draw contrasts between the facts and ideas in the articles and their lives and reality. Such a lesson clearly reflects a constructivist learning theory and can be considered a student-centered pedagogical strategy because it communicates respect for and affirmation of students' lived realities. However, this lesson fails to be liberatory because it fails to engage the students in critically examining the cultural and political context of the facts in the articles. In order to be an act of liberatory education, a lesson or learning activity must support conscientization. To do that, the discourse used and the questions posed by the teacher must explicitly engage students in interrogating the social, political, and economic forces that created the facts. This is what Freire meant when he advocated for a dialogic teaching-learning process as the heart of a humanizing and liberatory education. As he wrote, "True dialog cannot exist unless the dialoguers engage in critical thinking" and the goal of this dialogic process is the "continuing transformation of reality, on the behalf of the continuing humanization of man [sic]" (Freire, 2000, p. 81).

More than Methods: Philosophy and Beliefs Matter

Clearly, social justice and equity are goals for which many educational practitioners strive, and more than a few have turned to Freire's work as a guidepost. Even so, large-scale research data indicate that traditional, textbook-bound practices of knowledge transmission pervade classrooms (Cuban, 1996; Goodlad, 2004). Why has so little changed? Why does the "banking" model still hold such sway? Bartolome (1994) argues that it is the consequence of reducing teaching to methodological problems, particularly with respect to teaching students from subordinated cultures, such as African Americans. This method's "fetish," as she calls it, is a mechanistic orientation to teaching that disconnects pedagogical actions from their underlying philosophical and theoretical principles. Too many teachers refuse to confront the value-laden nature of teaching and therefore do not question the content of the curriculum. They are content to tinker with the processes alone.

Unfortunately, in the hands of some, Freire's articulation of a liberatory educational practice seems to have been befallen by such a fate. As Macedo (2006) points out, liberatory teaching is often reduced to a simple, singular focus on the dialogue method. There are two consequences of this reductionism. First, focusing on dialogue only as a method leads to classroom practices where "sharing experiences is often reduced to a form of group therapy that focuses on the psychology of the individual" (Macedo, 2006, p. 175). The focus of the student-teacher dialogue in this scenario is altogether different than Freire's, whose notion of dialogue involved constructing a shared, critical perspective on the world, including the oppressive social structures. A "group therapy" approach is a rather literal interpretation of dialogic as verbal conversation, rather than a more dynamic understanding that would frame dialogue as a shared engagement and interaction with ideas, whether the ideas are presented verbally or through various media. Moreover, this focus on individual psychology frames oppression or social injustice as an individual "problem," rather than as a consequence of the current inequity in the social organization of the culture at large. The second consequence that Macedo identifies is the tendency for such a "laissez-faire method of sharing experiences" to result in "a new form of paternalism." This is because it diverts learning away from engagement with the political and ideological analysis that might help African

Americans gain a more critical perspective on reality (Macedo, 2006, p. 181). We can see here how instructional method uncoupled from the underlying philosophical framework loses its educative aim, and thus its power to transform students' lives.

Research has shown that teacher beliefs and theories have profound effects on the enacted curriculum (Clandinin, 1985; Elbaz, 1983). Thus, it would seem that a teacher who wants to heed Freire's call to engage in a humanizing literacy practice should not begin such a journey thinking that it is a simple matter of adding a method or strategies to one's repertoire, or using a newly developed, packaged literacy curriculum. Rather, the journey seems best begun by critically examining one's own philosophical beliefs and personal theories about the nature of knowledge, literacy, learning, and teaching. This reflective examination and analysis can be a door to its own type of dialogic learning process for a teacher, if it allows her to link together personal understandings with powerful philosophical and theoretical frameworks such as those offered by Freire. But, the sojourner toward a liberatory and humanizing educational practice must be willing to confront honestly her beliefs and personal theories both about teaching and learning in general and about the lives, talents, abilities, and possibilities of the African American youth she teaches. She must learn to be comfortable with the value-laden nature of knowledge and learning inherent in the educational process and be willing to explicitly insert these issues into the literacy curriculum so that both she and her students can learn to "read the world." Finally, she must be bold and confident enough to discard the "banking" model of education that has so bankrupted generations of people of African decent.

The journey toward a humanizing educational practice that promotes equity and social justice for all children is one worthy of a life's commitment. But, it is not an easy journey. It seems even more daunting in the midst of the current climate of increased standardized testing and the related scripted teaching programs that are epistemologically grounded in a behaviorist paradigm. Nevertheless, for teachers committed to equity, the resurgence of the transition model can be the catalyst for embarking on the journey toward a "literacy of promise." I hope through this exploration of Freire's philosophy in connection to our growing understanding of learning and literacy instruction that I have provided both a desire and a space for others to join in this journey.

Questions for Discussion

1. In this chapter, the author argues that teachers should not be concerned solely with teaching methods, but should also consider the "philosophical and epistemological roots" that ground them. What is your reaction to this statement?
2. What are some of the beliefs and assumptions upon which current educational practices are based?
3. Describe your experiences with "banking education."
4. How does "banking education" act to perpetuate inequities in society?
5. In what ways do the "functional literacy" and "cultural literacy" models act to maintain the status quo?
6. Discuss the differences between the traditional "banking" model of literacy, and Freire's notions of a liberatory literacy that involves dialogue and is grounded in students' lives.

Extension Activities

1. Create a diagram that compares constructivist theory with Freire's ideas of a humanizing education.
2. Bring in collections of various texts: magazines, videos, newspapers, "junk mail," etc. Consider what these texts tell us about our society. Create collages that reflect certain ideological themes that emerge from these texts.
3. Using a current news article (e.g., one involving violence), ask students to read the text for different purposes. First, have students read to retain factual information. Then, have students personalize the text by discussing how the facts relate to their own lives. Finally, consider the socio-political context in which the text is embedded. What historic, economic, political, and social norms and events shaped the current event? What are the values, beliefs, and cultural assumptions inherent in the text? Consider reading the text through different "eyes": a CEO, a member of Congress, a laborer, a person in poverty.

References

Anyon, J. (1988). Schools as agencies of social legitimization. In W. F. Pinar (Ed.), *Contemporary curriculum discourses* (pp. 175–200). Scottsdale, AZ: Gorsuch Scarisbrick.

Bartolome, L. I. (1994). Beyond the methods fetish: Toward a humanizing pedagogy. *Harvard Educational Review, 64,* 173–94.

Bruner, J. (1987). *Actual minds, possible worlds.* Cambridge, MA: Harvard University Press.

Cadiero-Kaplan, K. (2002). Literacy ideologies: Critically engaging the language arts curriculum. *Language Arts, 79,* 372–381.

Clandinin, D. J. (1985). Personal practical knowledge: A study of teachers' classroom images. *Curriculum Inquiry, 15,* 261–385.

Cuban, L. (1996). *How teachers taught: Constancy and change in American classrooms, 1890–1980.* New York: Teachers College Press.

Elbaz, F. (1983). *Teacher thinking: A study of practical knowledge.* London: Croon Helm.

Finlay, L. S., & Smith, N. (1994). Literacy and literature: Making or consuming culture? In K. Myrsiades & L. S. Myrsiades (Eds.), *Margins in the classroom: Teaching literature,* (pp. 74–88). Minneapolis: University of Minnesota Press.

Freire, P. (1984). *The politics of education: Culture, power, and liberation.* Westport, CT: Greenwood, Bergin-Garvey.

Freire, P. (2000). *Pedagogy of the oppressed* (30th Anniversary ed.). New York, NY: Continuum.

Giroux, H. (1983). Theories of reproduction and resistance in the new sociology of education. *Harvard Education Review, 53,* 257–293.

Goodlad, J. (2004). *A place called school* (2nd ed.). New York: McGraw-Hill.

Macedo, D. (2006). *Literacies of Power: What Americans are not allowed to know.* Boulder, CO: Westview Press.

Moll, L. (2000). Inspired by Vygotsky: Ethnographic experiments in education. In C.D. Lee & P. Smagorsky (Eds.), *Vygotskian perspectives on literacy research* (pp. 256–268). Cambridge: Cambridge University Press.

Oakes, J. (2005). *Keeping track: How schools structure inequality* (2nd ed.). New Haven, CT: Yale University Press.

Scheurman, G. (1998). From behaviorist to constructivist teaching. *Social Education, 62*(1), 6–9.

Shepard, L. A. (2000). The role of assessment in a learning culture. *Educational Researcher, 29*(7), 4–14.

Shor, I. (1992). *Empowering education.* Chicago: University of Chicago.

Skinner, B. F. (1954). The science of learning and the art of teaching. *Harvard Educational Review, 24,* 86–97.

Vygotsky, L. S. (1978). *Mind in society: The development of higher psychological processes.* Cambridge, MA: Harvard University Press.

Wells, G. (1994). *Language and the inquiry-oriented curriculum.* Paper presented at the Annual Conference of the American Educational Research Association.

4

Resistance, Reading, Writing, and Redemption

Defining Moments in Literacy and the Law

SHERMAN G. HELENESE, LINDA A. SPEARS-BUNTON

AND KIMBERLY L. BUNTON

Introduction: Standing in the Need of Prayer

We may not ordinarily think of the symbiotic relationship between literacy and the law. What does one have to do with the other? Law is the people's official agreement to establish systematic rules of conduct and behavior to govern the affairs of a particular national body. Literacy is often narrowly conceptualized as an individual ability to read, write and speak a particular vernacular. Indeed, literacy is too powerful and complex to be reduced to "the mere knowing of letters, words and sentences" (Freire, 2000). Literacy is the catalyst to social justice and ultimately social change. In the tradition of Paulo Freire, a person is not literate until he or she has become politicized, that is, become aware of the impact of social, cultural and political realities on their lives (Freire, 2000). Literacy leads to *praxis,* informed action. Thus, a literate person is able to interpret and manipulate the various forms of verbal language necessary to unlock the key to societal freedom.

Reading involves a quiet, sedentary, somewhat innocuous cognitive act. Aspects of character, such as morality and ethical behavior—a person's goodness and even godliness have been attributed to the possession of literacy (Heath, 1996). Differences in wealth, social access and opportunity have been attributed to possessing and practicing literate behaviors. These include the technical aspect of decoding and constructing printed texts as well as ways of speaking, the language(s) spoken, and fluency in non-verbal behaviors such as mannerisms, dress, eye-contact and gestures. The acquisition of literacy has also been described as an indicator of one's work ethic in a capitalistic society such as the United States of America because it is necessary to invest time, energy, intellect and often material resources in order to acquire literacy and to secure access to schools and libraries. People who cannot read are often considered lazy or trifling; the notion of shame or diminished personhood is firmly attached to illiteracy. Possession of literacy has also been used to identify or ascribe social class and economic privilege, and to exercise the right and authority of the law to sanction human activity including reading, writing and speaking outside the people's official agreement. For African Americans, to not own literacy imputes stupidity as a person and irrelevant citizenry in the face of legal institutional structures designed to prohibit, criminalize and punish literate people of color.

Because mainstream literacy is so intimately associated with the American dream, literacy is often falsely and negligently referred to as one of the great equalizers. Literacy does breed competence and competence *suggests* intelligence (Corley, 2003). Thus, equalizer or not, literacy is a power tool to be respected (D'Amico, 2003), and a power tool so coveted that those who possess literacy often stoop to acts of oppression to prevent others from gaining access to the education necessary to obtain even minimum levels of literacy: "Poverty pimps to the extent that while proclaiming the need to empower students, [educators] are in fact strengthening their own privileged positions" (Freire & Macedo, 1998, p. 11). These acts, while more savvy and sophisticated than the overt slave owner, garner the same result: oppression. As a result, oppressors, such as slave owners, took great effort in protecting the privileged status quo by actively creating, supporting and maintaining discriminatory laws designed to prevent human *things* such as slaves from obtaining access to literacy forums.

James Baldwin (1971) argued that if we can change the way we think about the world, even by a little, we can change the world. It is unsurprising therefore, that the people of the slave-holding south agreed to restrict the conduct of chattel property as a preemptive measure to prevent any shifts in the locus of control and power.

> . . . it was unlawful, as well as unsafe, to teach a slave to read . . . "If you give a nigger an inch, he will take an ell. A nigger should know nothing but to obey his master—to do as he is told to do. Learning would spoil the best nigger in the world. . . . " if you teach that nigger (speaking of myself) how to read, there would be no keeping him. It would forever unfit him to be a slave. He would become unmanageable, and of no value to his master. As to himself, it could do him no good, but a good deal of harm. It would make him discontented and unhappy.
>
> (Douglass, 2004, p. 34)

Douglass (2004) unveils the promise of literacy among African Americans; hope and intellectual freedom are possible even in the face of unspeakable circumstances. Herein, Douglass exposes the myth that intelligence does not exist behind an African American face or that whiteness constitutes enhanced humanity, enlightenment or morality. Douglass helps us to see that access to literacy and critical literacy practices, including contemplation upon one's life circumstances and the sources of discontent and unhappiness, are necessary developments in the decolonization of the minds and bodies of oppressed people. Literacy among African American people has historically been far more than an antidotal, albeit remarkable, individual achievement; it has also been a community resource and a vehicle for a people's survival, voice and transformation. Even a cursory study of African American slave narratives (Craft & Craft, 2007; Jacobs, 2007; Moody, 1990; Northrup, 1969), journalism (Hutton, 1993), letters and diaries (Wells, 1995) speeches (Hamer, 1993; Malcolm X, 1992; Terrell, 2005), and fiction (Butler, 2004; Cooper, 1999) yields compelling evidence of an interrelationship among: (1) the dependency of White supremacist economic exploitation and control on African American labor; (2) severely limited access to economic and social opportunities; (3) regularized White on Black violence; and (4) the power of the law to restrict conduct and to sanction human activity. Reading and writing, according to the dominant rationality, was a highly political, socially dangerous act consistent with physical acts of resistance, criminality and revolution. Thus, as we consider the persistent political, social and economic struggles of African Americans, we come to see that much has been defined by a struggle for literacy; at the heart of that struggle is the struggle for human dignity, efficacy and authenticity. Social justice for all is rendered poignantly palpable.

Underscoring contemporary notions of social justice is the economic, sociopolitical and theological history of a nascent, capitalistic super-power complexly founded upon the ideology of human equality and democracy, yet grounded in conflicting perceptions of race, class, culture and gender. The struggle for literacy among kidnapped Africans in America parallels the struggle to overcome legal, social, political, and economic barriers that were instrumental in maintaining slavery and institutionalizing a permanent system of privilege. An ideology of White supremacy demanded consistent, brutal, legalized mechanisms for structuring the "stupidification" of African Americans (Macedo, 2006). This ideology spawned the construction of malevolent social, cultural and theological rationalities that thinly masked the contradictions, dehumanization and moral degradation of Whites (Douglass, 2004). Through language, law and social customs, populations of citizens accepted idiocy as normative and as necessary to meet an economic end. White supremacists zealously guarded the promise that literacy offered African American people to reclaim their voices, tell their stories and take their freedom. Even so, despite the threat of death, and legal sanctions involving maiming and dismemberment, history reports that many African Americans not only 'stole away' and learned to read and write, but taught others as well (Franklin & Moss, 2000; Franklin & Schweniger, 2000; Berlin, Favreau & Miller, 2000).

Running, John Hope Franklin reminds us, was the most common form of rebellion on southern plantations. Unlike the general population of enslaved persons, runaways suspected of being literate were described as "intelligent, artful, and plausible" men and women who appeared to be very truthful (Franklin & Schweniger, 2000). Many of these persons were believed to carry forged manumission papers and passes. Literate slaves and later literate freedmen and women were seen as a political, social and ideological threat. Slave owners spent considerable time and resources tracking down runaways carrying illegal knowledge in their minds and threatening the foundation of the southern economy with their determination to be free. African Americans' struggle for literacy and freedom was earmarked by several defining moments; these events played a major role in establishing the foundation for a more judicious political, social and economic environment for all Americans. Among African Americans, social justice and participatory democracy remains dependent upon access to an equitable education and meaningful literacy instruction. Herein, we consider the law as part of the complex matrix of what constitutes literacy.

In the course of American jurisprudence literacy has been a vehicle for social transformation and a weapon for hegemony. Hence the entangled and often mangled relationship of literacy and law is an unbridled kaleidoscope that charts the defining history of the African American struggle. This chapter highlights some of the most important moments in African American legal literacy history. Specifically, we explore: (1) the impact of literacy on the delayed emancipation of slaves; (2) the importance of The Reconstruction Era; (3) the advent of literacy requirements for voting rights; (4) judicial review of literacy requirements; (5) the Voting Rights Act of 1965; (6) the "Modern-Day Literacy Test" presented by present-day felon disfranchisement; and (7) the so-called educational liberation of African Americans in *Brown v. Board of Education*. In this way, we will be able to examine the intersections between literacy and the law and the ways in which the physical and intellectual freedom of African American people have been defined in this context.

Delayed Emancipation: Interpreting the Word of Freedom

The Negro will only be truly free when he reaches down to the inner depth of his own being and signs with the pen and ink of assertive selfhood his own emancipation proclamation.

(Martin Luther King, Jr.)

On January 1, 1863, President Abraham Lincoln signed the Emancipation Proclamation declaring slaves of the seceded states free from the bondage of slavery. The restricted liberation was directed exclusively to those states which had seceded the Union to free their slaves, and expressly omitted Union and border States. Moreover, the Emancipation Proclamation exempted parts of the Confederacy that had already succumbed to Northern control. Still, the Emancipation Proclamation marked the symbolic freedom of designated slaves and explicitly shifted the message of the war to human freedom. This message, however, was lost on all slaves, particularly those slaves directly impacted by its expressed language of freedom.

There are many factors to blame for this communication debacle, such as the malicious intent and conspiracy of southern slave owners and the Democratic Party to conceal the emancipation (Ponte, 2002), and the lack of Union military resources and manpower to spread the word and enforce the word of the emancipation (Franklin & Moss, 2000). Ultimately one must conclude that the deficient literacy level of slaves enabled the conspirators to conceal news of the slaves' sudden freedom for a whopping two and a half years. Slaves had no direct or indirect access to the Emancipation Proclamation. Moreover, had slaves been provided a copy or access to a publication containing the language of the Emancipation Proclamation, their ability to analyze and interpret the extent of their freedom would hinge on their individual ability to interpret the language of the legal document. For example, while the Emancipation Proclamation provides a restrictive application, it is also very vague and ambiguous regarding the new relationship between the former slave and master. In fact, if one is not sufficiently literate, some language may be construed to suggest the continuation of the submissive role of slaves. Specifically, the Emancipation Proclamation states:

> And I hereby enjoin upon the people so declared to be free to abstain from all violence, unless in necessary self-defense; and *I recommend to them that, in all case when allowed, they labor faithfully* for reasonable wages.

It can be argued the term "labor faithfully" suggests "stay put" and continue as is—no change. The term "reasonable wages" hints at an ambiguous employer/employee relationship without paid wages. Notably, the Emancipation Proclamation does not require any slave owner to pay wages to its former slaves for labor, it merely "recommends" it. Such situations make it easy to create confusion among the literate, let alone those without formal literacy training. In fact, there are ongoing legal debates regarding the term "reasonable" (Issacharoff, Karlan & Pildes, 2006). Reasonable is a subjective measurement that shifts with time and experience. More importantly, news of the emancipation was stalled heavily because of the overwhelming lack of literacy among African American slaves. People held as slaves could neither deny nor confirm the credibility of their slave owners. Reading the newspaper, mail or other forms of written material simply was not an option. Thus, news of the slaves' freed status traveled at a snail's pace.

In fact, it was not until roughly two and a half years later, after enactment of the Thirteenth Amendment which outlawed slavery in all states, that many of the slaves freed by the Emancipation Proclamation learned of their freedom. On June 19, 1865, Major General Gordon Granger landed at Galveston, Texas with news that the war had ended and that the enslaved were now free (see e.g. juneteenth.com). As his first act, General Granger read to the people of Texas, General Order Number 3 which began most significantly with

> The people of Texas are informed that in accordance with a Proclamation from the Executive of the United States, all slaves are free. This involves

an absolute equality of rights and rights of property between former masters and slaves, and the connection heretofore existing between them becomes that between employer and *free laborer*. [Emphasis added.]

Historically, this day has been memorialized as an African American holiday recognized in many, mostly southwestern, states as "Juneteenth." Yet, as with the Emancipation Proclamation, the same problem of language construction and interpretation subsisted with the Order: what exactly is a "free laborer"? Here, the liberation of slaves is left to the interpretation of the savvy and experienced reader, General Granger. It can be said that a "free" laborer is still a slave and free to go nowhere. As a result, "Juneteenth is recognised as symbolic of how slaves were denied literacy by their masters" (Ponte, 2002).

Stony the Road: Constructing the Word and the World

They will starve, and freeze themselves in order to attend school, so highly do they value the privilege of learning to read, write and reckon.
(Gutman, p. 112, in Berlin, 2000)

Uncertainty marked the lives of thousands of African American people. At the time of reconstruction, we see a nascent, post-war federal government grappling with the formidable task of situating former slaves into society. Scholars have variously described the status of African Americans following the civil war variously as "neither slave nor free," or almost free. Freedom was a journey mapped like a malignant maze and later codified into law—an agreement of the people—as the Black codes or Jim Crow Laws. Even so, schools for freedom initiated, financed and maintained by African Americans flourished.

Union victory in the Civil War ended de jure slavery in the United States via the Emancipation Proclamation in 1863; however, before the end of war the proclamation was relatively meaningless outside states under union control (Anderson & Moss, 1991). In addition to Texas, Arkansas and Louisiana continued slavery for several years after the end of the war as southern planters reconstructed their livelihoods with the benefit of free African American labor. Slavery left the majority of the African American population uneducated and illiterate (Douglass, 2004; Franklin & Moss, 2000; Franklin & Schweniger, 2000; Du Bois, 2007). The vitriolic deliberateness of denial of access to learning generally, and literacy specifically, served the social, political, economic and ideological ends of capitalism and hegemony well beyond emancipation and reconstruction. Millions of unlettered, dispossessed free men and women were consigned to agricultural labor on southern plantations, where white employers and school officials conspired to take African American children out of classrooms and place them in cotton fields (Chafe, Gavins & Korstad, 2003). Chain gangs, leased by the state to planters, consigned African American children as young as eight to long arduous sentences and short life expectancy.

Partnerships among schools, businesses and the penal system placed African American children and their vulnerable, newly freed community at a perennial, egregious risk. Faced with the loss of wealth generated by free African American labor, former slave owners sought to control African American labor by establishing a labor and social system as close to slavery as possible. The struggle over literacy was as profound as it has been prolonged.

Even so, the Reconstruction Era was the first time the United States unilaterally acted in an attempt to reverse the horrors of slavery by enacting civil rights legislation. Notable legislative enactments are as follows: (1) the Thirteenth Amendment; (2) the Civil Rights Act of 1866; (3) the Fourteenth Amendment; (4) the Fifteenth Amendment; (5) the Military Reconstruction Act of 1867; and (6) the Enforcement Act of 1870. All were enacted during the Reconstruction Era beginning in 1863 and ending in 1877.

Collectively, these Amendments should be considered the "human freedom" amendments. Taken together, this body of legislation is astounding. The constitution of the United States was changed to not only abolish slavery (Thirteenth Amendment), but also to grant citizenship (Fourteenth) and voting rights (Fifteenth) to former slaves. This legislation overturned a way of life and the United States military was used to enforce the rule of law. The citation below from a woman who lived through slavery and during reconstruction provides an excellent example of why the military was necessary and is a poignant critique of the misapplication of the rule of law.

In her interview recorded in *Remembering Slavery*, Harriet Smith narrates the circumstances of the murders of her husband and brother following the Reconstruction Acts of 1867:

> ... they didn't like people up to date you know ... a church man, an' a politic man too ... He had a good learning. And he round up the votes, and that's how they come to kill him ...
>
> (Berlin, Favreau & Miller, 2000, pp. 325–326)

A more comprehensive examination of the issues of literacy and the law after reconstruction will follow. For the moment however, it is important to note the correlation this former slave women makes with the practices of literate behavior—her husband had a good learning and he used that learning to speak in group settings and draw both African American and White votes. Both murders occurred in a small community where presumably everyone knew who the killers were. Moreover, while murder is illegal, Harriet Smith reports that the boy who killed her husband lived openly in their community and "they didn't do nothing, didn't hang him up" (p. 227).

Legally No Longer Slaves: The Thirteenth, Fourteenth, and Fifteenth Amendments

The Thirteenth Amendment to the United States Constitution was ratified in 1865. The Thirteenth Amendment prohibited involuntary servitude by explicitly stating: "[n]either slavery or involuntary servitude, *except* [emphasis added] as a punishment for crime where of the party shall have been duly convicted, shall exist within the United States, or any place subject to their jurisdiction"(U.S. Const. Amend. XIII, §1).

Shortly after the ratification of the Thirteenth Amendment the Civil Rights Act of 1866 was passed over President Johnson's veto (Paul, 1972). The Civil Rights Act of 1866 was introduced to ensure that (from a constitutional perspective) African Americans in America enjoyed the same autonomy as their White counterparts. Together, the Civil Rights Act of 1866 (section 1), and the Freedom Bureau's Act (section 7) in the same year memorialized the basic freedoms and rights that African Americans were often denied. It provided for:

(1) the right to make and enforce contracts; (2) the right to buy, sell and own realty and personality; (3) the right to sue, be parties and give evidence; (4) the right to vote (if certain minimum requirements were met); (5) the right to full and equal benefit of all laws and proceedings for the security of persons and property.

(Paul, 1972, p. 11)

The Fourteenth Amendment to the United States Constitution was ratified in 1868 (Paul, 1972). It prohibited governmental action which impaired life, liberty, or pursuit of happiness and states as follows:

All persons born or naturalized in the United States and subject to the jurisdiction thereof, are citizens of the United States and of the state wherein they reside. No state shall make or enforce any law which shall abridge the privileges or immunities of citizens of the United States; nor shall any state deprive any person of life, liberty, or property, without due process of law; nor deny to any person within its jurisdiction the equal protection of the laws.

(U. S. Const. Amend. XIV, §1)

The Fifteenth Amendment of the United States Constitution brings us to the very core of our focus on the promise of literacy because it sought to guarantee voting rights. The Fifteenth Amendment states that:

The right of citizens of the United States to vote shall not be denied or abridged by the United States or by any state on account of race, color, or previous condition of servitude.

(U. S. Const. Amend. XV, § 1)

It is clear that the primary intent of the aforementioned text was to guarantee voting rights to African American males who were either former slaves or descendants of slaves. The Fourteenth Amendment also empowered Congress with the ability to take the appropriate legislative steps to ensure compliance to this and every other amendment (U. S. Const. Amend. XV, §1, section 2).

The Military Reconstruction Act of 1867 was one of the legislative measures enacted by Congress to enforce the newly codified civil liberties bestowed to African Americans. The Act provided for African American male suffrage in the South and conditioned readmission of Confederate states into the Union upon compliance with the terms of the Act (Grofman, Handley & Niemi, 1994).

The Enforcement Act of 1870

The Enforcement Act of 1870 prohibited: (1) state officials from applying voting and election laws in a racially discriminatory manner; (2) physical threats and economic intimidation against voters; and (3) conspiracy to interfere with one's right to vote (Grofman, Handley, and Niemi, 1994). Congress appointed special supervisors to observe voting registration and election procedures in the South. As a result, in 1868 over 700,000 African American voters were registered to vote in the south (Grofman et al., 1994). The newly enfranchised voters successfully exercised their power to vote by sending fourteen African American representatives to the United States Congress and two African American representatives to the United States Senate. These constitutional enactments were necessary accessories of the Reconstruction Era. The necessity of legislation demonstrates how deep-rooted the anti-African American sentiment was among most White Americans.

Klan activity became so pervasive that Congress initiated a formal inquiry regarding its activities. In fact, Congress passed the Ku Klux Klan Act in 1871. This Act enabled federal law enforcement officials to intervene directly in local matters that allegedly involved civil rights violations committed by Klansmen. Thousands of Klansmen were arrested subsequent to the passage of these acts for violating the civil liberties of African Americans. Despite the implementation of the Constitutional amendments and various other federal laws, racism was rampant in the South. In the course of Reconstruction, the political willpower to effectively enforce the campaign against discrimination was suspended indefinitely. Reconstruction came to an end long before the work of social justice and democracy was achieved. This work is our inheritance.

The End of Reconstruction: The Resurrection of Southern Rule

The end of Reconstruction was earmarked by the Compromise of 1877 and the presidential election of Rutherford B. Hayes. Like the 2000 and 2004 presidential elections of George W. Bush, the presidential election of 1876 was marred by confusion. Presidential candidate Samuel J. Tilden captured the majority of the popular vote. Problems arose when the electoral votes in a number of key southern states showed that Hayes was the victor. The ballot-counting techniques of the southern states were disputed by supporters of Tilden (Foner, 2002).

Political supporters of each candidate argued that their candidate won the election. The matter, therefore, was taken to the United States Congress. Resolution regarding the election was complicated by the fact that Republicans controlled the Senate and the Democrats controlled the House of Representatives. The divide in political ideology and control made it impossible to recount the votes to determine the victor of the election. The legislative bodies created an Electoral Commission to address the issue (Foner, 1988). The Commission recommended the following compromise: that Congress certify the Republican electoral in favor of Hayes on the condition that Hayes adopted "the policy of leaving the South to work out its problems free from national interference by withdrawing the . . . army from [the South]" (Issacharoff, Karlan, and Pildes, 2006). The compromise was agreed upon, thereby effectively ending Reconstruction via the withdrawal of Federal troops from the South. Without federal protection and enforcement, African Americans were unable to practice the inalienable rights that White citizens enjoyed. Consequently, few African Americans were able to vote and even fewer African Americans made it to political offices. African American political representation was significantly curtailed.

Southern racism once again gained a foothold in the South via the emergence of Jim Crow laws. Jim Crow practices openly called for racial segregation in all public and private facilities. Jim Crow also went so far as to undermine the spirit of the Fourteenth Amendment by implementing literacy requirements. Many southern states passed literacy requirements because they knew that it would prohibit most African Americans from exercising their right to vote. The literacy requirement was an ingenious and pernicious method of discrimination because the majority of African Americans lacked formal educational training.

Discriminatory Intent: Literacy Tests and Voting

Beginning in 1890 with the state of Mississippi, White southerners instituted a plan of discriminatory intent to exclude African Americans from voting (Issacharoff, Karlan, and Pildes, 2006). Following Mississippi's lead, every state in the deep South either adopted a new constitution or rewrote an existing constitution through "disenfranchising conventions." The intent of the contrived conventions was unquestionable: "Discrimination!" exclaimed Carter Glass, a delegate to the Virginia Convention of 1906. "Why that is precisely what we propose; that exactly is what this convention was elected for" (Woodward, 1971, p. 321). Thus, the coordinated malicious campaign to diffuse the African American vote began and literacy became the weapon of discriminatory intent. A by-product of this discriminatory campaign, the now infamous literacy test, was manufactured to assess the literacy levels of potential voters and ultimately, determine whether voters were "learned" enough to vote.

On the face of it, literacy tests were applied across the board to all qualified registered voters. However, when applied to African Americans, literary tests were discriminatory because the test administrators often exercised their own discretion to adjust the difficulty of the test. Moreover, at the time more than 69 percent of African American adults in seven southern states that adopted literacy tests were illiterate. Thus, random or iniquitous application of the literacy tests would not be necessary to prevent much of the African American vote. "In one instance, a rejected African American applicant stated that the registrar 'said what I was saying was right, but it wasn't like she wanted me to say it,'" United States v. Louisiana, 225 F. Supp. 353, 383 (E.D. La. 1963), aff'd, 380 U.S. 145 (1965).

African American voters were up against a losing battle. Such tests were so difficult that if applied today most Americans would fail them. The activity box at the end of this chapter contains an example of a literacy test that was commonly given to uneducated African American voters.

The test systematically eliminated the vast majority of the African American electorate from voting. The effect of such tests forced African Americans away from the ballot booths. Consequently, less than five percent of eligible African American voters were even registered to vote until the passage of the Voting Rights Act of 1965 (Grofman et al., 1994).

Challenging the Validity of Literacy Tests

One of the first literacy test cases occurred during the Civil Rights Era. In *Lassiter v. Northampton* (1959), the plaintiff, an African American female, was denied voter registration when she refused to take the North Carolina literacy test. The plaintiff sought to have the North Carolina literacy test declared unconstitutional because it was discriminatorily applied to exclude African Americans from voting. North Carolina voting requirements also incorporated a grandfather clause. This restrictive code required that:

> Every person presenting himself for registration shall be able to read and write any section of the Constitution in the English language. But no male person who was on January 1, 1867, or at any time prior thereto, entitled to vote under the laws of any state in the United States . . . shall be denied the right to register and vote (North Carolina State Const. VI, §5 at 988).

This law required registered voters to read and write a section of the United States Constitution. Moreover the grandfather clause essentially applied to African American voters because most African Americans, given their previous condition of servitude, were unable to vote in any election prior to 1867. In determining the unconstitutionality of the North Carolina voter registration grandfather clause the Court relied on *Guinn v. United States* (1913). In *Guinn,* the Court held that grandfather clauses were repugnant to the Fifteenth and Sixteenth Amendments. The court also ruled that literacy tests were permissible because the Constitution of the United States empowers the States to establish their own voting qualifications. Most states legitimized the use of literacy tests by arguing that such tests are necessary to insure "an independent and intelligent exercise of the right of suffrage" (*Lassiter v Northampton County Board of Education,* 1959). The plaintiff in *Lassiter* offered no real proof that the North Carolina literacy test was applied inequitably. The Court, therefore, could not directly address the issue of whether the tests were discriminatorily applied.

Lassiter is an important case because it was decided before the passage of the Voting Rights Act of 1965 and in the midst of the Civil Rights Era. *Lassiter* demonstrated the court's willingness to seriously and impartially consider the discriminatory effects that literacy tests had on African American suffrage. Although the Court upheld the validity of literacy tests, it also held that such tests would be deemed unconstitutional if they were unequally applied against African Americans. Attitudes were changing regarding the status of African Americans; the issues of literacy, equal access and social justice were firmly situated as sites of socio-political struggle.

As the struggle for citizenry continued, literacy remained at the center of the battle. Other court challenges followed. In *United States v. State of Louisiana* (1963) the United States District Court of Louisiana decided that Louisiana's literacy test was unconstitutional. Louisiana required its citizens to take a literacy test to qualify for voter registration. Applicants had to read, write, and give an accurate interpretation of various sections of the state or federal Constitutions. The Court found that the literacy tests were discriminatorily applied against qualified African American voters. Furthermore, the Court held that the interpretation requirement of the test was "unconstitutional because of its unlawful purpose, operation, and inescapably discriminatory effect" (*United States v. State of Louisiana* (1963) 225, F. Supp. 353).

In *Katzenbach v. Morgan* (1966), the Court decided the issue of literacy tests as it applied to New York State's literacy requirement and the effect it had on the state's Puerto Rican population. New York State's English literacy requirement denied the right to vote to all persons who received the equivalent of a sixth grade education in a Puerto Rican school "in which the language of instruction was other than English" (*Katzenbach v. Morgan,* 655). Section 4(e) of the Voting Rights Act states that no person who has successfully completed the sixth grade shall be denied the right to vote because of their inability to read or write English. The issue in *Katzenbach v. Morgan,* was whether Section 4(e) of the Voting Rights Act of 1965 superseded the conflicting state law of New York. The court held that the Voting Rights Act of 1965 prohibited voting requirements which made one's ability to read and write English a condition to voting (*Katzenbach v. Morgan* at 641). In this case, we note the foreshadowing of contemporary battles about language dominance in schools. Herein, we come to understand that the exercise of civic rights was contested on cultural, racial and educational differences. White supremacists sought to retain literacy as the privilege of White, English-speaking males and rather reluctantly of females. The fact that such practices are in direct conflict with the principles of a nation founded on the notions of freedom, equality and Godliness seems to have had no merit among the many proponents of the literacy test.

Nevertheless, enforcement of the Voting Rights Act of 1965 continued to progress. Barriers to voting registry were removed on a state-by-state basis. The State of North Carolina challenged the validity of the Voting Rights Act of 1965. In *Gaston County, North Carolina v. United States* (1969), North Carolina sought the reinstatement of the literacy test. The Court denied North Carolina's request. The court found that it would be unfair to reinstate literacy tests because "[n]egroes ... have for decades been systematically denied educational opportunity equal to that available to the white population" (North Carolina v. United States (1969) at 289).

Modern Day Literacy Test: Felon Disenfranchisement

According to a recent study of the 2000 election conducted by Jeff Manza and Christopher Uggen (2006), if ex-felons had been permitted to vote in Florida in 2000, Al Gore would have handily won the state. As sensational as this may sound, the number of state and federal prisoners is upward of 1.4 million—excluding the additional two million prisoners housed in local jails (Manza & Uggen, 2006). Once released from prison, these felons either lose their voting rights altogether or face delayed access to voting while on parole.

Once convicted, felons automatically lose their voting rights in forty-eight states. In thirteen states, felons lose their right to vote permanently, such as Florida where some 500,000 felons are affected (Marquardt, 2005). The remaining states restrict felon voting rights during incarceration and during parole only. These felon voting laws have been compared to the literacy tests common during the Jim Crow era by linking the theme of discriminatory intent. Like literacy tests, felon disenfranchisement laws have a disproportionate application to African Americans, particularly African American males. According to Daniel S. Goldman (2004), the percentage of non-White prison inmates nearly doubled between 1850 (during slavery) and 1870 (after slavery). Goldman expressly states:

> By the start of the Civil War in 1861, slightly more than half of all states had broad felon disenfranchisement laws. Yet by the end of Reconstruction in 1876, nearly eighty-seven percent of states had felon disenfranchisement laws, and in the decades that followed, many states revisited, amended, or created new felon disenfranchisement laws (p. 625).

Adding cause and effect to the argument, Andrew Shapiro (1993, p. 538) writes:

Narrower in scope than literacy tests or poll taxes and easier to justify than understanding or grandfather clauses, criminal disenfranchisement laws provided the southern states with insurance if courts struck down more blatantly unconstitutional clauses.

Yet, the ease of justifying felon disenfranchisement continues. Indeed, felon disenfranchisement has withstood the test of time even with constant scrutiny from legal scholars, civil rights leaders and advocates, and other social justice cheerleaders. In "Felon Disenfranchisement: A Policy Whose Time Has Passed?" published in the Winter 2004 issue of *Human Rights*, Marc Mauer notes:

American disenfranchisement policies are extremely broad and can be traced back to the nation's founding, when the Founders carried over the concept of "civil death"—the deprivation of all rights, dating from medieval times—to people convicted of a felony (p. 16).

Richardson v. Ramirez (1974), is the leading precedent courts use to reject constitutional challenges to disfranchisement laws. In *Richardson v. Ramirez* the Supreme Court found that the Equal Protection clause of the U.S. Constitution does not require states to advance a "compelling" interest before denying the vote to citizens convicted of crimes. Specifically, the Supreme Court said that Section 2 of the Fourteenth Amendment reduces a state's representation in Congress if the state has denied the right to vote for any reason "except for participation in rebellion, or other crime," and distinguishes felony disfranchisement from other forms of voting restrictions, which must be narrowly tailored to serve compelling state interests in order to be constitutional.

However, the Supreme Court clarified its position eleven years later, in *Hunter v. Underwood* (1985). The Supreme Court unanimously declared that Section 2 did not protect disenfranchisement provisions that reflected "purposeful racial discrimination" that otherwise violated the equal protection clause. In other words, the Supreme Court left the door open for challenges to discriminatory application of the felon disenfranchisement laws. Moreover, the court was not willing to extend disenfranchisement laws to misdemeanor offenders. The court held unconstitutional a provision of the Alabama constitution that disenfranchised offenders guilty of misdemeanors of "moral turpitude" after finding that the intent of the provision had been to prevent African Americans from voting and that it continued to have a racially disproportionate impact (*McLaughlin v. Canton*, 1995).

Still, the impact of felon disenfranchisement laws on African Americans is devastating. This is so primarily because many falsely believe these laws to be race-neutral in application and impact. Quite simply, the number of African Americans currently incarcerated does not support this naïve belief. Clearly, Americans must be educated on the impact of felon disenfranchisement laws. Moreover, it is compellingly clear that neither literacy nor the law is race-neutral.

Closing the Educational Gap: Brown v. Board of Education

During the Reconstruction era, there emerged a concerted effort to educate former slaves. After years in bondage in which they were denied the opportunity to read and write, African Americans were hungry for literacy. So eager were African Americans to become educated that they began building schools, churches, and meeting halls even before the governmental assistance of the Freedman's Bureau. It was the Freedman's Bureau, however, that organized the educational efforts during Reconstruction. During the five years of its existence, the bureau built 4,300 schools, as well as Howard, Fisk, Storer and Hampton universities. Katz (1971, p. 242) writes that these schools were quite successful. One witness to a school in North Carolina observed that "'A child six years old, her mother, a grandmother and great-grandmother, the latter over 75 years of age. . . commenced their alphabet together and each one can read the Bible fluently.'" In Tennessee, an observer noted that "'The colored people are far more zealous in the cause of education than the whites. They will starve themselves, and go without clothes, in order to send their children to school.'"

Freedman Bureau efforts were greeted with animosity from the majority of White southerners. Opponents to African American education feared African American political dominance in the South; consequently, most African Americans were openly and not infrequently violently discouraged from becoming educated (Anderson & Moss, 1991). Added discouragement stemmed from the fact that most education centers were inaccessible, understaffed, and poorly funded, and therefore could not accommodate all the African Americans who sought to be educated. Despite these barriers, however, their zeal for education continued throughout the nineteenth century. A New England reformer, who traveled 3,500 miles through the South, writes in 1891: "In some sections, the eagerness of the colored people for knowledge amounts to an absolute thirst" (Katz, 1971, p. 353).

This quest for a quality education continued into the twentieth century. In 1951, thirteen courageous Topeka, Kansas parents sought to liberate their twenty children from the clutches of the inequitable Topeka school system by calling for the end of segregated education (*Brown v. Board*, 1954). The parents filed against the Board of Education of the City of Topeka, Kansas in the U.S. District Court for the District of Kansas. At the time of the filing, the Topeka Board of Education, under an 1879 Kansas law, permitted (but did not require) districts to maintain separate elementary schools for African American and White students in twelve communities with populations of over 15,000. The case of

Brown v. Board of Education was heard before the Supreme Court and combined three other NAACP sponsored cases: *Briggs v. Elliott* (filed in South Carolina), *Davis v. County School Board of Prince Edward County* (filed in Virginia), and *Gebhart v. Belton* (filed in Delaware). Ultimately, the Supreme Court ruled in favor of the parents, holding that racial segregation of students in public schools violates the Equal Protection Clause of the Fourteenth Amendment, because separate facilities are inherently unequal. Chief Justice Earl Warren wrote:

> Today, education is perhaps the most important function of state and local governments. Compulsory school attendance laws and the great expenditures for education both demonstrate our recognition of the importance of education to our democratic society. It is required in the performance of our most basic public responsibilities, even service in the armed forces. It is the very foundation of good citizenship. Today it is a principal instrument in awakening the child to cultural values, in preparing him for later professional training, and in helping him to adjust normally to his environment. In these days, it is doubtful that any child may reasonably be expected to succeed in life if he is denied the opportunity of an education. Such an opportunity, where the state has undertaken to provide it, is a right which must be made available to all on equal terms.

Brown set the stage for equity in education. Legally, African Americans were provided full access to educational opportunities afforded to Whites. The access was not without controversy. Though *Brown* laid the foundation and set precedent for all schools in America, many states and schools districts were vigorously resistant to the idea of integration.

In Virginia, Senator Harry F. Byrd, Sr. organized the Massive Resistance movement on February 25, 1956. The Massive Resistance movement was responsible for laws passed in 1958. Intended to prevent the integration of schools, the law legalized closing schools as a remedy to desegregation. In Arkansas, Governor Orval Faubus called the state's National Guard to block the nine "African American students" (Little Rock Nine) entry to Little Rock High School. President Dwight Eisenhower responded by deploying elements of the 101st Airborne Division from Fort Campbell, Kentucky to Arkansas and by federalizing Faubus' National Guard.

More than fifty years later, the *Brown* decision continues to face scrutiny and controversy. Both conservatives and liberals alike wrestle with the impact of this landmark decision. Catharine Prendergast (2003) contends in *Literacy and Racial Justice: the Politics of Learning after Brown v. Board of Education* that it is a shared understanding of literacy as White property which continues to impact problematic classroom dynamics and education practices. Literacy, Prendergast argues, has historically been recognized as "White property" throughout American history in its courts, laws, markets, and literacy initiatives. Prendergast opines that *Brown* awarded access to literacy in the schools to all Americans, triggering the site for literacy training to shift away from the traditional school setting and resulting in "white flight": "The ideology of literacy has been sustained primarily as a response to perceived threats to White property interests, White privilege, the maintenance of 'White' identity, or the conception of America as a White nation" (Prendergast, 2003, p. 7).

Providing evidence of her theory, Prendergast points to education initiatives with heavy literacy emphasis such as *No Child Left Behind.* According to Prendergast, *No Child Left Behind* is besieged with standardized tests, perfunctory approaches to literacy instruction, and systemic calls for assessment and accountability—all of which, she contends, use literacy to divide rather than unite. Thus, over a half-century later, *Brown* continues to befuddle even the most savvy and well-intentioned in its application.

Sankofa: We Have Come This Far

The literal meaning of Sankofa in the Adinkra language is to return (*san*) and go or seize (*ks*), what was left behind (*fa*). Sankofa, represented as a bird with its head leaning backward in the direction of its tail while flying forward, is a guide to the future and at the same time, it is a critically necessary reminder of the past (Willis, 1998). It is thus a fitting intellectual and metaphorical space in which to conclude the legal exploration of our journey toward a literacy of promise, and at the same time move forward and above the structural and ideological shackles which have circumscribed our past and threaten to nullify our future. Despite the spins and disgraceful twists of some political pundits, race really does matter in America (West, 2001).

The pervasiveness of racism in American society often undermined hard fought and long earned gains. Civil equality occurred, dissipated, reoccurred; some arguably contend that such liberties are once again being chipped away. Literacy however, persists as an ideological and pragmatic site in the struggle for social justice. The laws of the land, that is, the people's agreements, are marked by defining moments of conflict, contention, and confusion in a poignant struggle to be wholly free in a democracy.

From Reconstruction to the Civil Rights Movement, the means for emancipation developed its stronghold in literacy. The eloquent words of African American leaders such as Ida B. Wells, W. E. B. Du Bois, Septima Clark, Martin Luther King and hundreds of unsung heroes/sheroes served as the catalyst of the Civil Rights Movement and inscribed social change with human decency and justice. Education and literacy also led to empowerment by leading individuals to form political coalitions that fostered change. Thus for African Americans, literacy has served as a double-edged sword. Quite literally, literacy has meant life and death and, at times, despair and frustration. Literacy has also come to mean hope, empowerment, agency and social change. It may be argued that literacy is the pragmatic representation of the symbolic meaningfulness of Sankofa; a spiritual mindset which guides individuals to deliberate and to collect data before and during attempts to complete a task.

Political power and change in the United States was fostered by African American participation in the political process. In bondage, African Americans had no rights that any White person was obliged to respect. Emancipation and Reconstruction afforded African Americans some political and economic autonomy. This autonomy led to the creation of prestigious African American universities and colleges. These colleges nurtured the leadership to successfully challenge Jim Crow and organize considerable anti-discrimination campaigns. These challenges undoubtedly influenced the American judicial political system in its removal of the Jim Crow laws, overt racial discrimination, and voting literacy requirements. Literacy and the law remain inexorably intertwined in the African American struggle for social justice. In the worldview of Adinkra people, understood by millions of kidnapped west Africans, literacy is the seed the Sankofa bird carries in its mouth; it contains the essence of what is needed to succeed in our journey toward a literacy of promise.

Questions for Discussion

1. Literacy Test: determine your eligibility to vote. One incorrect answer disqualifies you from casting a ballot.

   a. Which of the following is a right protected by the Bill of Rights? (a) Public Education, (b) Voting, (c) Employment, or (d) Trial by Jury.

   b. The federal census of population is taken every five years. (True or False.)

   c. If a person is indicted for a crime, name two rights which he has.

   d. A United States senator elected at the general election in November takes office the following year on what date?

   e. A President elected at the general election in November takes office the following year on what date?

   f. Which definition applies to the word "Amendment?" (a) proposed change, as in a Constitution, or (b) making of peace, or (c) a part of the government.

   g. A person appointed to the United States Supreme Court is appointed for a term of _.

   h. When the Constitution was approved by the original colonies, how many states had to ratify it in order for it to be in effect?

   i. Does enumeration affect the income tax levied on citizens in various states?

2. In what ways might literacy be considered a "power tool" in contemporary America?

3. In what ways can it be said that tests continue to define winners and losers in our society?

4. According to the Thirteenth Amendment, what two definitions of free labor may be developed? In what ways does your definition apply to the separate but equal law?

5. Explore the laws governing the disenfranchisement of convicted felons. How are these laws similar to literacy tests?

Extension Activities

Explore the Massive Resistance Movement that was passed in 1958.

References

Anderson, E. & Moss, A. A. (1991). *The facts of reconstruction: Essays in honor of John Hope Franklin.* Baton Rouge, LA: Louisiana State University Press.

Aptheker, H. (1993). *Documentary history of the Negro people in the United States.* Minneapolis, MN: Tandem Library Books.

Ball, H., Krane, D., & Lauth, T. P. (1982). *Comprised compliance of the 1965 Voting Act.* CT: Greenwood Press.

Baldwin, J. (1971). Foreword. In L. Meriwether, *Daddy was a numbers runner* (pp. 7–9). NY: Pyramid Books.

Berlin, I., Favreau, M. & Miller, S. F. (2000). *Remembering slavery: African Americans talk about their personal experiences of slavery and freedom.* NY: The New Press.

Birnbaum, J., & Taylor, C. (2000). Introduction: The modern civil rights movement. In J. Birnbaum & C. Taylor (Eds.), *Civil rights since 1787: A reader on the black struggle* (pp. 327–330). NY: New York University Press.

Butler, O. (2004). *Kindred* (25th anniversary ed.). Boston: Beacon Press.

Chafe, W. H., Gavins, R., & Korstad, R. (Eds.) (2003). *Remembering Jim Crow: African Americans tell about life in the segregated south.* NY: The New Press.

Coleman, P. (1993). *Fannie Lou Hamer and the fight for the vote.* CT: Milbrook Press.

Cooper, J. C. (1999). *The wake of the wind.* NY: Knopf.

Corley, M. A. (2003). *Poverty, racism and literacy,* ERIC Digest No. 243, Charleston, WV: ERIC/CRESS, Appalachia Education Laboratory.

Cornelius, J. Duitsman. (2000). Literacy, slavery and religion. In J. Birnbaum & C. Taylor (Eds.), *Civil rights since 1787: A reader on the black struggle* (pp. 85–89). NY: New York University Press.

Cornelius, J. (1983). We slipped and learned to read: Slave accounts of the literacy process, 1830–1865. *Phylon,* 44(3), 171–186.

Craft, W., & Craft, E. (2007). *Running a thousand miles for freedom: Or the escape of William and Ellen Craft from slavery.* Charleston, SC: BiblioBazaar.

D'Amico, D. (2003). Race, class, gender, and sexual orientation in adult literacy: power, pedagogy, and programs. In *Review of Adult Learning and Literacy, Volume 4* (pp. 37–69). Philadelphia, PA: Lawrence Erlbaum Associates.

Diouf, S. A. (1999). American slaves who were readers and writers. *The Journal of Blacks in Higher Education,* 24, 124–125.

Douglass, F. (2004). *Life and times of Frederick Douglass written by himself.* Reprinted from the revised edition of 1892. Whitefish, MT: Kessinger Publishing, LLC.

Du Bois, W. E. B. (2007). *The souls of black folk.* NY: Oxford University Press.

Foner, E. (2002). *Reconstruction, pt. 2: America's unfinished revolution, 1863–1877.* NY: Harper Collins.

Foner, P. (1988). The International Slave Trade. In J. Birnbaum and C. Taylor (Eds.), *Civil rights since 1878: A reader on the black struggle,* (pp. 9–15). New York: New York University Press.

Franklin, J. H. (1993). The Emancipation Proclamation: An act of justice, *Prologue Magazine,* 25(2).

Franklin, J. H., & Moss, A. (2000). *From slavery to freedom* (8th ed.). NY: Knopf Publishing Group.

Franklin, J. H., & Schweninger, L. (2000). *Runaway slaves: Rebels on the plantation.* NY: Oxford University Press.

Freire, A. M., & Macedo, D. (1998). *Paulo Freire reader.* NY: Continuum International.

Freire, P. (2000). *Pedagogy of the oppressed* (30th anniversary ed). London: Continuum International.

Goldman, D. S. (2004). *The modern-day literacy test?: Felon disenfranchisement and race discrimination.* Stanford Law Review, 57(2), 611–656.

Grofman, B., Handley, L., & Niemi, R. G. (1994). *Minority representation and the quest for voting equality.* NY: Cambridge University Press.

Heath, S. B. (1996). Society and literacy. In R. Barr, M. Kamil, P. Mosenthal, & P. D. Pearson (Eds.), *Handbook of reading research, vol. II* (pp. 3–25). Mahwah, NJ: Lawrence Erlbaum Associates.

Hutton, F. (1993). *The early black press in America 1827–1860.* CT: Greenwood.

Issacharoff, S., Karlan, P., & Pildes, R. (2006). *The law of democracy: Legal structure of the political process* (2nd ed.). Eagan, MN: Thomas West.

Jacobs, H. (2007). *Incidents in the life of a slave girl.* Charleston, SC: BiblioBazaar.

Katz, W. L. (1971). *Eyewitness: The negro in American history.* NY: Pittman.

Lassiter v North Hampton County Board of Elections, 360 U.S. 45 (1959).

Lincoln, A. (1863). *The emancipation proclamation.* Washington, DC: The National Archives and Records Administration.

Macedo, D. (2006). *Literacies of power: What Americans are not allowed to know.* Boulder, CO: Westview Press.

Manza, J., & Uggen, C. (2006). *Locked out: Felon disenfranchisement and American democracy.* NY: Oxford University Press.

Marquardt, S. (2005). Deprivation of a felon's right to vote: Constitutional concerns, policy issues and suggested reform for felony disenfranchisement law. *University of Detroit Mercy Law Review, 82*(2), 279–302.

Mauer, M. (2004). Felon disenfranchisement: a policy whose time has passed? *Human Rights, 31*(1), 16–18.

Moody, J. K. (1990). Ripping away the veil of slavery: Literacy, communal love, and self-esteem in three slave women's narratives. *Black American Literature Forum, 24*(4), 633–648.

Northrup, S. (1969). Twelve years a slave, narrative of Solomon Northrup. In G. Osofsky (Ed.), *Puttin' on ole massa: The slave narratives of Henry Bibb, William Wells Brown, and Solomon Northrup.* NY: Harper and Row.

Paul, A. (1972). *Black Americans and the Supreme Court since emancipation: Betrayal or protection?* NY: Holt, Rinehart & Winston.

Ponte, L. (2002). *Juneteenth.* Retrieved on July 28, 2007 from http://www.frontpagemag.com/Articles/ReadArticle.asp?ID=1116.

Prendergast, C. (2003). *Literacy and racial justice: The politics of learning after Brown v. Board of Education.* Carbondale, IL: University of Southern Illinois Press.

Shapiro, A. (1993). Challenging criminal disenfranchisement under the voting act: A new strategy, *Yale Law Journal, 103,* 537–556.

Terrell, M. C. (2005). *Colored woman in a white world.* NY: Prometheus.

Wells, I. B. (1995). *An intimate portrait of the activist as a young woman.* NY: Beacon Press.

West, C. (2001). *Race matters* (2nd ed.). NY: Vintage Books.

Willis, W. B. (1998). *The Adinkra dictionary: A visual primer of the language of the Adinkra.* Washington, DC: Pyramid.

Woodson, C. G. (2006). *The mis-education of the negro.* San Diego, CA: The Book Tree.

Woodward, C. V. (1971). *Origins of the new south, 1877–1913.* Baton Rouge, LA: Louisiana State University Press.

X, Malcolm. (1992). *The autobiography of Malcolm X.* NY: Ballantine Books.

II
Realizing a Literacy of Promise through Literary Texts

5

"Educational, Controversial, Provocative, and Personal"
Three African American Adolescent Males Reflect on Critically Framing A Lesson Before Dying

JULIA JOHNSON CONNOR AND ARLETTE INGRAM WILLIS

The white people out there are saying that you don't have it— that you're a hog, not a man. But I know they are wrong. You have the potential. We all have, no matter who we are . . . I want you to show them the difference between what they think you are and what you can be.

(Gaines, 1997, p. 191)

During the 1999 spring semester we undertook a research project that explored critically framed reader response in a secondary English classroom in a local public high school. Along with the assigned classroom teacher, we co-taught a semester-long "Minority Authors" elective, a de-tracked English class of twenty-four juniors and seniors.

After the first class, Mrs. Smith proclaimed "It is so nice having y'all here, I don't have to work so hard to gain their trust." We mulled over her statement, not having experienced anything quite as profound as trust, and waited for our senses to be heightened throughout the semester. It was a statement, nonetheless, that we would recall, much like one by Shakespear (1999). Eileen Shakespear relied upon a cultural broker because she was able to facilitate small discussion groups where African American male high school students talked in "an open and uninhibited exchange" (p. 82). Both Mrs. Smith (a pseudonym) and Shakespear seemed to presume that there would be a more open dialogue among African Americans. We kept these thoughts in mind as we interacted with students, watched them grow, and learned along with them. However, we did not envision their response to us as a matter of trust; we understood their response as respectful and hopeful.

We observed early on that the majority of the African American male students (seven in total) were performing superbly in class. The "light in their eyes" (Nieto, 1999) was unmistakable. Outwardly, they appeared to be the exact same students that mainstream society regards as "at-risk," with "behavioral problems," and generally in need of control, fixing, or alternative education. However, in our class these students were succeeding. That is, they were reading, and contributing to the classroom community's knowledge without behavioral problems.

This chapter is part of a larger study on critically framing reader response to multiethnic literature in the high school. Here, we focus on two different yet related questions. First, we wanted to understand what was happening or working differently in this class for the African American males. Critically framing literacy, in any class, can be a risk, as students respond personally to the text. It can be a greater risk when in a diverse setting you engage a text that clearly discusses issues of race and institutional racism. Second, we wanted to better understand how the African American males would respond to a critically framed reader response unit for the novel *A Lesson Before Dying* (Gaines, 1997). In this chapter, we share three case study portraits of African American males as representative of the group, and as representative of the complexities that surround their engagement within the context and the text.

Ethnographic data including participant observations, videotaped class sessions, audio-taped interviews and student responses to literature, as well as student artistic and written work were collected over fifteen weeks. Minority Authors met daily at a large public high school in a mid-western college town. Using the constant comparative method (Bogdan & Bilken, 1992; Glaser & Strauss, 1967), the interviews were transcribed, analyzed, and categorized based on the content and themes in students' responses.

The specific class was entitled "Minority Authors"; Mrs. Smith taught the class for ten years prior to our intervention. The class's title was misleading, however, because the course focused exclusively on African American literature. This may be a reflection of the fact that the school and department label courses, but teachers maintain academic authority over the content of the course. Mrs. Smith's rationale for this practice was that students who typically enroll in her class were African American students who were not exposed to a significant body of literature written by African Americans in their other English classes. She reasoned that if she did not offer them the opportunity to read broadly within the African American canon, they would not have the opportunity in high school.

The class of twenty-four high school juniors and seniors was taught by a veteran, European American high school teacher and the two African American researchers. Students in this elective class represented a range of academic histories—learning/behavioral disorder, honors, advanced placement and mid-level courses. The class was comprised of nine female and fifteen male students; twelve students were African American, ten were European American, one was Asian American and two students identified themselves as bi-racial (African and European American). Students' families ranged from affluent and middle-class to working-class poor. Within the classroom, over half of the African American students either spoke only Ebonics[1] or switched between Ebonics and the standard English register. Korean was the first language of our sole Asian American student.

Critical Theory: Lessons in Literacy and Social Justice

The purpose of critical theory is to "improve human existence by viewing knowledge for its emancipatory or repressive potential . . . Critical theory holds that knowledge is socially constructed, contextual, and dependent on interpretation" (McLaren & Giarelli, 1995, p. 2). Neither critical theory, critical literacy theory or pedagogy is monolithic. Rather, within the general framework, critical theory offers a flexible, yet focused theoretical lens for a scholar seeking to understand the complexity of race, literacy and social justice within the context of school and schooling. The most important tenets of critical theory for the present study include: (1) the critique of cultural, social, and historical events in society; (2) the impact of events on individuals and groups; (3) the struggle against social injustice; and (4) the hope of emancipation from oppression. In this chapter we extend our notions of critical theory, and critical literacy, to critical race theory. Race for this study was central. Thus we posed questions about how to apply critical literacy theory and pedagogy in a secondary English classroom. The class lessons in our study centered on a text written by African American writer Ernest Gaines; this text invites readers to engage issues of race with particular and compelling historical and contemporary relevance to African American people.

Our understanding, interpretation, and adaptation of notions of critical literacy pedagogy were inspired by the work of Freire (1986), Giroux (1988), Macedo (2006), and Shor (1992). Other philosophers, social activists, and teachers who inspired us include Septima Clark (1962), Anna Julia Cooper (1990), W. E. B. Du Bois (1953), Myles Horton (1990), and Carter G. Woodson (2006), who are seldom named among critical theorists, but whose lives and works exemplify critical theory. Like many in the latter group, we also have extended our concerns to embrace racial and social issues. Building on the work in law, educational researchers who wish to broaden understandings of the changes in political, legal, and social policies affecting people of color have labeled this way of thinking *critical race theory* (Ladson-Billings & Tate, 1995). In the field of literacy, where becoming literate is an intensely social and political process, critical race theory legitimizes a focus on racial issues as a means of understanding the interconnectedness and influence on literacy, language, teaching and social justice.

Readers, Race and Response: Framing Literacy

The literary canon operates as a vehicle for perpetuating hegemony within many high school English classrooms. The canon largely excludes or marginalizes the experiences of various racial, ethnic, cultural, religious, and linguistic groups living for many generations in the United States (Jordan & Purves, 1993). Rudolfo Anaya (1992) refers to this exclusion of diverse groups of authors as "censorship of neglect" as these selection choices are deeply linked to both political and social implications. Scholars like Jordan, Purves, and Anaya insist that students have opportunities in school to transact with literature outside of the Eurocentric canon and engage in interpretations of multiethnic literature. This literature serves as a constant reminder that ethnic groups within this country have perspectives, values, traditions, and worldviews which are often distinct from the mainstream.

Studies exploring ethnically/racially diverse students' responses to multiethnic literature indicate that personal connections between the reader and the text support the student's ability to identify with the characters, theme(s) and world views presented by the text (Athanases, 1998; Spears-Bunton, 1990). Among the adolescent readers in Spears-Bunton's (1990) study, there was a pronounced shift in the way adolescent readers talked about people who were racially different from themselves; over the course of the study they moved from the language of distance—us, ours, them and they—to I, me and we when talking about characters in the text and about their peers. Responding to "works by an ethnically diverse group of authors can engage equally diverse groups of students and teach across the lines that divide about profound human experiences" (Athanases, 1998, p. 291).

Many scholars argue that response occurs within a triad including the reader, the text and the context (Rosenblatt, 1994; Probst, 1994). Importantly, the primary site for response—the classroom—may be influenced by the dynamics of the interactions between the text and the reader. This seems to be particularly pronounced when the world view of the text explores difficult issues of race from the perspective of an authentic blackness. That is, typically silent African American students became active participants in class activities and performed "equally well" on class work and tests (Spears-Bunton, 1990, p. 573). The narrowing of the gap among students could partly be attributed to how "*House* opened a door through which an African American student could explore the symbolic referents in both African American and European American fiction" (p. 574). Matthews and Chandler (1998) noted that "Caucasian males, who were previously active participants in class, seem to withdraw from discussions, while African American females, whose voices we have not often heard, come alive. They raise questions, offer answers, and give their opinions" (p. 85).

While a growing body of research on reader response and multiethnic literature in the high school exists, few studies examine the complex and varied nature of the responses of students of color to diverse literary texts (Fairbanks, 1995; Lee, 1995; Spears-Bunton, 1990, 1992). Particularly rare are studies that explore ethnically diverse students' responses to "parallel cultural literature." Mingshui Cai and Rudine Sims Bishop (1998) define parallel cultural literature as "literature written by authors from parallel cultural groups to represent the experience, consciousness, and self image developed as a result of being acculturated and socialized within those groups. In this sense, parallel literature is the literature of a cultural group" (p. 66). Parallel cultural literatures are written by inside members of particular cultural groups and in essence subsequently belong to each respective group. Further, while Rosenblatt's (1994) transactional approach to reader response gives us a viable conceptualization of the reader as a human actor who evokes and re-creates the text, more research is needed that investigates approaching the teaching of literature critically (Willis, 1998; Willis & Johnson, 2000b) and transactions with parallel cultural literature by students of color.

Much of the early research on reader response to multiethnic literature is centered on personalized interpretations of the text and generally ignored profound cultural, historical, and political information significant to the texts. We argue that without this information, students are not fully informed and "understandings of ideology, culture, class, society, and gender remain fundamentally unchanged and unchallenged" (Willis & Johnson 2000a). Our project unites notions of teaching and reading multiethnic literature using critically framed reader response. Thus, our critically framed reader response theory acutely reexamines Bleich's (1978) response heuristic to include additional cultural, historical, and political interventionist materials necessary for an increased comprehensive reading of both the text and the world in which the text is situated. A critically framed reader response acts as an informed way both to teach and read multiethnic texts and contributes in compelling ways to the promise that literacy offers to help people move toward personal agency and social justice.

We undertook this study with the belief that there were political and social events within US history that were poorly understood, and in some cases, not known by students. In general, these events centered on our nation's ugly history of racism. We selected a novel that would allow for a more in-depth discussion of racism historically and contemporarily. The particular novel we selected permitted us to extend conversations about race to issues of social justice.

Portraits: Three African American Male Readers

The case study portraits of three African American males presented herein reflect on both their life experiences and the curricular intervention of critically framed reader response. It is our purposeful and conscious intent to disrupt hegemonic, uninformed discourse and stereotypes that continue to portray African American male adolescents as monolithic and unidimensional (see Hines, 1997; Sheehy, 2002). For instance, Hines (1997) describes David and Kevin, two African American male adolescents using the following flat and stereotypical descriptors: "living in a housing project," "refused to act like white students," they were "resistant," "oppositional students," "headed for failure" (pp. 116, 117). In a similar example, Sheehy's study lists an African American male participant and then fails to present him as a complex human being. By foregrounding the voices of the students, we seek to offer a more complex and genuine understanding of adolescent male African American readers.

We elected to focus on the responses of three African American males for two reasons: (1) their responses were representative of the range of responses of all students; and (2) we wanted to examine more closely the divergent responses among African American males. Two separate sets of interviews were conducted with each of the students early in the study and later, after the students had completed reading *A Lesson Before Dying*, and had been exposed to the interventionist materials. In both interviews, students were asked to reflect on their world views, past English classes, and thoughts on responding to literature. While both interviews included the same questions, the post intervention interviews also asked students to analyze various aspects of a critically framed reader response. We include the data collected during both interviews in an attempt to offer a much richer, more in-depth presentation of these three young men: Vincent, Ahmad, and Clarence.

Vincent

A senior enrolled in Minority Authors, Vincent stood about 5′ 10″, had a slender frame, dark brown skin, and the ability to code switch between Ebonics and the standard register. His trademark bottle of cocoa butter (to relieve any ashy, dry skin) and round bristle brush were always kept close by his side in the school bag he placed next to his desk. During class discussions, we would often notice Vincent rubbing cocoa butter into his hands and brushing his evenly cut, close to his head, hair (aka a "medium even Steven" to bring out his waves). Vincent tended to wear a mix of casual blue jeans and shirts or slacks and sweaters. In his spare time, he enjoyed "Reading, watching TV, playing video games . . . and watching movies." He also was committed to "being part of the church."

Vincent was president of the school's African American club and a school leader; despite his love for basketball, he was not involved in any sports. Throughout his high school career he had been tracked into mid-level classes. Unlike a number of his classmates, Vincent never once voiced disappointment at how a class entitled "Minority Authors" was actually "African American Literature." He exhibited a very strong sense of self as an African American male and seemed able to negotiate the school terrain without voicing the need to "act white" (Fordam & Ogbu, 1986). Vincent planned on getting a job after graduation to support himself.

Vincent's life experiences included tragic events. When asked to describe his perfect day, he quickly responded, "A perfect day would be for me to have a mother with me. A real mother with me . . . She passed away. She had colon cancer." He went on to explain how his mother had become ill while she was pregnant with him and died shortly after he was born. He lived with his father his entire life and has "had like three or four stepmothers since then . . . I've had some bogus stepmothers." It appeared as though he never quite bonded with any of the mother figures that came in and out of his life. His current stepmother gave birth to a little boy during the time of the study. Vincent was proud to be a big brother.

Vincent's life also included opportunities to live outside of the United States. He spent much of his childhood moving from city to city because his father was in the military. When asked about his knowledge of the world, Vincent had literally seen the world: "I got to go to Germany, and I've been to Turkey, and I've been all over the world, and I've seen so many people." He articulated a real sense of global issues when he described his perfect world as one with "no hate; perfect world, everybody get along, Black and White. No fights, no crimes, no tears, no depression, none of that . . . we'll have a way of government that everybody enjoys."

When asked to describe his best friend, he replied, "I got a lot of those." He just couldn't describe only one, so he described a close male and female friend—both of whom had been his friends "through thick and thin." The social roles in our classroom did not appear to bother Vincent; he was quite participatory and actively involved in most discussions. When asked about his thoughts on the influence of social roles in the class, he simply said, "I enjoy doing social things. I enjoy classrooms."

Our interviews also sought to get a sense of what Vincent thought about past English teachers and English classes in general. Vincent could name one particular English teacher who he thought was good because in her class, "we read and do a lot." Conversely, he could not name an English teacher he did not enjoy: "I haven't had any worse English teacher. I like English. I try to make it good." When asked about English as a subject, Vincent answered, "I like English, because I'm good at it. I like the literature the best, I guess." He would often have to "read and write papers. Lots of papers . . . " in most of his past English classes at Main. However, he voiced a preference for "group work. I don't like writing."

Talking about his past experiences with reading and responding to texts, Vincent reported enjoying reading "fiction books, wilderness. I like Latin authors . . . I read a lot of poetry . . . I read a lot of comics—Calvin and Hobbes. I have all their books." In his past English classes, Vincent mentioned being asked to respond to texts by writing "book reports, essays, and papers." Additionally, when asked if his responses to text have changed since he had been in high school, Vincent reflected: "I've grown a lot in my little English stage . . . I could say I was the same; I'm not the same. It's like my knowledge has improved maybe. I've expanded maybe. I guess I'm more mature. I know of the grades and the system, what I'm supposed to do. I guess I've changed." Finally, for Vincent, liking a book provided the impetus to seek information about and beyond an individual text: "If I really liked it [a book], I'll go to or go look around to see if there's some more stuff I can learn about." Overall, Vincent enjoyed English class, read various genres outside of class, preferred not to write, and had, in the past, searched for information related to but external to a text. In classes dominated by the canon, Vincent has been required to write in formulaic text-based ways that did not allow him to draw upon his world knowledge or personal beliefs and values.

Ahmad

Ahmad was a senior enrolled in the Minority Authors class. In class, Ahmad spoke a standard variety of English and was always very serious in his demeanor. Light-brown-skinned with a small frame, Ahmad was shorter than most of his male peers in the class. He kept his hair cut very close to his head and at times looked almost bald. While Ahmad's real name sounds Muslim in nature, he was a devout Christian (fundamentalist and Pentecostal). When asked what he read outside of school, Ahmad remarked: "I'd say the only thing I read is my *Bible* . . . Like right now I kind of memorized scripture to help me out here today."

He is the oldest of three younger siblings and his mother is a teacher at a local middle school. Ahmad dressed in very simple shirts and pants—often tee-shirts or sweatshirts and jeans. Occasionally, he wore his track team warm-up suit on days when the track team had a meet. Soft-spoken in class, Ahmad began the year only occasionally contributing to discussions, yet he would always agree to read passages from texts out loud if asked. He sat in the most central desk in the classroom, was always prepared for class and was rarely absent. Ahmad planned on going to a local community college after graduation, transferring to a university, and eventually pursuing a career in "art, I mean I like drawing and doing stuff with art. There are a couple of things I could do with it, like computer graphics, or like interior design, or something like that." Ahmad exhibited a strong sense of self. Grounded in his Christianity, Ahmad's religious devotion seemed to allow this reflective and thoughtful young man to move comfortably throughout the school, without appearing to feel pressure to conform to either stereotypes of young African American males or to social pressures of teenagers.

When asked to reflect on both what would be his perfect day and his perfect world, he said he would be doing "something to have fun, maybe go out with my friends, or that I'm around like the people that have the same voice I do." He continued by saying "I like going to different places, as long as I could . . . go to this one church." His perfect world "would be, of course, like everybody would be happy, but particularly if I got happy, I mean . . . giving other people some of myself. I'm not thinking about myself. I'm thinking about the world for other people. I think that if everybody felt that way, it [the world] would be better." Ahmad went on to mention how he liked "driving" and "going to movies with people" in his spare time. Christianity seems to inform aspects of both Ahmad's perfect day and his perfect world.

Sharing his thoughts about his friends and the ways in which the social roles in the classroom influenced his willingness to share his thoughts, Ahmad reflected: "I don't think I have a best friend; I mean I have a lot of good friends. I have friends in different cities." Ahmad went on to report that he did not have a group of friends at Main High School, but rather found his group of friends at his racially mixed church. Although Ahmad was soft-spoken and tended to keep to himself in class, he offered great insight into the nature of social roles in the classroom: "I mean, it depends on the people. There are certain people that it would be easier to talk around." When asked how this statement related to our Minority Authors class, Ahmad replied easily, "I know a lot of people [in the class]. It's not really hard." This statement implies that Ahmad knew people in the class (perhaps from past classes) and this fact made sharing easier. Ahmad wanted us to know the following regarding him and verbal communication: "That's one of the ways I'm trying to better myself. I mean I'm not that good of a communicator, but I'm always trying to grow in my articulation. Like being able to express myself. I don't know. When I was younger, I didn't have like a lot of friends, and like right now, I'm still like learning how to make a friend." Thus, while he felt comfortable with the social roles in our class, he was personally working on improving his communication skills.

We also asked Ahmad to share his thoughts on past English classes, teachers, and responses to literature. Ahmad's typical English class included studying vocabulary, writing papers, reading different books, and giving reports and presentations. Ahmad frankly told us he disliked the work involved in writing, but felt confident in his ability to write a paper: "when I need to write, I can do it . . . it's pretty much easy for me. I can put something together, and get good grades." One particular teacher was his favorite because "she had high expectations. I mean things I appreciate in a teacher like relatability and like ability to teach." Interestingly, this same teacher was also his least favorite because "she was very strict." In the past, Ahmad responded to literature by giving reports, writing short paragraphs, and writing essays. However, he prefers creative responses to literature "because I can express myself. I mean like with drawing, that's like I can express myself completely." When asked in the past to respond to literature, Ahmad didn't like "the nervous part of the presentation" and found he also disliked "the work part of the writing."

Finally, Ahmad discussed how his knowledge of the world helped him to understand what he reads. When asked if he ever searches for additional information outside of, but related to a text, he simply said, "No." However, Ahmad was reflective when asked about to what extent his own knowledge informs his reading: "I might look at those and see how they relate and see how they affect me, and try to relate that to what I'm reading, or what the situation is, like some person might react the way I would . . . Pretty much how it affects me." As was the case with Vincent, Ahmad was a mid-level student who had characterized his experiences in English classrooms as places where students read, write, and present book reports. Although he enjoyed writing and felt confident in his abilities as a writer, he preferred to express himself through art.

Clarence

In class, Clarence spoke only a standard form of English. His deep chocolate-colored skin seemed well matched by his slightly athletic 5'10" inch frame. Clarence played on Main's varsity baseball team and was a member of the Asian American club. He preferred to wear name brand "preppie" clothes from Abercrombie and Fitch and J. Crew.

Highly paid professionals, Clarence's parents were alumni of a historically Black college; they lived in one of the city's wealthiest communities. Their neighborhood has its own golf course and country club. This position of privilege extended into school as he was both the senior class officer and had been enrolled in advanced placement (AP) classes at Main High School. In contrast to his parents' education, Clarence insisted on attending a predominately White, large mid-western university.

When he talked about a perfect world, Clarence spoke about his desire for one race and the absence of nuclear weapons. He was the only student to mention a preference of one race. For him, a perfect day would have nice weather and with the company of friends. He talked about waking up late, going to a local bistro for broccoli cheese soup and chicken salad on croissant sandwich, driving to a mall in a nearby large city, and coming "home to a nice party." In his spare time, Clarence enjoys "partying," "playing baseball," and "listening to music." He listened to "mostly hip-hop, classic rock, and hard rock" music and particularly liked the Dave Matthews Band and Rage Against the Machine.

When asked about his friends, Clarence discussed his best friend, a European American senior, who was also enrolled in our class. Clarence stated that the two had not planned their schedules together, instead "it just worked out that way." As we inquired about social roles in the classroom and how they influenced his willingness to share in class discussions, unasked, Clarence made clear distinctions between his past AP classes and our Minority Authors class. In his AP classes, Clarence reported he was "more reluctant to give my response sometimes, because like it might not be right . . . [the teachers] want to hear the right answer . . . They want to know, like what is your personal perceptions on things, but like when we have class discussion, like they want to know the right answer."

In contrast, Clarence very openly talked about the influence of other students on his perceptions of our Minority Authors class— "some of the people in the class are just like I feel like I'm totally blowing off, because I'm not taking advanced literature or something like that. I'm taking minority literature. Like, I like the class. It just feels weird that I've never been around those students . . . I feel different from them, but in a way, I mean, I'm just exactly like them." Even so, in our de-tracked class of racially and ethnically diverse students, he reported that he liked "listening to the people in the class." Clarence was not asked to make a distinction between his AP classes and the Minority Authors class, yet he very obviously separated the two in his discourse. Moreover, he separated "minority literature" from his "advanced literature" classes. Importantly, Clarence discussed the role of the teacher—"they want to know the right answer"—in the context of the social roles in the AP classes, while focusing on his peers in his reflection on the social roles in the Minority Authors class.

When asked to reflect upon his experiences in past English classes, teachers, and responses to literature, Clarence recalled his American Literature class (an interdisciplinary course that combines literature and history courses) as his favorite because "we looked at a lot of stuff, like stuff that influences, like, our lives and how we got to where we were, and I like reading books about like history." His favorite English teacher was the woman who taught his American literature class because "she had the best curriculum. She had American studies and she challenges you . . . makes you think about like what you're reading about. She doesn't make it easy, and it's known as a tough class, and she challenges you."

Clarence shared a personal story when asked about his least favorite English teacher. He remembered being a young child in his early grades whose family had just moved to a small town—the home of a small state university. Before making this move, he remembered, "I was in the gifted program. And I was an exceptional kid, and . . . when we moved to [city] Illinois, and my first teacher [name], my English teacher, said I had reading disabilities, that I couldn't read." He attributed her "assumptions" to the fact that he "was the only African American student there . . . she thought I had a learning disability or something and put me in the lower level, LD, and it didn't make sense. I ended up like Illinois scholar . . . and she looked kind of stupid."

Aside from American literature, Clarence reported that he likes to read a lot of magazines and newspapers, "like I still like to read stuff that pertains to me." Specifically, Clarence mentioned reading *Newsweek*, stories with morals in them, and autobiographies. Clarence's comments suggest that he enjoys both reading and classes that focus on history and current events. The final area of discussion in our pre-intervention interview focused on Clarence's preferences in responding to literature and how he becomes more informed about issues outside of the classroom. Clarence preferred to "write papers . . . like write a book report . . . but not necessarily just writing them . . . maybe you can write your response to something, like creative, like give some personal view." When asked if he ever wrote about materials that he read independently, Clarence indicated that "I might write a poem about things I hear about . . . I might talk about something I've read." Clarence's performance in our class was consistent with these statements as Clarence opted to write a poem as a response to the literature and very often expressed himself verbally in the class. Clarence stated that he stayed informed on issues by watching "CNN and very often, but just watching documentary type shows."

Unlike Vincent and Ahmad, Clarence had been enrolled in AP English classes throughout high school. His experiences in such classrooms afforded him freedom and opportunities for personal expression to literature. Although neither a strong nor reflective writer, he was very comfortable writing in various response formats. He also did not hesitate in sharing his conservative views during class discussions.

Text and Context: Critically Framed Reader Response in an Intervention Curriculum

After spending the summer of 1998 reading approximately ten African American novels, the researchers and Mrs. Smith all agreed to read *A Lesson Before Dying* with the "Minority Authors" students. The novel is set in a rural Louisiana town in the late 1940s when a poorly educated, young Black man, Jefferson, is sentenced to death for a crime he did not commit. During Jefferson's trial, the court-appointed, White defense attorney labels Jefferson as a "hog"; it is this label that Jefferson's godmother, Miss Emma, wants disproved. Miss Emma asks for the help of the most educated Black man in the town, Grant Wiggins, the school teacher and narrator of the novel, to help Jefferson "die as a man." By the end of the novel, these two men and their community share astonishing lessons of both wisdom and fearlessness. The socio-cultural, political and race issues combined with the poignancy and timeliness of this novel provided a compelling opportunity for constructing an informed reader response while leaving much space for students to analyze what society could be.

Central to a critically framed reader response is providing students with additional, external information related to the novel's themes. This extra information enhanced and expanded the information base students were able to draw upon in their reading of both the text and the world in which the text is situated. Our motivation in selecting the following interventionist materials were to evoke and encourage a critical, present day, and realistic extended reading of *A Lesson Before Dying*.

The cultural, historical, and political information added to the unit included:

- two videos (*The Scottsboro Boys* and *Dead Man Walking*);
- four guest speakers (The Honorable Judge Richard DeLamar who spoke about the death penalty in Illinois, Dr. William Fowler who lectured on the Miranda rights, Dr. James Anderson who shared his reflections of growing up as an African American young man in the Jim Crow south, and Dr. Daria Roithmayr, who argued that race is a factor within the criminal justice system, especially in death penalty cases);
- additional literary genres (the poem "If We Must Die" by Claude McKay and the short story "Sanctuary" by Nella Larsen);
- a transcript from an episode of Oprah Winfrey interviewing Ernest Gaines about *A Lesson Before Dying*;

- a letter from a death row inmate;
- instructor information (on two of the central themes in the novel—the death penalty and Christian holidays) gathered from a variety of sources.

In our intervention model, we have also allowed for student choice on selected activities. Aligned with social constructivist theories of teaching and learning and critical pedagogy, student choice invited individual voices, beliefs, experiences, and opinions. For the final project, students were permitted to choose from the many forms of response used throughout the course of the semester (written, oral, dramatic, and artistic).

Critically Framed Lessons: Learning Following *A Lesson Before Dying*

Vincent

"I don't want you to go. Stay. Why do you have to go?" were the first sentences that Vincent spoke in his second interview. Our fifteen weeks together were coming to an end. He described the unit as "enlightening" and thought the teachers used "class discussions, group work, research papers, public speaking— all that good stuff" in our teaching of the unit. Further, Vincent commented: "You know, we've read books before in English class, and you kind of read them and you might see the video of that book, but it's not really natural, normal for the teacher to kind of bring in more videos, to kind of complement that. It was a first, and it did bring out some view-points, and it helped a lot for you to really get into it, recognize what was going on, look deeper into the book."
    Vincent's reading of the book and going deeper extended beyond the class as he reported talking about the book and capital punishment with a law student who attends his church. He was quite a verbal student which he described by stating: "I had fun talking . . . I spoke a lot. I usually talk when I have something to say . . . So it was fun. I enjoyed it. It was my best class. I looked forward to class."
    Vincent also was asked about the additional information used during the unit. He found the guest speakers to be the most helpful additional source of information to his reading of the text because "it got real at that point. When you spoke to the judge, you kind of realized that this kind of thing does happen . . . All of that kind of got real, and you kind of had to listen to that. I thought the public speakers were good." By participating in the unit, Vincent stated that "it brought to my attention the—kind of sit back and think about the court systems, and kind of where we are now . . . in general, I think I was opened up to some issues that I hadn't thought about in a while, or not ever before. The book brought that stuff to my attention." Vincent thought the videos "all tied together" with the book and specifically,

[the videos] brought realism and reality back to what I mean—the book is fictional, but it happened, was real *Scottsboro Boys* and *Dead Man*

Walking... that just brought everything up front and personal ... That informed me from Jefferson's point of view. You kind of look at Matt (is that his name?) in *Dead Man Walking*. You kind of see the differences and the similarities. I mean, it's [*Dead Man Walking*] set kind of present [time], but he went through the same things that Jefferson went through.

Vincent was asked to reflect on the various forms of response used during this unit. Vincent was pleased with "the audio thing" [his readers' theater he recorded on audiotape] and the "image theater." Vincent recorded a portion of the text as his final project. His reading captured the tone, style, and language of the text and time. He stated that he enjoyed the written responses and longer essays the least. Importantly, he thought his responses to literature had changed over the course of the unit: "I used to read to read it, and thought 'that was a good plot, that was a good story,' but now it's like I'm looking at each sentence like this: 'Is this what the author wants us to think? Am I supposed to go deeper into this?' ... so I look more into books now, I think."

Finally, we sought to get a sense of what Vincent thought about having two African American women teaching the unit and if he could identify with any themes or characters in the book. He had this to say: "Yeah, I think it made a difference. When [name of actual classroom teacher] is teaching, I don't know if they listen a lot. I don't know if they listen ... It's just sometimes better, I think, for the own race to teach, because they kind of bond a little better. You know, it's kind of better, so I think it makes a difference sometimes."

He also could identify with themes in the text and explained one such example: "Still, White people think they're better than Blacks, but I don't know if we'll ever be on the same level. We are on the same level they are, but I don't know if everybody recognizes that. They need to, but they won't." Throughout the class, Vincent remained comfortable in discussing race and demonstrated both cultural sensibilities and racial consciousness.

Ahmad

Asked to think once again about how the social roles in the class influenced his willingness to share and he now felt, Ahmed mused, " ... lately I've been a little more comfortable, like talking in front of like more people, instead of just one." Further, when asked about his perfect world for a second time, Ahmad had this to say: "Everybody would be innocent, kind of like little kids. Um. Everybody would love each other equally. Everybody would know God, everybody would love God." In describing how he felt the unit was taught, he said, " ... it got to different points of view and different experiences from different people, from different backgrounds." For him, the unit was "educational, controversial, provocative, personal."

Reflecting on what additional information was most helpful to informing his responses, readily Ahmad recalled the guest speakers and the videos. Dr.

Anderson's presentation on growing up in the South during the time of the novel seemed to have particular significance for Ahmad. "We got to see like first hand what people went through and what they have experience with . . . hearing history first hand from somebody else is just kind of cool." He also shared the types of information he gained from the videos: "from the *Scottsboro Boys*, I learned how hard it was for like Black people to get a fair trial and to get off death row. Um, from *Dead Man Walking*, I kind of saw what the guy [being executed] went through . . . what his family went through."

The interviews also attempted to get feedback on the various forms of responses allowed over the course of the unit. Ahmad also enjoyed two particular forms of response: "The dramatic was kind of fun because you got to work with the group, but I don't know. I like drawing the best." When asked what he learned from participating in these various response formats, he articulated, "I kind of learned how to—I don't know—dig deep and you know, like express myself if I don't have an idea."

When questioned about whether or not he felt having two African American teachers made a difference in the teaching of this class, Ahmad replied, "I don't know. I don't know if it would be any different, . . . but you guys were more flexible and tried to understand people." In addition, Ahmad felt as though he identified with one of the protagonists, Grant: "Well, I mean I understood Grant. I don't think I really looked like anyone else as much as I look at Grant, but I just see like his attitude. I see where he's coming from, like how he's been degraded, how his people have been degraded for so long, and doesn't want to be part of it. He doesn't want to be hated like that." Finally, Ahmad wanted to share an added important reflection he had: "Hmm, well, I didn't think it would happen, but I kind of—I don't know—learned a lot more about my culture in this class."

Clarence

When questioned about his perfect world for the second time, Clarence had this to say: "I don't know what a perfect world would look like to me, but what comes to mind is . . . racial harmony . . . multiracial children and multiracial people. And less war, no war." Asked about how he thought the course was taught, Clarence replied, "I think that we took a very in depth look at the literature . . . we looked at all aspects, not just like from what was actually in the book but all the issues that the book touches upon . . . I thought it was very good 'cause we looked at the death penalty and all the different aspects of it. And the pros and cons and the good stuff." Clarence went on to describe the unit as "enlightening."

Since the unit attempted to improve the depth of student responses by offering additional information external to the text, Clarence was also asked to reflect on how he was informed by the additional information. Overall, Clarence found the additional information, "made you look like deeper into the actual text." Clarence found the guest speakers to be the most helpful in informing his responses to *A Lesson Before Dying*. Specifically, he "liked Judge DeLamar, he like taught some, said some things that I really didn't know about pertaining to the death penalty in Illinois." He added how, in general, the four guest speakers, "made you think of all the details that were going along with the whole death penalty thing and Jefferson being on death row and the judicial side of it. And it made me like put into perspective, like if this could happen in, like in Illinois at this time, which is no. And, well I guess no."

The two videos also informed Clarence's reading of the novel. "I didn't know the story of the *Scottsboro Boys* and I think it was very important that I learned it, being an African American male in the United States. And from *Dead Man Walking*, it just kind of gave you like a good look into what a person goes through on death row before they are being executed." While Clarence found the guest speakers (particularly the judge) the most helpful in informing his responses, he also gained information from the videos.

Another aspect of this research project sought to investigate various mediums through which students could respond to literature. Clarence liked "the dramatic one the most because it was just a little bit different. I like something different, of all the years of English where you have to do written responses." Conversely, he was not as interested in completing artistic responses to literature: "I just wasn't very motivated to do artistic responses as much [as the dramatic response]." Clarence stated that written responses "taught me how to portray my feelings in short paragraphs."

Clarence was asked, again, to think about the social roles in the class and if having this unit taught by two African American teachers made a difference. To explain how the social roles in the classroom influenced his willingness to share his thoughts, Clarence explained, "Well, I think sometimes, like I wouldn't say things 'cause I didn't think anyone was really listening . . . I think that my peers weren't listening, so it really wasn't that important. And I'm not trying to teach the teachers. You guys don't need to be taught, do you?" Clarence reasoned that the teaching of the unit was biased because two African American teachers were teaching it: "I think it definitely did because I don't know if it was exactly bad, but I think that sometimes like the message like you are only portraying one side of most of the issues . . . I think you guys were portraying one side and only taught one side to it."

When questioned as to which side he thought we portrayed, Clarence answered, " . . . the pro-life side." Perhaps the most detailed discussion during our interview occurred when Clarence was asked if he personally identified with any themes or characters in the novel. "Maybe Grant, a little bit. I did think about Grant, I could put it into my own perspective as in he was pressured into helping Jefferson." Clarence goes on to explain his position:

He like sometimes felt like he was, since he was educated, he was like better than the rest of the African Americans in the quarter and stuff. I don't necessarily think of myself as being better, but I have trouble, like, I don't know, say like helping others like to better themselves . . . I love helping others, but like I just have trouble when someone says, 'Hey you're Black and somewhat accomplished, you need to help the other Black kids that aren't as accomplished.' I don't like it being a Black thing. 'If you're black and you have some sort of education, you're supposed to help other Blacks.' . . . you should help, like being a humanitarian. Helping like these people in general . . . Just because I'm Black doesn't mean I have to help Blacks . . . you should help people in general, not just Black people.

Herein, Clarence appears able to identify with how Grant, who was seen as educated because of a college degree and status as a teacher, was pressured into helping Jefferson. Clarence personally could identify with this situation and preferred that help be offered to all communities in need.

Black and Brown and Tan: Divergence Among African American Male Respondents

On the surface, the portraits of these three African American young men may appear quite similar. Vincent, Ahmad, and Clarence are all African American men, all seniors in high school; they share similar socioeconomic backgrounds ranging from middle- to upper-middle-class. All live in two-parent homes (Vincent and Ahmad lived with both their biological parents and a step parent), while Clarence lived with his biological mother and father), and all three planned on attending college (Vincent and Ahmad to community college and Clarence to a four-year university). Based on this information and in a class of twenty-five students, it is quite likely that a teacher could see these three individuals as more alike.

However, these three young men had very different voices, life experiences, and past English classes. Vincent lived with only memories of his mother; had traveled to various parts of the world; was president of his school's African American Club. He read fiction, poetry, and comic books outside of class, and dreaded the common practice of writing reports, essays, and papers in English class. Ahmad, the soft spoken Christian who read the Bible and memorized scriptures in his free time, was consciously working on improving his communication skills among his peers, and although confident in his ability to write, also disliked writing. And finally Clarence, who experienced a life of economic privilege, chose a preppy dress style, desired one multiracial race, felt "different from" the students in our de-tracked and ethnically diverse class, and chose to respond to literature in creative, non-scribal ways that went beyond writing.

The diversity present among Vincent, Ahmad, and Clarence was present in their reflections on a critically framed reader response. Vincent and Ahmad found the guest speakers and videos most improved their responses, while

Clarence found the guest speakers (the judge specifically) to be most informative. Consistent with Vincent's verbal proficiency and dislike for writing, Vincent most enjoyed readers' theater and least enjoyed lengthy essay assignments when responding to the literature. Ahmad, who was a skilled artist, most enjoyed responding to literature via art. Finally, Clarence most enjoyed dramatic responses to literature.

While Vincent identified with the theme of race relations between "Whites" and "Blacks," both Ahmad and Clarence stated that they could identify with the character of Grant in the novel—but for very different reasons. Ahmad identified with Grant's desire to not be "degraded" as an African American male, while Clarence identified with the way in which Grant was made to help Jefferson simply because Grant was African American and educated. Vincent felt he bonded better with teachers who shared his race, Ahmad suggested the African American teachers were flexible and understanding, and Clarence felt that having African American teachers resulted in only one side being portrayed and taught. Thus, while agreeing on guest speakers and videos as the most informative types of additional information, all three young men preferred different forms of response, used distinct rationales for identifying with the same character, and thought dissimilarly about having African American teachers.

On a Well Lighted Path: Critically Framed Response

In thinking about why learning needs to be more centrally connected with multicultural education, an image came to me: the light in the students' eyes when they become excited about learning. There is nothing quite as dazzling as this sight. Once we have seen the look of discovery and learning in students' eyes, we can no longer maintain that some young people—because of their social class, race, ethnicity, gender, native language, or other difference—are simply unmotivated, ignorant, or undeserving. The light in their eyes is eloquent testimony to their capacity and hence their right to learn, and it equips educators with the evidence and courage they need to defy the claims that some students are more entitled than others to the benefits of education.

(Nieto, 1999, p. xix)

The "light" that Sonia Nieto (1999) speaks about is dear to educators. As teachers who share literature with students, we particularly cherish our responsibility to offer students the opportunities to read both texts and read the world in which the text is situated. Clearly a challenge, the reward of student excitement, hearing their voices and witnessing their brightness is profoundly important if the promise of literacy is to be realized and social justice is to be lived in our world. The light in the eyes of students, like Vincent and Ahmad, who perhaps we do not regularly witness arriving at academic achievement in the English classroom as often as we desire, shines for all of us.

Race was a central aspect to nearly everything about the class—the race of the students, the race of the teachers, the race of the researchers, the racial nature of the literature selected. Not only was race central, but it mattered in intimate, complex, and subtle ways.

The words of these three young men are in accord with the findings of other studies (Athanases, 1998; Henly, 1993; Matthews & Chandler, 1998; Spears-Bunton, 1990) which demonstrate that reader response is an effective instructional strategy in teaching multiethnic literature in the high school. Through the use of reader responses, all three students made reference to their ability to aesthetically transact with *A Lesson Before Dying*. However, this study also suggests that a student's transaction with a text is influenced by much more than simply the reader, the text, and the teacher (Probst, 1994; Shelton, 1994). Aligned more with the findings of Sipe (1998) and Spears-Bunton (1990, 1992), these data suggest that students' transactions with texts are influenced by the context of the reading and the race of the student. Comparative case studies confirm the research of Spears-Bunton (1990) and Henly (1993) on the complex, individual, and varied nature of the transactions with text by students of color (who share the same racial background). How one teaches a text and the critically framed instructional material used to scaffold instruction, are both key factors in a reader's response to a particular literary work.

Important too, is how a teacher positions herself within the context. We elected to position ourselves as "warm demanders," to use Irvine and Fraser's (1998) moniker. We held high expectations for the students. We communicated to all students a language of anticipation, that is, anticipating the students would complete the assignments. For example, we stated in non-threatening tones "I expect you to read the following pages and come to class prepared to discuss them tomorrow" or "You will write a four page paper about your family." One of the students, in disbelief, said, "you must think we are in level 3 (AP) classes." Even the classroom teacher said, "It is just amazing how much they will do for you. They do it because they know you don't really know which level they are on." True, their labeled levels were of no import to us. We believed we could raise the standard of performance for all students, by engaging them in the text by critically framing instruction. We were not disappointed.

During our time in "Minority Authors" we noticed increased levels of participation and engagement by the African American males. Affirmation of them as capable learners may have contributed to an enhanced level of confidence: that they can share opinions/interpretations, that they can add to a discussion, and that they can add to how classmates are reading and understanding the text in English classrooms. Many of these levels of participation, documented on videotape, fall under an intangible category. For instance, classroom conversations increased in length and dynamic, with Ahmad, Clarence and Vincent often leading the discussions. On one occasion, during an exchange program with students from a predominately African American magnet high school in Chicago, students visited the classroom and our students continued their very candid conversations about the intersection of race and the criminal justice system. Other examples of intangible evidence of engagement included: the respectful climate and mood of the classroom, the overall preparedness of each focal student for each class discussion and assignment, and the freedom to choose a preferred response format without fear of rejection of their ideas. Vincent produced an audio reading of a passage from the text that captured the intonation, tone, and flow of the language and culture that is superior to the merchandised audio book version. Ahmad translated his interpretation of the text into a series of artistic representations from various characters' positions.[2] Clarence and two other students produced a video depicting a crime and the resulting execution of the defendant to support their position on capital punishment.

The responses of Ahmad, Clarence and Vincent indicate that their engagement with literature was altered during our study. We find that when personal and cultural knowledge is invited into the classroom discussion of the literature, engagement increases. We observed that opportunities to use personal and cultural knowledge, when transacting with the literature, became more layered as students were invited to share stories that helped them make links to ideas, events, and language/dialect in the text. In one instance, students were asked to interpret the following passage filled with cultural specificity and dialogue (Gaines, 1997, pp. 11 and 12). Our interpretations are included in italics:

"Ain't you gon'n speak to Miss Emma?" she said.
(This statement is made with attitude, not quite scolding, but poignantly instructive. Generally, African American folk know that you are obligated to speak to an elder when you know s/he is in the house, especially if you can see them physically.)

"I was going to. I was just looking over some papers."
(He offers a weak excuse for not doing as asked immediately.)

"She want talk to you."
(The implication is that she wants to talk to you about something important and you should move now to see what that might be.)

"Sit down Grant," my aunt said.

"I can stand, Tante Lou."
(Grant is uneasy in his response because he wants to take a stand as an adult while trying to remain respectful to his aunt's command.)

"Sit down," she said.
(What is implied by her direct command is that Grant is not too grown to be told what to do, and to do it immediately with no backtalk or excuses.)

Most African American students seemed to understand the above text without need of interpretation, however, inviting them to publicly interpret and share their interpretations with their classmates increased their level of engagement. They smiled and laughed as they recalled similar instances from their own lives. Although the statements above reflect a seemingly simple set of sentences, they carry great cultural information about African American communication patterns and expectations that were part of the home lives of many students.

Vincent, Ahmad and Clarence had different experiences in English classrooms prior to this course. Clarence had experienced opportunities to respond to texts in multiple ways and openly share; Vincent and Ahmad's experiences had been largely confined to completing worksheets and some small group work. During this project, however, their personal and cultural knowledge was welcomed, appreciated, and expected to add to everyone's understanding of the novel. Vincent describes the method as 'enlightening' as he looked forward to class where he could speak because he was interested. Ahmad said that the class was structured like one of the higher-level courses where the expectations are also high. In general the students appeared to enjoy digging deep into text, being asked to think deeply about the story, and learning through literature, about African Americans.

Critically framing reader response to the text, *A Lesson Before Dying*, invited students like Vincent and Ahmad to share the light in their eyes. As Nieto (1999) points out, creating critically framed multicultural learning communities can reveal these veiled lights in students' eyes. In witnessing Vincent and Ahmad's radiant essence, we knew we had uncovered a defining moment.

Questions for Discussion

1. Discuss the criteria used by educational institutions to group, sort, and categorize African American male students. How does this categorization process reinforce stereotypes? In what ways does the class described in this study help to eliminate stereotyping?
2. Re-examine the students' responses prior to and after the unit of study. In what ways did the study lead them to think in different ways?
3. In what ways did the videos and guest speakers contribute to a critical analysis of the text?
4. How do the forms of student responses reported in this chapter differ from traditional responses associated with "schooled literacy" (Chapter 1)?
5. In what ways does this chapter offer new insights into how complexities of race, class, and gender intersect with and influence students' responses?

Extension Activities

1. Work with a group of students to develop criteria for selecting novels and other literary works for class study. Use the criteria to choose a novel to read as a class. Together, design a unit of study that incorporates community speakers, videos, and related literary texts.
2. Consider Howard Gardner's theory of multiple intelligences. Brainstorm various ways that students might respond to literature.
3. Select a literary work (e.g., a poem) and respond to it in various ways (e.g., dialogue journals, drama, visual representations, musical renditions). Which form of response did you prefer? Why?

Notes

1. Ebonics referring to "Black sounds . . . an all encompassing, non-pejorative label, the term Ebonics refers to the language of West Africa, Caribbean, and U.S. slave descendants of Niger-Congo African origin . . . includes both the verbal and paralinguistic communications of African American people, this means that Ebonics represents an underlying thought process. Hence, the nonverbal sounds, cues, gestures, and so on that are systematically used in the process of communication by African American people are encompassed by the term as well" (Smith, 1998, p. 54).

2. To listen to and view examples of Vincent and Ahmad's responses, see http://www.reading online.org/articles/art_index.asp?HREF=willis/index.html.

References

Anaya, R. (1992). The censorship of neglect. *English Journal, 81,* 18–20.

Athanases, S.Z. (1998). Diverse learners, diverse texts: Exploring identity and difference through literary encounters. *Journal of Literacy Research, 30*(2), 273–296.

Bleich, D. (1978). *Subjective criticism.* Baltimore: Johns Hopkins University Press.

Bogdan, R.C., & Bilken, S.K. (1992). *Qualitative research for education: An introduction to theory and methods.* Boston: Allyn Bacon.

Cai, M., & Sims Bishop, R. (1998). Multicultural literature for children: Towards a clarification of the concept. In A. Soter & T. Rogers (Eds.). *Reading across cultures* (pp. 57–71). NY: Teachers College Press.

Clark, S. (1962). *Echo in my soul.* NY: Dutton.

Cooper, A.J. (1990). *A voice from the south.* NY: Oxford.

Du Bois, W.E.B. (1953). *The souls of black folk.* CT: Fawcett.

Fairbanks, C.B. (1995). Reading students: Texts in context. *English Education, 27*(1), 40–52.

Fordham, S., & Ogbu, J. (1986). Black students' school success: "Coping with the burden of 'acting white.'" *Urban Review, 18,* 176–206.

Freire, P. (1986). *Pedagogy of the oppressed.* NY: Continuum.

Giroux, H. (1988) *Teachers as intellectuals: Toward a critical pedagogy of learning.* Critical Studies in Education Series. NJ: Bergin & Garvey.

Glaser, B.G., & Strauss, A.L. (1967). *Discovery of grounded theory: Strategies for qualitative research.* Chicago: Aldine.

Henly, C.P. (1993). Reader-response theory as antidote to controversy: Teaching *The bluest eye. English Journal, 82*(3), 14–19.

Hines, S. (1997). *Factors influencing persistence among African American upperclassmen in natural science and science-related majors.* Paper presented at the annual meeting of the American Educational Research Association, Chicago, IL.

Horton, M. (1990). *The long haul: An autobiography.* NY: Doubleday.

Irvine, J., & Fraser, J. (1998). Warm demanders. *Education Week on the WEB* [Online]. Retrieved July 28, 2007, from http://www.edweek.org/ew/1998/35irvine.h17.

Jordan, S., & Purves, A.C. (1993). *Issues in responding to culturally diverse texts: A preliminary study.* SUNY: National Research Center for English Learning and Achievement. Retrieved July 28, 2007 from http://cela.albany.edu/issrespon/index.html.

Ladson-Billings, G., & Tate, W. (1995). Toward a critical race theory of education. *Teachers College Record, 97*(1), 47–68.

Lee, C.D. (1995). A culturally based cognitive apprenticeship: Teaching African American high school students skills in literary interpretation. *Reading Research Quarterly, 30*(4), 608–630.

Macedo, D. (2006) *Literacies of power: What Americans are not allowed to know.* Expanded Edition. Boulder, CO: Westview.

Matthews, R., & Chandler, R. (1998). Using reader response to teach *Beloved* in a high school American studies classroom. *English Journal, 88*(2), 85–92.

McLaren, P., & Giarelli, J. (Eds.) (1995). *Critical theory and educational research.* Albany, NY: State University of New York Press.

Nieto, S. (1999). *A light in their eyes: Creating multicultural learning communities.* New York: Teachers College Press.

Probst, R.E. (1994). Reader-response theory and the English curriculum. *English Journal, 83,* 37–44.

Rosenblatt, L. (1994). *The reader, the text, the poem: The transactional theory of the literary work.* Carbondale, IL: Southern Illinois University Press.

Shakespear, E. (1999). What I'd tell a White gal: What my Black male students taught me about race and schooling. In S. Warshauer Freedman, E. Radin Simons, J. Shalhope Kalnin, A. Casareno, & the M-Class teams (Eds.), *Inside city schools: Investigating literacy in multicultural classrooms* (pp. 77–88). NY: Teachers College Press.

Sheehy, M. (2002). Illuminating constructivism: Structure, discourse, and subjectivity in a middle school classroom. *Reading Research Quarterly, 37*(3), 278–302.

Shelton, K.Y. (1994). *Reader response theory in the high school English classroom.* Unpublished master's thesis. Wake Forest University, Winston-Salem, NC.

Shor, I. (1992). *Empowering education: Critical teaching for social change.* Chicago: University of Chicago Press.

Sipe, L.R. (1998). Individual literary response styles of first and second graders. In *National Reading Conference Yearbook* (pp. 76–89). Chicago: National Reading Conference.

Smith, E. (1998). What is black English? What is Ebonics? In T. Perry & L. Delpit (Eds.), *The real Ebonics debate: Power, language and the education of African-American children* (pp. 49–58). Boston, MA: Beacon Press.

Spears-Bunton, L.A. (1990). Welcome to my house: African American and European American students' responses to Virginia Hamilton's *The House of Dies Drear. Journal of Negro Education, 59,* 566–576.

Spears-Bunton, L.A. (1992). Literature, literacy, and resistance to cultural domination. In C.K. Kinzer & D.J. Leu (Eds.), *Literacy research, theory, and practice: Views from many perspectives.* Forty-first Yearbook of the National Reading Conference (pp. 393–401). Chicago: National Reading Conference.

Willis, A. (Ed.) (1998). *Teaching and Using Multicultural literature in grades 9–12.* Norwood, MA: Christopher-Gordon Publishers.

Willis, A., & Johnson, J. (2000a). "A horizon of possibilities": A critical framework for transforming multiethnic literature instruction. *Reading Online* [On-line]. Retrieved July 28, 2007, from http://www.readingonline.org/articles/willis/index.html.

Willis, A., & Johnson, J. (2000b). Reader response and social action. *National Reading Conference Yearbook, 49,* 356–366.

Woodson, C.G. (2006). *Mis-education of the negro.* San Diego, CA: The Book Tree.

Literature cited

Gaines, E.J. (1997). *A lesson before dying.* New York: Vintage Books.

Hamilton, V. (2006). *The house of Dies Drear.* New York: Simon & Schuster.

McKay, C. (1922). If we must die. In *Harlem shadows: The poems of Claude McKay.* New York: Harcourt, Brace and Co.

Morrison, T. (1972). *The bluest eye.* New York: Pocket Books.

Morrison, T. (1987). *Beloved.* New York: Knopf.

6

The Obscured White Voice in the Multicultural Debate
Race, Space and Gender

LINDA A. SPEARS-BUNTON

Reading literature from multiple perspectives is an important avenue toward empowerment for both teachers and students. The process of listening to voices different from our own and experiencing the myriad of possibilities presented by the human experience, leads toward a higher-level literacy. Literacy, grounded in multiple perspectives, may instigate empowerment as readers begin to (1) generate questions; (2) draw comparisons from their reading and life experiences; and (3) think independently. This chapter presents a captured glimpse of the process of empowerment among school children, and demonstrates how empowered teachers can effect reform through literacy instruction.

The observations presented here are based upon a naturalistic study that examined the interrelationships among culture, literature and literacy in order to develop a description and an understanding of how African American and European American students transact with European American and African American literary texts. The school in which the data were collected is an inner city school serving two neighborhoods, Sternville and Riverview.[1] There is a history of racially motivated animosity between them. Data were collected among twenty-eight poor and working-class African American and European American students and one veteran European American teacher over the course of an entire school year. The research focused on a Junior Honors classroom, and examined particular kinds of events, i.e. literature teaching/learning and response, from the perspective of the students. Ethnographic data including interviews, observations and case study portraits were collected. The research explored the affective dimensions of response, specifically the reader's volition and motivation for engaging or resisting the world of the text when juxtaposed against the cultural knowledge of self and others.

Student response initiated with students expressing their liking or disliking of the text. Liking/disliking is the paradigm for response established by the adolescent readers. Two distinct categories of response emerged from an analysis of the data; these fell along a continuum of the liking/disliking response to both African American and European American literature texts. These categories are: (1) alignment, a proximal relationship reflecting where readers positioned themselves in relation to the text; and (2) valuation, reflecting the importance of the text in reference to the reader's own experiences and perceptions of what is important. The study sought to understand reader-response within a larger socio-political context, and considered text, context and individual readers as integral dimensions of the reading-responding process. In the study, transgressing a tradition of invisibility and silence about race and gender signaled the emergence of a more empowered community of readers.

Introduction

What happens to a Black kid who never gets to read a book written by a Black author? How do the White kids feel about the emphasis on Black literature?[2]

Paula's (pseudonym) question gives voice and immediacy to many high school English teachers who begin to infuse non-canonical literature into their curricula. Paula's decision to make African American literature an integral part of her curriculum rested upon her double-edged question: What are the consequences of a mono-cultural curriculum upon Black and White students? In her school there was a subtle mandate to avoid the mention of cultural/racial differences. As a European American female teaching both European and African American students—and the elite track—Paula faced challenges from students as well as administrators. Paula decided that the establishment of symmetry in the curriculum was worth the effort, facilitating a love for reading was a worthwhile instructional goal, and that engaging the conflicts of race within the classroom was a viable way of resolving them. These decisions led to a dynamic transformation in the teaching/learning process in her class.

For Paula, teaching and learning were interrelated acts of both empowerment and liberation from ignorance which she defined as "a consequence of being improperly taught." In this sense, ignorance was related to the hegemonic, mono-cultural content of traditional English curricula at both the university and the high school level. Paula vowed that neither she nor her students would be as ignorant at the end of the school year. Moreover, Paula found the curriculum, represented by the class anthology, to be problematic. Flipping through her new class anthology, she commented with disgust: "look at this, there is almost nothing about Blacks, even in the time lines!" Through Paula, we come to see that the traditional curriculum may disempower teachers and students by presenting them with a skewed view of the human experience. Paula's new discoveries, combined with her passion for teaching and learning, seemed to propel her to act. Literature was her weapon; a revised pedagogy was her operating strategy.

For Paula, reading, teaching and responding were interrelated, active processes that could engender the emergence of both individual and collective empowerment, social consciousness and social change. Her classroom became a site for individuals to act as agents for social change against a historical context of racial and sexual segregation, paternalism and silence (Blauner, 1999;

Franklin, 1993; Giroux, 1993; Kincheloe, 2002; Weiler, 1988; Wright, 2004). Taken together, the stories of Paula and two of her female European American students help us to understand that reading, exploration and response to literature can be revolutionary; it can be the catalytic and cathartic force that provides the impetus for personal and social change.

This chapter positions Paula's question somewhat differently: "What happens to a White kid who never gets to read a book written by a Black author?" I will argue that America is a racialized and gendered society. Yet, the canon provides scant attention to issues which have powerfully shaped our nation's social, economic and political ideologies. The canon continues to influence the way(s) we think about and treat people defined as "Others." Moreover, the social positioning of European Americans as an elite yet "unraced" group of people severely limits their attempts to understand the world and an individual's place within it (Frankenburg, 1993; Gilligan, Ward, Taylor & Bardige, 1990; Morrison, 1993; Weis, 1988). Within the multicultural debate, this very social positioning may silence or obscure European American female voices. That is, while the effects of a mono-cultural curriculum upon students of color are rather obvious, there is a danger of overlooking the needs of the socially stratified elite to examine, articulate and analyze issues that are complex, and for many, frightening. As an institution within American society, racism affects the oppressor as well as the oppressed. Overcoming historical and contemporary racist attitudes and dispositions requires crosscultural knowledge, multiple experiences, a good deal of self reflection and an astute and courageous guide.

The notion of race is a powerful social and political force woven into the fabric of American society, and embedded into the consciousness of American people. America is a raced society in the sense that people are described and defined in language, law, social policy, and custom in racial terms. Relationships between people are partially determined by our perception of what we think the other person is. Even "a drop" of African blood can be socially and politically important because we have been socialized to "know" the difference between racial groups, and these differences have been internalized into our cognitive processes (Aboud & Skerry, 1984; Rothenberg, 1988; Rotheram & Phinney, 1987). Racialization subjectifies "race" because it is based on the belief that the distinctive characteristics found among human beings determines their respective cultures and circumscribes their humanity (Du Bois, 2007).

Without an understanding of the cultural knowledge and attitudes students bring to a text, research and pedagogy will fail to make multicultural education a viable and permanent part of the school curriculum. This is critical because the development of multiple literacies fosters the emergence of the kind of literacy which moves beyond de-coding and deconstruction of printed texts, and toward questioning and examining taken-for-granted assumptions (Edelsky, 1999). Without a critical examination of the consequences of a mono-cultural curriculum upon European American students, research and pedagogy can unconsciously foster ambivalence and confusion among these students. A mono-cultural curriculum limits opportunities to examine the equation that constitutes the human experience and creates a false standard of cultural superiority.

This chapter examines the struggles of European American female students moving toward more culturally inclusive understandings. Their struggles, guided and supported by Paula, were remarkable in intensity and complexity. The portraits of the young women presented herein are illustrative of how difficult it is to change, to question and to challenge taken-for-granted attitudes and assumptions, especially within families and communities that resent new knowledge and undermine the struggle. I will argue that teachers can act as ambassadors, utilizing literary texts as material for debate, negotiation, imagination, delight and self discovery.

Reader Response: The Discourse of Empowerment

The process of reader-response as social discourse was initiated by Paula. Paula took three describable steps towards becoming empowered as a reader and claiming empowerment as a teacher: (1) she read avidly as a scholar seeking knowledge and understanding; (2) she shared her reading with friends, colleagues, and students; and (3) Paula read with dual purposes: (a) she read for personal satisfaction and to expand her limited knowledge; (b) she read with an eye towards selecting materials for her students.

Paula's reading/responding processes are closely akin to Rosenblatt's (1995) theory of reader-response. Reader-response theory offers a viable way of looking at the interaction of the reader with the text by giving us a theory-driven conceptualization of the reader as a human actor who evokes and recreates the text. These elements include: (1) prior experiences and literary conventions that the reader uses in order to construct meaning from a text (meaning construction encompasses the recursive and reflective dimensions of response); (2) the affective dimensions of response, specifically the reader's feelings about the text and character identification; and (3) the posture the reader takes towards the text which determines whether the text is read for factual information (efferent posture) to be used in other contexts, or for the experience of living through the text (an aesthetic posture). Paula's story indicates that the paradigm for anti-hegemonic response—re-reading the word and the world—is established by the teacher who claims empowerment for herself, values the content of this learning, and invites students into the process of constructing knowledge.

Response to a literary text is both cumulative and recursive, and evolves as the reader transacts with the text, reflects upon his/her experience of it, and then participates in discussion as part of a larger community such as a classroom (Fish, 1980; Langer, 1988; Wolf, 1988). Literary discussion may also be tempered by gender and cultural affiliations. The reader's background knowledge consists of the gestalt of the reader's lived culture as well as knowledge gained vicariously from reading. The scholarship in reader-response indicates that response to a literary text is both a process and a consequence of the reader's personal engagement with the text (Beach, 1983; Galda, 1983; Rabinowitz, 1998; Rosenblatt, 1995).

Literature and response are socio-cultural products that have socio-cultural results. Differences in cultural perspective will affect the text evoked by readers (Brewer & Ohtsulka, 1988; Halasz, Laszlo & Pleh, 1988; Purves, 1981; Purves & Rippere, 1968; Rosenberg, 1988; Steffensen, Joag-Dev & Anderson, 1979). Readers may separate or align themselves from the text in ways similar to the way they separate culturally different people from themselves; readers use the language of "I," "me," "us," "White people" ("Black people"), to indicate cultural inclusiveness and identity, or them, they, their and Black people (White people) to indicate cultural exclusiveness or distance from self. A consideration of the cultural self moves beyond traditional reader response theory to a critically framed reader response. Culture is central, rather than tangential, to the affective domain of response.

The literary text offers readers a sensual/emotive stimulus giving readers images with which to think (Bruner, 1987). Charged with the responsibility of transmitting cultural history and perpetuating the dominant culture's attendant suppositions of morality, aesthetics and traditions, the canon—the officially sanctioned set of literary texts judged to be standard and universal—has been assiduously guarded. Historically, the composition of the canon has been defined and delineated by those who rule; traditionally those who rule have not been people of color or women. Thus, there was little impetus to seriously consider the cultural perspective of "Others." The multicultural debate may be part of the process of challenging hegemony and moving toward a more balanced, honest and egalitarian curriculum that befits a democratically organized society. The balance of this chapter examines some of the ways in which a teacher and her students chart a course toward this end.

Good Students, Good Readers

For purposes of discussion and analysis, student respondents have been divided into two broad categories: (1) students who were described by Paula and themselves as "good students" and "good readers"; and (2) students who were described by Paula and themselves as good readers who were "not-so-good students." I will focus primarily on the former category because among the students I studied, the reading-responding experiences of Courtney and Lucy (two of the six "good student/good readers") reveal the potential for trans-formation and empowerment through literature. Both students articulated goals beyond high school; however only Lucy initially reported that she liked to read. Prior to the beginning of the study, both students reported that they had never read any African American literature.

Lucy

In small group discussions, Lucy was invariably the leader. Following Paula's brief introduction of me and the research, she walked up to me and announced that she and her best friend Courtney wanted to volunteer "to help me with my work." In an early interview, I asked her why she agreed to participate in the study. She replied in her typical forthright manner, "you looked scared to death so I figured you could use the help." A native of Sternville, Lucy was the oldest of six siblings. During our interviews, she commented that her family might not be pleased with her considerable success in school, but declined to elaborate further. Paula described her as "very smart," but somewhat bittersweet and was "surprised" that she volunteered to participate in the study.

A school activist, Lucy was a journalist for the school newspaper and an outspoken member of the student government association. She said that she believed that being a good student went beyond getting good grades; it meant being involved in school activities and making things better. Lucy spoke lovingly about reading and especially enjoyed mysteries and romances. She reported that she had always liked to read. I enjoyed watching her face as she talked about texts she liked because she became so deeply engaged in the books she was reading. However, when we talked about cultural/racial differences in fictive, historical or contemporary people and their circumstances, particularly at the beginning of the study, her talk was hesitant and her typically self-assured demeanor slipped momentarily. Later in the study, Lucy spoke about these issues spontaneously with passion and urgency. Lucy and Courtney provided me with a privileged look at the worlds of Westmoreland HS and Sternville from the perspectives of European American females. Over time, we developed a comfortable relationship. They kept me up to date on what was going on in school and in Sternville.

Courtney

Courtney described herself as a good student and an effective school activist. She said she liked to know that she could make a difference in her school and in her community, and was comfortable taking charge of things. A native of Sternville, Courtney came to Westmoreland as a ninth grade student. She liked both her school and her community because she had family roots in both places. Three of her older sisters had attended Westmoreland, and many of her childhood playmates were currently enrolled. The youngest of a large family, Courtney felt that she had a very good life because she was loved by a family who provided all of her material needs. Courtney reasoned that "being a good student was important because it would allow her to make more choices about what to do with her life."

Courtney emphatically claimed to dislike reading. She said that the books she was asked to read for school were frequently hard to understand. In these cases, she enlisted the help of her stepfather, and forced herself to complete the reading assignment. Independently however, Courtney reported that she read mysteries, romances and biographies. Probing this contradiction, I asked her "what is the difference between the books you read for school and the books you read on your own; reading is reading, isn't it?" Courtney explained that reading for school typically meant reading something an adult assigned and that an adult would be interested in, not a teen. Moreover, she stated that school reading was typically accompanied by time constraints, deadlines and inevitably a test. She was always worried that she might not remember something important for the test. Thus, literary response was trivialized and reduced to learning a series of automatic features about the text.

The question of cultural/racial distinctiveness in literary texts initially made Courtney uncomfortable. When I introduced the subject of racial perspectives in literature in our second interview, she remarked, "that was such a long time ago, there's no sense in talking about it; we should just get on with it." I sensed that she was not quite convinced by her words; the uniqueness of the interview context and the presence of an African American adult may have been disquieting for this polite and cooperative young woman.

Over time, Courtney shared intimate details of her personal, family and school life with me. On excursions into Sternville with her, I was an obvious, but courteously treated guest. It seemed important to her that people in her community "get to know and to like you." Inside of school, Courtney and Lucy shared yearbook and prom pictures, "girl-talk" and often invited me into their small groups. When I agreed, they kept me on task; when, as often happened, I needed to spend time with other students and their groups, they understood, although they warned me that my reputation could be ruined by some of the company I kept.

Distancing: European American Students

Among the European American students, alignment, where readers positioned themselves in relation to the text, was characterized by distancing. This was indicated by: (1) silence, whereby typically vocal students were reluctant to participate in class discussions about African American literature texts; (2) a reluctance to discuss difference portrayed in African American literature texts; and (3) expressions of discomfort with the participation of African American students in literature activities. Importantly, these students distanced themselves from the issue of cultural differences by insisting that cultural experiences had only historical significance and were consequently lacking in immediate or personal relevance. Given the traditional school curriculum in both English and history in which these students previously "learned" about Black history only during the month of February, such a position is understandable.

In terms of valuation, there was a gradual change toward a reassessment of previous stereotypical perceptions of both groups with the exposure to African

American literature. Over time, European American female students began to personally identify with the actions, attitudes and attributes of African American fictive characters. Later, they began to critically examine assumptions about race and culture within their community and family. These European American female students added their voices to those of their African American peers and challenged the content of the curriculum.

Closing the Cultural Gap: Becoming Empowered Readers

The European American students initially assumed a cultural sameness, riddled with ambiguity and contradiction, between themselves and their African American peers. These students, exemplified by Lucy and Courtney, struggled with the ambiguities of race in themselves and within their community. Each student began our discussions of cultural difference with a nearly identical statement: "We're all the same. They got their culture and we got ours. They just have different hairstyles and eat different foods, like chitterlings." None of the students specified a White food or a White hairstyle; they did not single out specific attributes of whiteness. When probed about distinctive White characteristics, Courtney replied, "well, you know, just regular food." No respondent could recall ever seeing chitterlings or seeing a Black person eating them. Even taking into account the presence of an African American adult, and the relative strangeness of talking openly about cultural differences in this context, the similarity in the language about difference is striking. Listening and trying to hear the taken-for-granted assumptions among these European American students, we come to understand the powerful role skewed public knowledge about people plays in shaping responses to differences.

The European American students reading African American literary texts evidenced some similarities with their African American peers. Most notable was the liking response, and specific behaviors that proceeded liking. These included: (1) a verbal acknowledgement—"I like the book"; (2) taking over ownership of the reading event(s); and (3) allocating special times to read and the completion of reading assignments ahead of schedule.

There were, however, critical differences between the two groups of students, and these differences shared a relationship with the culture, race and gender of the respondent. Whereas the African American students of both genders initiated discussions about culture, European American students tended to avoid cultural discourse. Two examples excerpted from separate interviews with Tasha (an African American) and Courtney illustrate this point:

> I would read about struggle—how long it took to fight for what we have now . . . because this is where our heritage comes from . . . It'll [African American literature] be different in language and the way people live or the customs they live by . . . (Tasha)

I think that slavery and everything—it seems like such an old issue. I think there's no sense talking about the past. I don't like to be in a position where you have to pick from side to side what you are. We should all be just equal Americans, not African Americans . . . they're the same as us. (Courtney)

While both Tasha and Courtney made distinctions between the past and the immediate present, their association with the past and their expectations about what can be gained from examining the past are strikingly different. Tasha's expectation was that African American literature would present history, culture, ways of living, struggle and survival. Courtney's expectation was that Black literature was about slavery. Although Courtney said "they're the same," she acknowledged that slavery made some differences; she did not venture to explore what these differences might be. Tasha affirmed that the past was connected to her present situation and concerns. Courtney distanced her present situation and her cultural group from "them" and from a past that lacked personal relevance for her. An underlying assumption in Courtney's reasoning—at this particular point—was that talk about difference and talk about the past was the problem. In this logic, silence or distance were both solution and resolution.

The More I Know, the Better I Feel: A European American Female Revision

Over time, across multiple texts, and in the more private domain of the interview, the European American female students incorporated their analysis of African American literary texts into their analysis of their community, their families and a critique of the larger society. For example, when asked to talk about her reading of *The House of Dies Drear* (Hamilton, 2006), Courtney smiled and settled back in her chair. What follows is Courtney's personal response.

Oh, I could just see those caves. I can imagine running across that river there and getting to that house. I would have explored every one of those caves and I would have been so glad to be there and to be safe . . . You know, maybe Black literature should be set aside, special like, so I can see it better for myself.

Courtney's response to *House*, her choice of language about the text, suggests that she engaged the text in a personal and affective manner. She visualized herself in the novel's caves; she conceptualized a flight to freedom as a heroic act that she could personally participate in. So close was her identification with Thomas that when he dropped a flashlight in one scene, Courtney reported that she "grabbed his hand and ran." Identifying with the plight of a runaway slave and the curiosity of an African American child, Courtney found wonder, security and perhaps a quintessential truth about humanity's great quest for freedom. Moreover, she began to revise her thinking about cultural differences among people and among literary texts. Black literature as a genre, she reasoned, had intrinsic value for her. Her references to African American texts changed from comments about what "they [teachers] wanted [students] to read and understand" to observations on how she felt about her reading. Her references to "them" (African Americans) were replaced with "I would have run, I would have felt glad and safe." As we closed our interview, she indicated that she would "love to visit a house" like the one described in the novel. She and Lucy planned a special shopping trip to purchase the sequel "because we have been arguing about what's in that trunk. Lucy thinks it will have maps, journals and treasures the slaves used to help others run away; I keep filling it up and emptying it out. I don't know what I want to be in there!"

Lucy struggled with the ambiguities of race and gender at home and at school. The highest ranked junior in the school, she began receiving scholarship invitations in early October. She would be the first high school graduate in her immediate family; her family wanted her to help at home with the younger children and perhaps send one of her brothers to college. As noted previously, Lucy's sense of cultural differences in fictive, historical and contemporary people was "basically, we're all the same; they got their culture and we have ours; they just eat different food like chitterlings and have different hairstyles." When I asked her how she had come to know these things she replied: "Well, you just know some things and you can easily see the hair—it's kinda—curly?"

After the class had read and discussed Jacobs' *Incidents in the Life of a Slave Girl* (1987), I asked Lucy, "if you had been a slave, here in this city, what would you have done?" She paused a bit, and responded, "well it would depend on how I was treated." Her statement seemed to be both a question and a statement. Responding, I replied, "well, like the old doctor who owned Harriet Jacobs, he wanted her body." Without hesitation, and with considerable forcefulness, Lucy replied, "I would have run, and I would have taken my children!" Lucy's remark is a striking example of the critical importance of a personal, affective response to a text.

Lucy's response invites us to consider what would have been acceptable human bondage to an intelligent and independent young woman. When asked, she could not say. Lucy's response underscores how the status of whiteness as opposed to blackness in the larger society, and the dominance of that position within the traditional curriculum, contributes to inane assumptions of cultural sameness (somewhere, under the skin where it can not be readily observed) and simultaneously reinforces diametrical differences. Lucy, with her excellent grades and her passion for learning and knowing did not have a vocabulary with which to talk about difference. Quoting Paula, "that's a shame . . . a doggone shame." Yet given the cultural hegemony of American society in general, and the traditional school curriculum in particular, unexamined contradictions tend to be the norm, and for some, appear to make a good deal of sense. That is, although the European American students typically asserted that they did not like the traditional literature required for class, these texts presented a view of life that the dominant social order dictated they were supposed to read, to value, to understand and to embrace as their own.

The classics—presented in the class anthology, from the Planters and Puritans to Hemingway—represent at least one version of American values, aesthetics, ethics and truth. Like Paula, students may read these texts and wonder where African American and Native American people were for four hundred years, but they may graduate from high school with honors, and never hear the voices of the "Others." Thus, curricular marginalization of people of color may not appear problematic to dominant members. Equally problematic for Lucy and Courtney was the fact that they genuinely liked the second novel Paula assigned, *The House of Dies Drear*. They seemed disquieted by the fact that they liked a "Black" book and disliked *The Scarlet Letter* (Hawthorne, 1978), a "White" book.

The infusion of African American perspectives into the curriculum through literary texts initially created tensions among European American students. The presence of blackness presented by African American literary texts in Paula's classroom seems to have precipitated a shift in the position of power. Paula called my attention to different seating arrangements and a shift in class behaviors, remarking:

> Have you noticed the seat changing going on in here? Have you noticed that the Black kids are talking more and the White kids are almost quiet? Do you think that the Black kids feel that they have more right to speak when the topic is about Black literature? Do you think the White kids resent it? . . . Well there it is. I knew there was racism in this school and in this class. Better that it comes out in the open so that I can deal with it!

There seemed to be an ideological as well as a geographical shift among the students. Further, both African American and European American female students tended to isolate Jake, a self-proclaimed "White, male chauvinist, superior being" who swore that he and his friends "proved all women (including his mother) were prostitutes," and that "all literature was lies." Jake maintained his hard-line approach; the students seemed to tire of his jokes and the diversions from classwork they often occasioned; they avoided (when possible) small group work with him. Lucy and Courtney criticized him regularly.

The African American literature offered African American students an unusual opportunity to celebrate and to affirm blackness in school. Conversely, the centrality of African American perspectives in texts placed European

American students in the position of sometimes being tangential, rather than central, to the world of the text and the classroom. These tensions contributed in important ways to the emerging social critiques of both African and European American students.

Student Centered Social Critiques: Text, Talk and Analysis

Student social critiques that emerged from this study focused upon those areas of society where adolescent students accumulated much of their experience; specifically, their cultural/racial group, community, family, friends and curricular experiences. These students were both products of and participants in social transformations. The students not only engaged in social commentary, but openly criticized and made judgments about taken-for-granted social "truths" and the value of particular social customs, laws and practices. Critical comment emerged from student participation in literate activities. Reading, interpreting and analyzing literary texts, and making judgments about the appropriateness and inappropriateness of the behaviors of fictive characters are important indicators of what constitutes empowered readers. In Paula's class, engaging the contradictions and challenges presented by discourse about race, culture and gender led the students toward a literacy of promise.

In general, the social commentaries articulated by the students were couched in their aesthetic responses to African American literary texts. Lucy and Courtney, in a focus group interview in which *The Color Purple* (Walker, 2003) was the overall topic, articulated a social commentary upon both race and gender issues in their community, family and friendship groups. The following excerpt illustrates this point:

Lucy: My boyfriend is always trying to tell me what to do. He didn't want me to go on the field trip the other day . . . He hates Black people because he was beaten up by someone Black. He hates Liz because she went with Troy.

Courtney: There are a lot of fights around here about that—White girls dating Black guys.

Lucy: The White boys really rag out White girls who date Black guys. They call 'em every dirty name in the book. But they don't put down White boys who go with Black girls.

Courtney: . . . they never say anything when it's the other way around. My brother-in-law was a Grand Dragon in the Klan. He's calmed down now that he has a wife and child, but he's a real racist, and my sister is getting more and more like him . . .

Courtney: . . . these gangs, like the KKK and everything . . . I mean they're not necessary. They are people who had a hard life, like my brother-in-law, and they just take it out on Black people.

Both Lucy and Courtney reported that they had taken some abuse from White friends because of their friendship with Blacks. Lucy added that "my boyfriend wants me to drop out of honors because Troy and Len are in the class and we do a lot of things together outside of school." She continued however, "I'm not dropping honors and nobody can tell me who to have for friends!" The above interview, which occurred near the end of the study, was the first time these young women directly and explicitly addressed the issue of racism among Whites. In this interview, they moved toward rather than away from discourse about cultural/racial differences, and analyzed particular and personal racial attitudes of Whites they knew as being problematic. They described racism as a "White" problem.

The conversation in this interview was passionate. Before we closed our interview, both young women said they would remember the reunion in *The Color Purple*. When I asked why, Lucy responded, "because it was so special and it made me cry. It makes me cry every time I read it . . . " Finally, I asked, "do you think a White author could have written this book?" Simultaneously they replied, "no," with Lucy explaining: "I don't think a White person would understand. I think a White person would focus more on White people and abuse." Watching their young faces, I reflected that these young women have complicated lives and complex social situations to work their way through. At the same time, I reflected upon how much hope and how much potential was housed in their excellent minds, honest voices and generous hearts. I wondered who would help them.

The articulation of social critiques by students led towards a different kind of literacy—different in intensity and degree, insofar as reader affect contributed to a re-reading of the world and the reader's socio-cultural place in it. What this means in terms of the kinds of literate activities that may facilitate student learning in school and the role of the teacher and the curriculum in the multicultural debate will be the focus of the conclusion of this chapter.

An RX for Teachers: Cultural Consciousness/ Cultural Exchanges

Affective reader-response can initiate powerful meaning formations for the individual respondents and a community of readers. The notion of cultural consciousness establishes a distinction between being talked to and being talked about. "Talked about" implies a one-way monologue: one that is seen through the eyes of others and which offers an inadequate and distorted self consciousness (Du Bois, 2007). In the traditional canon, African Americans are described and talked about by others. Morrison (1993) has argued that

the presence of Blackness in America has fed white literary imaginations for centuries. For the most part, the literature of the United States has taken as its concern the architecture of a new white man . . . Playing in the dark, the constructed white man is able to position himself against a choked Africanist presence. Black characters exist at the pleasure of and to serve the needs of their White creators; rarely do the characters in these texts express their vision of the world in ways that reflect an authentic Blackness.

(p. 15)

Among the adolescents in the study, we can see some of the consequences of inadequate knowledge of self and others. The teacher and some of the students defined themselves as ignorant, despite or perhaps because of their schooling experiences.

"Talking with" suggests a dialogue—an exchange of ideas, feelings and responses; it is an interactive relationship with shared understanding and references. Gaps, or information that the narrator or story teller leaves out, may be inferred in culturally appropriate or inappropriate ways (Genette, 1983; Steffenson et al., 1979). However, both appropriate and inappropriate cultural extensions of a literary text provide for teachable occasions for extending readers' cultural knowledge within a community of readers when managed by a teacher who actively engages student discourse. Paula steadfastly sought ways to explore conflicts and contradictions with her students, not to silence or intimidate them, but to make conflict the subject of debate. At one point, she remarked, "I hate silence. I like to know what they are thinking."

Clearly, the teacher is a critical element in the journey toward a literacy of promise. It is equally clear that a teacher who has claimed a responsible and scholarly approach toward learning and social justice, offers the best opportunity for adolescents to become empowered readers/learners. The opportunity to explore a multiplicity of cultural perspectives and to participate in cultural exchanges adds to readers' repertoire of responses about books, difference and people. The curriculum, therefore, ought to provide adolescent readers with a broad basis for reading and responding to texts that includes multiple opportunities for cultural exchanges.

In order for empowerment to occur, multicultural education must become a viable process of educating people for the twenty-first century. The practice of merely "mentioning" cultural difference and ignoring the basic content of the curriculum must be revised. The traditional chronological order of the American literature curriculum, with its emphasis on the emergence of America as a new, strong and European American male nation, must likewise be revised because it is inadequate. Time ordering encourages teachers to cover material rather than to engage students in learning; huge cultural omissions are often the result. A logical alternative is thematic ordering, for example justice, freedom and survival. In this way, students can look at the emergence of America and the world from the perspective of all the social actors in historical events, including those who did not conquer, yet whose presence and voices contribute to world civilization.

Toward an Empowered Literacy: Risk and Reward

Moving toward a literacy of promise is not without risk. Tensions may be partially attributable to the historic reality of many cultures living side-by-side for several centuries and sometimes imitating each other in selective ways, but rarely fully comprehending the extent and meaning of their differences. When the cultural dynamic, created and vitalized by the community, comes together, readers, texts and social contexts cannot be easily appropriated and exploited by European Americans, who have been socialized in language, social custom and schooling to accept, unexamined, the essential rightness and superiority of whiteness. Within the context of American social, cultural and political history, African Americans have been cast as strangers and sometimes exotic (Abrahams, 1994). Thus, the presence of an authentic blackness defined and described by culturally conscious African American literary texts, may confound and disturb European American notions of self and the other. This confusion among European Americans encouraged distancing, and in some cases fear and a caustic devaluing of African American and female perspectives.

In the same vein, the experiences in Paula's classroom indicated that African American students need the assistance of the curriculum and the teacher as ambassador to assist them in their journey toward writing a revised epistemology of America and their place in it. As Len, an African American male student, put it:

> If them dudes hanging over there on that corner could read something about their history and their culture, they would know that hanging on the corner ain't so cool. It ain't what Black is really about.

Students involved in socio-cultural exchanges in an honest and safe environment, can articulate and explore their understanding, and receive support for their revisions.

Among well-intentioned European American students, the bestowal of White attributes—"They are like us"—bespeaks a socialization that both denies difference and denigrates the "other." Statements such as, "they are like us," are generous, but biased and emerged from student attempts to articulate in positive terms attributes that they have learned over time are negative. Such statements should be signals for the ambassador/teacher that work needs to be done.

When other perspectives were regularly sought, students' responses became more layered; they included alternative perspectives provided by African American literary texts and African American readers. Giving African American perspectives a voice and a respected place in the curriculum seemed to dissipate African American readers' anger and frustration, while at the same time empowering them to ask questions of their teachers and peers. Hearing, sharing and adding to the symphony of voices in texts and in African American people seemed to dissipate European American females' fear of difference, while at the same time empowering them to question socio-cultural relationships in their school and community.

This chapter argues that a fundamental grounding in multicultural education can mitigate the superficial and simplistic knowledge of self and others that students acquire when the curriculum lacks substantive content. Simply mentioning difference or telling school children to "treat everybody right" fails to prepare students for participation in critical, global discourse. Further, silence does not resolve cultural ambiguity, contradiction or conflict; silence may lead to further conflict. Importantly, this chapter argues that we need not think of multicultural education as something to be done for children of color. Rather, it is clear that multicultural education is critical for European American students who need considerably more than chitterling knowledge, good hearts and good intentions to survive the harsh reality of racism in their families and communities. Fortified with knowledge and free of fear and ambiguities, students like Courtney and Lucy can be powerful agents for change among the Americans with whom they come into contact. America cannot afford to leave such children at risk.

Questions for Discussion

1. In what ways does racism affect "the oppressor as well as the oppressed?" Think about the ways racism places White children at risk.
2. How did African American literary texts affect the students of color in Paula's class? How did these texts affect the White students?
3. What are your favorite books? Consider why you like them. In what ways could you relate socially and culturally to the texts?
4. Consider your own required reading list in high school. How would you characterize the majority of the books you read?
5. Can you recall any books that were written by authors of color?

Extension Activities

1. Survey your high school library or local bookstore. How many books are included that have been written by persons of color? Are these books "authentic" to their representative cultures?
2. Conduct research on famous African American authors. Read their autobiographies.
3. Analyze traditional novels for bias. In your analysis, you might consider the following:
   - who has the power;
   - the beliefs and values of the protagonists;
   - whose ways of "being in the world" are valued, and whose are marginalized;
   - the ways in which persons of color are portrayed;
   - the underlying ideology of the text (for example, individualism/ individual achievement characteristic of middle/upper-class Whites versus group identity/group achievement characteristic of many populations of color).

Notes

1.   All names of identifiable places and people in this chapter are pseudonyms.
2.   This question was posed by Paula Reynolds (a pseudonym) at the beginning of a year long, naturalistic research study. The question framed her curricular choices and pedagogical choices.

References

Aboud, F.E., & Skerry, S.A. (1984). The development of ethnic attitudes: A critical review. *The Journal of Cross Cultural Psychology 15*, 3–34.

Abrahams, R.D. (1994). *Singing the master: The emergence of African American culture in the plantation South.* New York: Penguin.

Beach, R. (1983). Attitudes, social conventions and response to literature. *Journal of Research and Development in Education 16*(3), 47–54.

Blauner, B. (1999). Talking past each other. In F. L. Pincus & H. J. Ehrlich (Eds.), *Race and Ethnic Conflict, 2ⁿᵈ edition* (pp. 30–40). Boulder, CO: Westview.

Brewer, W.F., & Ohtsulka, K. (1988). Story structure, characterization, just world organization, and reader affect in American and Hungarian short stories. *Poetics 17*, 395–415.

Bruner, J. (1987). *Actual minds, possible worlds.* Cambridge, MA: Harvard University Press.

Du Bois, W.E.B. (2007). *The souls of black folk,* NY: Oxford University Press.

Edelsky, C. (1999). On critical whole language practice: Why, what, and a bit of how. In C. Edelsky (Ed.), *Making justice our project: Teachers working toward critical whole language practice* (pp. 7–35). IL: NCTE.

Fish, S. (1980). *Is there a text in this class?* Cambridge, MA: Harvard University Press.

Frankenburg, R. (1993). *White women, race matters: The social construction of whiteness.* Minneapolis, MN: University of Minnesota Press.

Franklin, J.H. (1993). *The color line: Legacy for the twenty-first century.* Columbia, MO: University of Missouri Press.

Galda, L. (1983). Research in response to literature. *Journal of Research in Education 16*(3), 1–7.

Genette, G. (1983). *Narrative discourse: an essay in method.* Ithaca, NY: Cornell University Press.

Gilligan, C., Ward, J.V., Taylor, J.M., & Bardige, B. (Eds.) (1990). *Mapping the moral domain.* Cambridge, MA: Harvard University Press.

Giroux, H.A. (1993). *Living dangerously: Multiculturalism and the politics of difference.* New York, NY: Peter Lang.

Halasz, L., Laszlo, J., & Pleh, C. (1988). The short story: Cross-cultural studies in reading short stories. *Poetics 17*, 297–303.

Hamilton, V. (2006). *The house of Dies Drear.* New York: Simon & Schuster.

Hawthorne, N. (1978*). The scarlet letter.* New York: Dorling Kindersley Publishing.

Jacobs, H.A. (1987). *Incidents in the life of a slave girl: Written by herself.* Cambridge, MA: Harvard University Press.

Kincheloe, J.L. (2002). *Teachers as researchers: Qualitative inquiry as a path to empowerment, 2ⁿᵈ edition.* New York: Routledge.

Langer, J.A. (1988). The role of literature in cognitive development. In *Reading, writing and civic literacy: A conference report.* (Co-sponsored by Law and Citizenship Unit, St. Louis Public Schools, Missouri and the School of Education, Suny, Albany.)

Morrison, T. (1993). *Playing in the dark: Whiteness and the literary imagination.* NY: Knopf Publishing Group.

Purves, A.C. (1981*). Reading and literature: American achievement in international perspective.* Urbana, IL: NCTE.

Purves, A.C., & Rippere, V. (1968*). Elements of writing about a literary work.* Champaign, IL: NCTE.

Rabinowitz, P.J. (1998). *Before reading: Narrative conventions and the politics of interpretation.* Columbus, OH: The Ohio State University Press.

Rosenberg, S. (1988). Personality and affect in Hungarian and American short stories: A replication and extension. *Poetics 17*, 385–394.

Rosenblatt, L. (1995). *Literature as exploration, 5th edition.* New York: Modern Language Association.

Rothenberg, P.S. (1988). *Racism and sexism: An integrated study.* New York, NY: St. Martin's Press.

Rotheram, M.J., & Phinney, J.S. (Eds.) (1987). *Children's ethnic socialization: Pluralism and development.* Newbury Park, NJ: Sage.

Steffensen, M.S., Joag-Dev, C., & Anderson, R.C. (1979). A cross cultural perspective in reading comprehension. *Reading Research Quarterly, 15*(1), 10–29.

Walker, A. (2003). *The color purple.* San Diego, CA: Harcourt Trade Publishers.

Weiler, K. (1988). *Women teaching for change: Gender, class and power.* South Hadley, MA: Bergin & Garvey.

Weis, L. (Ed.) (1988). *Class, race and gender in American education.* Albany, NY: State University of New York Press.

Wolf, D.P. (1988). *Reading reconsidered: Literature and literacy in high school.* Albany, NY: College Entrance Exam Board.

Wright, G.C. (2004). *Life behind a veil: Blacks in Louisville, Kentucky 1865–1930.* Baton, Rouge, LA: Louisiana State University Press.

III
Realizing a Literacy of Promise through Oral and Popular Texts

7

Ebonics and the Struggle for Cultural Voice in U.S. Schools

IRA KINCADE BLAKE

". . . Then we have question and answer period. When I raise my hand, Mrs. — almost always calls on me . . . I always know the answers . . . She never lets my friends (two African American females) answer a question. When they raise their hands, Mrs. — always asks them if they want to go to the language lab." (Interviewer: What do they say?) "No." . . . (Interviewer: Does Mrs. — ever ask you if you want to go to the language lab?) "No." . . . (Interviewer: Why do you think she doesn't?) "Because I don't talk the way they do." (Interview: "What do you mean?)" I speak correct English; they don't." (Interviewer: How does it make you feel when your teacher asks your friends if they want to go to the language lab?) "Mmm, I don't like it very much. She should give them a chance to answer the questions, too. They could get them right."

(Excerpt from interview about everyday school
activities with seven-year-old African American Mica)

The use of language to dis-invite African American children from full participation in the educational process is illustrated in the above scenario on several levels. The most obvious level excludes Mica's friends from sharing in the genuine teaching/learning opportunities that occur in their classroom. A more subtle level presses Mica either to accentuate or to lessen the linguistic differences between her own speaking and that of her friends. The latter would likely jeopardize Mica's invitations to participate in the classroom in the future. The former might harm her affiliation with her friends. Although Mica did not report any tensions with her friends, the eventuality of such tensions is palpable and captured in labels such as "Oreo," which is ascribed to persons seen as possessing more mainstream than African American traits. While this text focuses on the challenges of teaching African American high school students, this chapter intentionally begins with childhood. The reader must keep in mind that children enter formal education excited and fully equipped to use their home language as a tool for mastering the activities there. From the beginning, the treatment of their home language influences their perceptions of themselves as good or bad learners, particularly in formal schooling contexts. Over a period of thirteen years, if they remain in school, African American children and youth typically can learn more about what is "wrong" with their language than receive valuable instructional and personal support to apply what they bring to the classroom to realize more of their human potential. In terms of their home language, teachers often understand little about and provide little practical insight into its distinctiveness and similarity to the version of American English favored in schools. What is really at issue is whether the home language of African American children has any place in school, and if so, should it be leveraged in school learning?

Giving African American Children Their Voice in School: The Oakland School Board Resolution

On December 18, 1996, the Oakland School Board in California unanimously adopted a resolution to address the types of experiences described above as well as the generally limited understanding of the nature of language and its relationship to formal education (Perry & Delpit, 1998). The board acknowledged and ascribed legitimacy to *Ebonics*, the native language of many Oakland school children (Fields, 1997) and a large percentage of African Americans. Nationally, African Americans as a group are disproportionately working-class and poor, and typically live in separated neighborhoods and inner city residential complexes (Logan, 2001) where the spoken language commonly includes several Ebonics features which mark their speech's distinctiveness from Standard American English, the preferred English variety of schools (see Gadsden & Wagner, 1995; see also Rickford, 2005). The board's main objective was to use Ebonics (better known as Black English and African American English) as an instructional tool to facilitate the academic performance of African American children and to assist them in learning the language of wider communication, Standard English.

Not unexpectedly, the resolution tapped a pervasive wellspring of criticism and apprehension, the agents of which represented a rare U.S. melting pot of consensus. This pot included the opinion of prominent African Americans such as the liberal Jesse Jackson in the midst of expected Anglo American conservatives such as Rush Limbaugh. However upon reflection, the blending of liberal and conservative positions on language is not really surprising at all, if one considers how various ways of speaking and writing, thinking and behaving have been marked and reinforced in the historical, social, economic, and educational relations among various racial and ethnic groups in the United States. Among U.S. citizens who have historically experienced much of American society at the margins, non-mainstream ways of speaking, writing, thinking, and behaving often trigger a host of negative, unhealthy stereotypes. For a disproportionate number of African Americans, particularly those living in urban/rural communities and labeled working-class and poor, these stereotypes have constrained further already limited, tenuous opportunities (cf. Logan, 2001).

Historically, the speech of most African Americans has been characterized as "something less than language" (Champion & Bloome, 1995), unlike the Standard American English variety that is taught in traditional American schools and used as the primary mechanism for most instructional transactions. African American adults and children alike have heard the speech of Blacks labeled bad English, broken English, and poor grammar. Such stereotypic descriptions not only permeate the mainstream of American society but are also prevalent in the African American community. Thus, the reaction within the Black community to the idea of using Ebonics in the schooling of Black children was expectedly heated. However, the language controversy actually reflects a more profound, systemic social state of affairs. By examining the additional factors of culture and race, their continued role in modulating the opportunities of African Americans can be better understood.

School as Cultural Battle Ground

A review of American education places language difference, cultural membership, and racial identity at the center of our understanding of varied performance on any measure. Whether we consider achievement on standardized tests, special educational services, drop-out rates or graduation rates, a strong relationship exists between linguistic, social, racial, and cultural differences and measures of educational quality. Positive relationships typically associate White, middle/upper-class privilege and its characteristics with greater academic success, while negative relationships usually signal associations between non-White, working-class statuses, their linguistic and cultural characteristics, and academic under-performance. The historical persistence of these relationships, and the pervasive legislative and social refusal to engage in genuine, pragmatic dialogue about their redress, represent the codification of cultural, linguistic and racial inequity in the United States.

Powell (Chapter 1) offers a process perspective on the hegemonic educational structure, using James Paul Gee's (cf. Gee, 2001; Bartolomé, 1998) conception of discourse (limited to specific linguistic forms) versus Discourse (as the speaking, thinking, behaving, and valuing that signal group membership). She argues that the traditional engagement of formal literacy in schools (current *schooled literacy*) has accomplished at least three negative results. First, it marginalizes the distinctive ways of speaking, behaving and thinking that children learn at home (home Discourses). Second, it is possibly "creating failure" for students who understand and practice their cultural knowledge and ways. And finally, the school's traditional practices reinforce the prestige associated with the "Discourse of power" and other cultural practices of the White, middle/upper-class experience, and proffer potential acceptance if one conforms. The experiences of Mica and her friends bring to life these consequences and how they impact the personal lives of African American children.

Schooling, particularly schooled literacy, has been a tool for facilitating and constraining learning opportunities for African American children by labeling a single Discourse as superior to others. Moreover, schooled literacy has maintained an oppressive racial and cultural tone that typically excludes the linguistic sounds and forms, meanings, and behavioral ways associated with African American experience as it maintains the privileged status of White, middle/upper-class experience. The greater social and educational challenge then is how to integrate students' language and cultural experiences in ways that support student achievement but also promote the understanding and value of distinctive human experiences.

One step in this direction is an articulation of the differences in human behavior and learning that result from distinctive cultural and racial experiences. Language represents a significant nexus for understanding how a hegemonic culture facilitates and inhibits learning within a culturally and racially diverse social space.

Setting the Record Straight First: Language Matters but Culture and Race Can Matter More

Americans have been socialized to believe that learning to speak Standard American English helps to eliminate many barriers to a better social and economic life. Personal testimonials and research attest in various ways to this as a pervasive belief, and in many cases, as proven fact. However, the cause and effect line is not always a straight one. Language as speech can and often does take a back seat to one's cultural and racial identity. What is important about the following example is that it took (and continues to take) place at the national level, exemplifying the relative roles of language, culture and race as modulators of opportunity in U.S. society.

In an article that focused on President George W. Bush's speech proficiency titled "Confronting 'NOO-kyuh-luhr' proliferation a lost cause" (*The Gazette*, Sunday, October 13, 2002, A21), the relationship between ways of speaking, race, culture and the power structure are evident. At issue is President Bush's pronunciation of the term "nuclear." Although a usage panel convened by a major dictionary overwhelming rejected President Bush's usage as unacceptable Standard American English pronunciation, the article strains to explain that Bush's pronunciation "is not uncommon, even among *prominent* and *educated* people" (column 1, paragraph 3, italics added). Legitimacy is forced by stating that three of the last U.S. presidents (Dwight Eisenhower, Gerald Ford, and Jimmy Carter) expressed this variant. Thus, the breaching of prescriptive rules for the Standard American English version spoken by White, middle/upper-class users are treated as tolerable when a person's culture and race signal privilege.

During his presidential campaign, the criticisms levied at President Bush's nonstandard use of American English pronunciation and grammatical structures were catalogued nationwide across all forms of public media. However, despite his use of "bad" English, he has suffered few obstacles to the best social and economic opportunities in American society. To demonstrate the superordinate importance of race, I will cite the case of Mr. Smit (a pseudonym), a hard-working male of African descent. Although for several years, Mr. Smit has helped his employer exceed a number of publicized company goals (which also resulted in increased revenues), he was not allowed to represent the company on a local TV program because of his "bad" English. Mr. Smit's exclusion was intentional for the reason mentioned, even though the TV program had explicitly requested his presence. The question then is under what circumstances is linguistic difference significant enough to derail merited opportunity for public representation and recognition? For example would Mr. Smit have been perceived similarly if English had been viewed as his second language?

Mr. Smit's way of speaking is grounded in the range of his cultural experiences, just as President Bush's is. However, President Bush's upper-class White privileged status insulates him from any direct penalties for demonstrating less than the desirable Standard American English features. As indicated above, President Bush may have suffered some teasing, but he generally was given the benefit of the doubt (i.e., that an individual is of importance, has valued characteristics and meaningful experiences to contribute) and fairly allowed to pursue self advancement. Also, I am sure that, unlike Mr. Smit, President Bush has rarely felt compelled to acknowledge that he "doesn't talk so good." Again, despite the linguistic forms of his discourse, the privileges associated with his identified group's Discourse were not reduced. The same was not granted to Mr. Smit, a member of a racially different and non-privileged speech group, despite no less a demonstration of commitment, belief in the American work ethic, and verifiable productivity. Importantly, one would assume that President Bush's children, like him, have not had their opportunities to succeed curtailed. Contrasting, historical practice suggests that the opportunities of Mr. Smit's children will be systematically impacted, as his were, if their speech contains many features associated with Ebonics.

President Bush demonstrates that ways of speaking should not be taken as evidence of lazy tongue, poor education, and less intelligence, characteristics typically attributed to persons such as Mr. Smit. President Bush's speech illustrates that, at the highest level of public power and visibility, each of us is a product of life experiences, and those experiences claim us as participants in obvious and subtle ways. At the same time, his treatment reveals that racial and cultural hegemony begets more privilege through permission to display behaviors customarily deemed unacceptable.

Turning squarely to language, what does it really mean to have a different way of speaking? More specifically, why is variation in speaking and its relationship to schooled learning so important to understand? How does variation in speaking influence learning in a context that promotes only one way of speaking? And finally, how do such limitations affect learners? This chapter addresses these kinds of questions, with the objective of demonstrating that the context for acquiring a first language results in at least two important developments: (1) the *structural* aspects of home language, which include the sounds, words, and grammar; and (2) the *functional* aspects of home language, which include how meaning, understanding and expression are ascribed to the physical and social realities of everyday experiences. In Gee's (1989) framework, language structure would be identified with *discourse*, or "connected stretches of language that make sense" (p. 6), while language function falls within *Discourse*, which are "*saying(writing)-doing-being-valuing-believing combinations . . . ways of being in the world*" (p. 6).

Language, then, is an extraordinary tool that enables us to create and share our intentions as it shapes our view of what to weigh as more or less valuable in our experiences. The Oakland School Board attempted to broaden the focus, to do more for African American children than to give them better access to a mainstream education. The board was determined to legitimize the cultural heritage and experience of the children by acknowledging the unique origin of their home language. Importantly, research does support the use of home language as a gateway to schooled literacy and formal learning (see Perry & Delpit, 1998; Smitherman, 1981). Moreover, when modulated like culture and race, language has profound effects on children's developing beliefs about who they are and can learn to be; what they do and can learn to do; with whom they can share and learn; and ultimately, to what they can aspire.

The Discourse of African Americans: Controversial by Any Name

As suggested earlier, the language of African Americans has been called different names at different historical periods. In addition to the term Ebonics there is African American English, Black English, Black English Vernacular, Black Dialect, and African American Vernacular English. Regardless of the appellation, discussion has always been contentious. There are two fundamental and related controversies regarding the distinctive spoken language of the majority of African Americans (Labov, 1995; Rickford, 2005), who live in largely mono racial urban areas separated from mainstream, non-Hispanic White suburban neighborhoods (Logan, 2001). The heart of the first blends the social and political. Is African American English, as "most speakers of Standard English think . . . just a badly spoken version of their language, marred by a lot of ignorant mistakes in grammar and pronunciation, or worse than that, an unimportant and mostly abusive repertoire of street slang used by an ignorant urban underclass" (Pullum, 1999, pp. 39–40)? The second focuses on the language origin and linguistic systems. If African American speech is not merely "a street version" of American English and is, as linguists inform us, a legitimate form of human languages, where does it come from? Each question will be addressed.

The study of the speech of African Americans has a long tradition (see the seminal work of Lorenzo Dow Turner, 1949, titled *Africanisms in the Gullah Dialect*). However, interest in its relationship to educational, social and economic access and mobility in U.S. society was heightened during the Civil Rights Movement of the 1960s. Of particular concern was the underachievement of African American children in school. As a result, many scholars and educators were looking for information that could be translated into instructional strategies to improve African American school performance (Bereiter & Engelmann, 1966; cf., Feagans & Farran, 1982). Since teaching and learning in school rely primarily on speaking, writing, and reading in Standard American English, comparative descriptions of Standard American English and the speech of African Americans were valuable in pinpointing substantial language differences. However, explanations of differences were typically grounded in a hegemonic, Anglo-American perspective, where the pronunciation and grammatical forms used by African Americans were labeled deficient or pathological. The goal, then, was one of remediation: to eliminate the non-standard forms permanently from their speech, replacing those forms with Standard American English ones.

In the early 1970s, linguists provided major insights into the nature of human language in order to counter prevalent language myths (see Wolfram, 1998). During that time, the speech of African Americans was best known as Black English. Research demonstrated that, similar to all languages, Black English was systematic and rule-governed. In relation to Standard American English, Black English was different not deficient, dispelling the linguistic inferiority myth. In terms of the grammaticality myth, researchers (e.g., Dillard, 1972; Labov, 1973; Smitherman, 1977/1986) described key differences which occur in the *patterning* of sounds and other grammatical structures between Black English and Standard American English. For example, when two consonants that are voiceless stops (such as /s/ and /t/) occur together at the end of a Standard American English word (e.g., *test*), the final consonant is not pronounced (*tes*). An example of grammatical structure is the use of *be* to mark an event or state that occurs habitually (*They be coughing when the teacher come in the room* in Black English v. *They always begin to cough when the teacher enters the room* in Standard American English). In addition to linguistic forms, ways of using language to express one's thoughts and to decipher the speech of others comprise a Discourse kit (similar to Gee's *Identity kit*). This kit serves as the anchor for expression about and interpretation of the world through a group's cultural viewpoint.

From discourse to Discourse: A Cultural Conceptualization of Language

Every dialect, every language, is a way of thinking. To speak means to assume a culture.

(Frantz Fanon, 1967)

Fanon's statement succinctly captures the integral relationship between language and culture. Culture is the paradigm for experiencing the personal, social and physical dimensions of one's world. Language reflects the manner in which those dimensions have been coded and assigned degrees of meaningfulness by an individual's culture. For children, the kind of ecological experiences that a child's parents, siblings, relatives, and preceding generations have had all contribute to the kind of language learned, the types of behaviors valued, the kinds of beliefs held, and the communally held blueprint for living. In other words, what group members do provide the basis not only for "*what* is to be learned but also *how*" to determine the worth of different features of what is experienced (Blake, 1999). Bloom (1993) characterized this process as a "tuning in" to certain aspects of the environment. This valuation, in turn, globally influences children's personal beliefs, attitudes, feelings, and behaviors. Thus, the manner of expression and many of the ideas, feelings, attitudes, and behaviors are shaped largely through the actual interactions with others in situational contexts. Reciprocally, children's interpretations of the expressed ideas, feelings, attitudes, and behaviors of others are in line with culturally sanctioned meanings and are reinforced by adults to be such.

Derived from these experiential dynamics are the fundamental tools for learning—informally and formally—which equip children to construct a reality of their own that is typically culturally coherent with the one continually offered by the community members around them. All children, then, bring this equipment—a cultural backpack with its complementary Discourse kit—for participating in the world of school. No matter how amenable children are to acquiring the potentially new ways of communicating, preferring, believing and behaving, they must leverage what they have already experienced in their home community. Consequently, teachers must pay attention to what children's ways of speaking, thinking, and behaving signal about the content of their Discourse kits and the customs, values and beliefs within their cultural backpacks (Labov, 1995; Simpkins & Simpkins, 1995). Beyond the linguistic forms of Ebonics, what comprises the Discourse kit of African American children?

Smitherman (1977/1986) speaks of "language and style," where Black speech reflects "a [cultural] point of view, a way of looking at life, and a method of adapting to life's realities" (p. 3). The Discourse kit is shaped by dimensions of an African American worldview which is grounded in the ancestral African background, the experiences of slavery, racism, and discrimination, and marginal social integration. In addition to the phonological and grammatical features of Ebonics are a number of communicative devices. I will identify several; however, the work of Geneva Smitherman presents one of the more complete, accessible descriptions. One device is *Tonal Semantics* where rhythm and intonation make "songified patterns of speech" through which "the sound of what is said [is] . . . just as important as the 'sense'" (p. 135). Dr. Martin Luther King's famous "I have a Dream" speech provides an excellent example. Another is *Signification,* a common form of verbal insult accompanied by humor. Although signification can occur as a one-liner, a much discussed form that incorporates *Rhyming* and *Rapping* (two other tools) is *the Dozens* where African American males participate in competitive turn-taking of verbal insults (e.g., *Yo momma so big she wear a sign that say "wide load"*). Another discourse form is *Call and Response* where the speaker and audience carry on a conversation. The audience responds to the speaker's comments using a variety of phrases, vocalizations and gestures. Call and response is most readily observed in the Black church where the congregation will frequently respond to the minister's comments with *"Amen."*

Sensibly, when children are in settings (e.g., school) that require learning unfamiliar content they use implicit, familiar strategies and interpretations that are culturally grounded in at least two fundamental ways: (1) to determine what is worthy of knowing; and (2) to select the manner in which it will be understood and used most effectively. Here the emphasis is not only on readily identifiable cultural products (e.g., discourse as forms and grammar of Ebonics), but also the social practices or subjective cultural products (e.g., Discourse as tonal semantics) that shape the manner in which expression and interpretation in Black English is framed. Therefore, simply acquiring aspects of Standard American English (SAE) discourse does not mean proficiency in SAE Discourse. Acquiring SAE Discourse involves learning or assuming the "identity kit" of those in power—complete with the beliefs, values, and cultural assumptions of that Discourse. Consequently, bringing the phonological and grammatical forms (discourse) of African American English into the classroom is only part of what is needed to create an inclusive learning environment that broadly values the African American child's experience as important learning and a starting point for mainstream forms of learning. We must also value that child's Discourse.

The Cultural Backpack: Rules for World Engagement and Survival

Within the mainstream psychological and educational literature, there appears to be doubt that African American behavior is anything other than Anglo-American with the differences often euphemistically attributed to the effects of poverty. Previously, Mitchell (1982, p. 28) captured this belief by reiterating Glazer and Moynihan's 1963 assertion that "the Negro is only an American and nothing else. He has no values and culture to guard and protect." This perspective captures an ethnocentric attitude that persists, no matter how subtle, in the social sciences today: African Americans, like other indigenous minorities, are less competent versions of mainstream Anglo-Americans, but, they are, nevertheless, solely products of the American experience. The differences in performance between indigenous minorities and mainstream Anglo-Americans have been attributed to a number of factors, namely intellectual deficiency and environmental deprivation (Hale-Benson, 1986; Moore, 1982; Thomas, 1983).

"Culture, based on socioeconomic status rather than common history, became the superordinate factor in the explanation of ethnic differences and [mainstream] failure" (Mitchell, 1982, p. 28–29). For an extensive review of the theories and politics about the language of African Americans, see Morgan (1994) and Gadsden and Wagner (1995).

In order to understand why African American children perform the way they do, a closer look into the African American cultural backpack is useful. But first, a brief answer to the generic question, *How do children learn?* is in order. A helpful analogy is the two-sided coin, while keeping in mind that human development and behavior are fundamentally complex and result from the *interplay* of multiple internal and external variables, including physiology, emotion, personality, environmental context, social relations, economic conditions, and cultural experiences (see Cole, Cole, and Lightfoot 2005). On one side is the active role of children in the learning process, i.e., children bring their biology to the process—intellectual potential that sets boundaries for how well and how much they understand; maturational timetables that enable them to take advantage of certain experiences; and personality traits that make their development a personal and individual one. So we get a sense that learning style is influenced by the personal characteristics of the individual. On the other side of the coin are a wealth of environmental and social variables that have been associated with the kind and manner of children's learning. Some of these factors are nutrition, physical environment, family configuration, rank among siblings, parental education, parental employment, marital status, socio-economic class, race, ethnicity, and culture (see Huber, Pewewardy, & Parscal, 1991; Scott-Jones, 1984). As indicated, race, ethnicity, and culture are but a number of factors in a large, complex learning picture. As they develop, children not only learn in school but within families and communities, all of which "are interconnected and embedded in the larger economic, institutional, and ideological patterns of society" (Scott-Jones, 1995, p. 103). Accordingly, instructional strategies must address each child as both an individual and a cultural member. Even so, research has shown that race, ethnicity, and culture do have a significant, noteworthy impact on learning (see Ball, 1995; Jones, 2004; Shade, 1992) as historical modulators.

In particular, members of the social group assist children in dealing with information in ecoculturally effective ways. Hence, distinctive learning styles are shaped by children using their own capacities to function in the world as well as by the direct and indirect teaching of adults and older children. Adults and older children can be considered *masters* of the successful ways of saying, doing, thinking, believing, and valuing (Gee's Discourse) in their particular cultural context. As masters, they mentor young children (*apprentices*) in how to use the content of daily experiences in their home culture. I mention this specifically because the explanations of poor Black children's performance in mainstream contexts are taken often to reflect a restricted ability in conceptualization

(Jensen, 1969; Sigel, 1990). Because most measures and investigations are based primarily on comparison with another cultural experience, not enough is known about distinctive preferences for higher order thinking skills in African American children. The manner in which such skills are utilized in a range of situations must be explored within the African American experience before such a conclusion can be drawn.

Some "ways of knowing" are more effective in certain cultural environments. Accordingly, children learn to pay close attention to culturally valued features of the environment, rely on specific sensory modalities to support this attention, and organize resulting knowledge in a way that enables them to effectively participate in that particular experience. They also learn to spontaneously approach any environment with the assumption that their style of learning about the world, learned in their primary cultural context, will work in all situational contexts. It is important to note that styles should not be viewed as mutually exclusive, but as continuous with the differential weighting of features that create consistent, habitual style variations. An example is the learning of math facts by a "visual learner." Although the visual learner's preference for memorizing math facts might be flash cards, if cards are not available, a secondary strategy such as verbal rehearsal, practicing the facts out loud, might be used instead. This change in approach might increase the time and effort needed to learn the facts since the preferred style of learning is not available. The point is that a range of learning skills is available to children. However, the manner in which those skills configure for effectiveness is influenced by the degree of cultural support and practice they receive. Importantly, children come to use culturally supported learning styles spontaneously, because of their routine effectiveness. Thus, these are the learning styles they rely on in new learning contexts such as school. And until they as students become aware that their culturally supported styles are not effective, they will continue to use those styles. Their ability to shift to a more effective style will occur more efficiently and effectively with details about what they typically do as well as explicit guidelines about the adjustments they need to make.

How does culture foster a preferred way of interacting with and responding to the environment? What aspects of culture shape learning style? If we keep in mind that culture is that part of the environment that is human made (Herskovits, 1948), we can view a group's culture as that set of responses to perceived and real needs created by the dynamics between them and the environment. These responses or products are two types: objective and subjective. Examples of objective products are computers, pencils, and overhead projectors; examples of subjective products are racism, democracy, and academic standards. Although objective products may become less functional and replaced with new, more efficient versions, subjective products die hard. Such products represent the shared knowledge and learned meanings of people; these persist over time, produce the sharing of attitudes, social representations and values, and foster shared behavior patterns that reflect these values (their Discourse).

Tools in the Backpack: The African American Belief System

Undergirding African American culture is a belief system comprised of a set of subjective products that frame how to participate in and react to the world. Several scholars propose that this system is rooted in traditional West African culture (see Boykin, 1986; Dillard, 1972; Smitherman, 1977). Nine basic beliefs are summarized in the literature (adapted from Boykin, 1986 and Willis, 1992). *Spirituality* refers to a conviction that powers greater than man are at work in the universe; *Harmony* represents the belief that all components of existence are connected through balance and rhythm, making man and his environment interdependent; *Movement* is rhythm based on nature's cyclicity, important to life and reflected in music, dance, and other forms of nonverbal communication; *Verve* signifies that movement has a psychological dimension of an alertness in perceptual orientation where several stimuli are simultaneously attuned to; *Affect* refers to a joining of expressiveness and sensitivity to emotional cues with reasoning and problem solving; *Communalism* elevates relations with others over self; *Expressive Individualism* indicates that a person's unique style, flavor and spontaneity in an activity are valued; *Oral Tradition* denotes the importance of information that is learned and transmitted orally; and *Social Time Perspective* indicates that time is viewed cyclically and nonlinearly in relation to the participants in events. This belief system is seen as the foundation for how African Americans think about and participate in the world—i.e., their cultural cognitive orientation, or *cognitive style*. Herein, we are not speaking of a rigid orthodoxy which reflects the ways of thinking and knowing among all African Americans. Consider for example Drs. Angela Davis and Condoleeza Rice. The public ways in which these southern-born African American women participate in the world through career, intellectual and political choices is indicative of radically divergent belief systems.

Even so, research argues that the aforementioned beliefs are the basis for a habitual way of perceiving, organizing and remembering information about the world (Shade, 1992; Willis, 1992). For example, African Americans in research settings have been shown to rely on cues from the environment rather than develop structure by themselves. They look for a dynamic interdependence among components of the environment. For example, African Americans will monitor changes in sounds (e.g., background music) and insert their spontaneous responses (e.g., dancing or singing) into an ongoing, unrelated activity (e.g., a homework session). Moreover, African Americans have been characterized as people-oriented. An individual's life and experiences are bound to the community of which he/she is a part—family, friends, church, and neighborhood. In the words of one of my African American students, "Out of the *we* comes the *me*." This is a proverb she has heard from her grandmother repeatedly throughout her life. The student, in turn, approaches the world from within this framework and what it means for both personal and social effectiveness. In addition, African Americans are said to be intuitive thinkers, valuing the role that personal experience plays in understanding the way the world operates. They also respect the likelihood of some causes of events as being other than logical, which acknowledges the spiritual component of their belief system and its influence in conceptualizing and acting in the world. And last, African Americans focus on the social material in context as a primary source of information. They are sensitive to other people's behavior, feelings, and expressions.

Related to the way one thinks about the world is the way one gathers information to use when thinking about the world—i.e., *learning style*. Willis (1992) proposes reciprocal roles for cognitive style and learning style. Guided by the evidence from studies of African Americans and the belief system, she derives four key characteristics of an African American learning style. It tunes in to the *Social/Affective* information present in a context, looks for *Harmonious* relationships between features, relies on the *Expressively Creative* skills of the user to support learning, and uses *Nonverbal Communication* to confirm and express learning. Evidence for distinctive cognitive and learning styles in African Americans represents the operationalization of a cultural world view (Shade, 1982, 1992; Willis, 1992). A note of caution is required here. We must acknowledge individual differences in light of group patterns. In other words, an individual's own preferences for perceiving, conceptualizing, and interacting with the world may be distinctive, in particular ways, from his/her group's identified pattern of preference. Moreover, the converse is true as well: a member of one racial/ethnic group can exhibit a style considered characteristic of members of another racial/ethnic group. Styles are on a continuum; despite cultural preferences, no single group has a monopoly on one, regardless of historical circumstances and ecocultural demands.

The Revelation of Cultural Backpack in African American Discourse: Evidence from Preschoolers to High Schoolers

Cultural patterns of behaviors in African American children of different ages demonstrate the existence of culturally specific content guiding interaction with the world. Looking first at a longitudinal, observational study of African American mother-child dyads (Blake, 1993), the purposes (i.e., functions) served by both mother and child speech reflected a social emotional orientation for communication. The children, who were aged 19–27 months and videotaped with their mothers once a month, were learning to use language to manage relationships between persons, and mothers were reinforcing such uses through elaborated verbal and nonverbal participation in activities that supported personal knowledge and interpersonal relationships (e.g., doll play). A content analysis revealed that the mothers were apprenticing their children in elements of their *primary Discourses* (Gee, 1989). For example, Affect and Communalism were displayed through the children's personal, affective expressions (e.g., *scared, like, want*) and were frequently encouraged by the mothers. Also, the mothers attributed personal feelings to the doll (e.g., *Is the baby crying?*) during the children's play and evaluated the children's behavior (e.g., *That's a nice boy*). The verbal dialogue around activities with high social value such as dancing (reflecting Expressive Individualism) and the verbalization of the names of relatives and friends (Oral Tradition) was extended by the mothers' frequent spontaneous commenting, unlike their specific, narrow instrumental use of language when the child was engaged in object-based activities such as putting together a puzzle. And finally, the mothers often marked time or an event not by day or hour, but with the appearance, disappearance or reappearance of a person (e.g., *We'll go get tacos next time Ira come over*; Social Time Perspective). The children were learning the cultural worth of acts of expression and interpretation that emphasized a preference for feelings and attitudes about aspects of the world.

In an ethnographic study of personal narratives, Potts (1989) found that working-class Black preschoolers emphasized personal evaluation (Affect) when recounting experiences. Evaluative devices such as conditional statements and intensifiers (e.g., *even*) express the "personal meaning of the experience being recounted" (Potts, 1989, p. 56). He concluded that types, frequencies and patterns of evaluation were cultural rather than simply personal, and hence necessary for effective storytelling. Brice Heath's (1983) ethnographic work on language socialization within a rural, working-class Black community provides similar information about Black children's acts of expression. She found that the Black children entered school with little experience in listing and labeling objective information in the environment. Instead, they expressed reason-explanations and metaphorical uses of language. Heath also reported the commonplace occurrence of multiple interactors (Verve) in addition to dyadic exchanges. In another study of narratives, Wolf and Hicks (1989) examined the play narratives of two seven-year-old girls, one middle-class White and the other working-class Black. Among the distinctive features reported was the Black girl's narrative recounting of a short film as a "highly evaluated story" in which she retold events from the perspective of one of the film's characters and created a "*participatory* stance towards events" for the characters.

Spears-Bunton (1993) used multiple methods to investigate reader response in Black and White high school students. She found that Black high school readers frequently expressed personal relationships by aligning themselves with their interpretation of the text and extending their valuations to the larger Black population. For example, in responding to Nathaniel Hawthorne's *The Scarlet Letter*, Black students aligned themselves with Hester Prynne, advocated for her against the abuse and misuse of Reverend Dimsdale, and extended those opinions to real life experiences within their community. Based on a content analysis, Spears-Bunton concluded that the students' responses were grounded in their cultural knowledge for interpreting experiences within their respective groups. In a study of self-concept as learner and future time perspective in an alternative high school, Doucette-Gates (1992) used a sentence completion task to study future time perspective and found that African American adolescent males more often expressed their future goals in terms of interpersonal relationships rather than individual accomplishments.

Taken together, these findings about language acts of expression and interpretation reflect a preference in African American culture for personal expressiveness and viewing one's own experience as interdependent with that of others (Abrahams, 1974; Boykin, 1986). The manner in which language is used facilitates such interpersonal understanding and reinforces the cultural worth associated with interpersonal relations. Thus, the emphasis in acts of expression and interpretation appears to be congruent with aspects of the broader cultural orientation described by Boykin (1986) and Willis (1992). This is further supported by Abrahams' (1974) ethnographic study of a Black community in which he discovered the "tremendous importance placed upon friendships, and rivalries, loves and animosities" (p. 2). Moreover, the significance of learning and teaching about the personal (me) and the interpersonal (we) is embodied in the extended family configuration found among many Black families (Boyd-Franklin, 2003; Harrison, Wilson, Pine, Chan, & Buriel, 1990; McAdoo, 1999).

When School Disallows Diverse Cultural Backpacks

We must contemplate the potential outcomes of a persistent, distinctive world view for African American children in mainstream settings. How does such an orientation influence African American children's learning in school? One possibility is the directing of the children's perceptual processes toward interpersonal content and contextual information whereby a person's actions and states can be evaluated. This proposition is a critical one because the dominant orientation for school at present is one that emphasizes objective relationships rather than interpersonal ones, and facts rather than opinions and judgments (Cazden & Dickinson, 1981; Heath, 1983). An example is stating the fact that *the sky is blue* (observable fact) rather than opining that *the sky is nice* (personal evaluation). Thus, the orientation that children use in the school context can influence what they perceive as important for learning and shape the acts of expression and intention they display within that context. This, in turn, affects the teacher's assessment of what children know, and often what teachers think children can learn. Recalling Mica's friends, not only would it have been appropriate for the teacher to listen inclusively with respect to the form of their comments but also to the manner and content that they expressed. This may be crucial for teacher–learner relationship, because most instruction occurs through language. Importantly, if the teacher and learners unknowingly continue to approach a learning activity with divergent frames for interpretation and expression, at the very least, frustration will obstruct positive, effective teaching/learning transactions.

Leveraging African American Discourse in the Classroom: Opportunities for Cultural Voice in Learning

If the culture of the teacher is to become part of the consciousness of the child, then the culture of the child must first be in the consciousness of the teacher.

(Basil Bernstein cited in Gilyard & Stix, 1997, p. 1)

Bringing the phonological and grammatical forms (discourse) of African American English into the classroom is only part of what is needed to create a learning environment that broadly values the African American child's experience as important learning and to identify starting points for mainstream forms of learning. Elements of culturally preferred ways of speaking, thinking and behaving (African American Discourse) must be incorporated as well. Through the incorporation of elements of Ebonics as expressions of cultural practices, African American children will have a cultural anchor for generating more equitable opportunities to participate in classroom learning. However, this position is not really new but an expansion of previous ones.

Over decades, some elements of African American discourse (typically phonological and grammatical features) have been used in the formal instruction of language arts (Baratz & Shuy, 1969; Hoover, 1998; Hoover, Dabney, & Lewis, 1990; Simpkins & Simpkins, 1981). And despite belief to the contrary, there is reasonable, supportive evidence that the use of information about Ebonics does produce more effective strategies for facilitating the school learning of African American children (see Rickford & Rickford, 1995). There is also information available about how the differences between African American Discourse and Standard American English Discourse influence communicability (cf., Blake, 1999; Kochman, 1981). The problem is the persistent unwillingness to legitimize meaningful differences resulting from African American experience that obstructs such programmatic efforts, thereby continually derailing the engine for educational, hence social, reform for African Americans.

In order to better facilitate the learning of African American children, we need to understand and be able to strategically use elements from their cultural backpack in school learning. Problems arise, as for other children, when African American children cannot link their cultural and linguistic practices to new learning opportunities in ways that receive adult reinforcement. As cultural actors, they identify schemas, play out scripts, and experiment with information grounded in their cultural experience. Even the distinctive acts and thoughts attributed to an individual (such as nonconforming behaviors) take place within the framework of culture. Thus, even when individuals attempt an adjustment to the demands of various social spaces, they first make adjustments thought to be appropriate (or inappropriate in the case of intentional nonconformity) in their own cultural place. Therefore, what individuals do, think and feel is what they have learned is culturally valued; and when they express themselves personally that expression also relies on (either adhering to or rebelling against) those cultural standards.

What specific ways can teachers leverage the Discourse practices of African American children? Rather than demonstrate the full range of culturally meaningful Discourse devices that can be used to affirm African American children's Discourse and culture, as well as to build bridges between their experiences and the Standard Discourse, the multiple ways a small set of Discourse devices can be incorporated into curricula will be demonstrated.

Children of all ages love the creativity of word play. Famous African American poets such as Paul Laurence Dunbar have written in both Ebonics and Standard American English. An example of his use of Ebonics is represented in a few lines from the poem *A Negro Love Song:*

Seen my lady home las' night,
Jump back, honey, jump back.
Hel' huh han' an' sque'z it tight,
Jump back, honey, jump back.

In his poem *Good-Night*, Dunbar demonstrated his linguistic flexibility by writing in Standard American English:

The lark is silent in his nest,
The breeze is sighing in its flight,
Sleep, Love, and peaceful be thy rest.
Good-night, my love, good-night, good-night.

Not only should teachers be able to instruct in the similarities (e.g., rhyming) and differences (e.g., pronunciation) in particular features of each language use but also to illustrate that linguistic proficiency in both magnifies one's opportunities for self expression. Students can later engage in writing their two poems about a single topic, using targeted features from each language. Subsequently, they can read the poems aloud (or perform them) and explain why they selected their specific topics.

With formal training in pronunciation and instruction in appropriate use of grammatical features in Ebonics, school teachers could then expand assignments on poems to include a richer, more explicit contrastive analysis of key Ebonics and Standard American English features. A related assignment might be a family biography which incorporates interviews with family members where the final report includes both home and school languages. Such an assignment is an opportunity to empower all students' learning through the inclusion of aspects of their personal and cultural lives.

Importantly, programs incorporating Ebonics-linked instruction have demonstrated that African American students can learn to use Standard American English (or school language) more proficiently. For example, the DeKalb Country School System in Georgia instituted a successful *Bidialectal Communication Program* which explicitly teaches students to use home speech and school speech selectively, depending on situational context (Cumming, 1997). Multiple media are used, including videotaped vignettes which students later analyze for effective and ineffective (rather than correct and incorrect) speech use. Rickford's (2005; Rickford & Rickford, 1995) extensive review of programs which use home languages (called *vernaculars*) to teach school languages demonstrates the substantial improvement in literacy scores when children's home languages are used, affirmed, analyzed, and discussed pedagogically by the teacher. In addition to programs which leverage African American English in Standard American English instruction, Rickford highlights similar efforts around the world: those using vernacular Swedish in Sweden, Creole English in Trinidad, and vernacular Norwegian in Norway.

Wyatt (1995) provides additional suggestions based on her observations of students' authentic use of language in everyday activities. She demonstrated that African American children as young as preschoolers infuse peer dialogue with elementary forms of adult speech events such as *Rapping* and playing *the Dozens*. Wyatt's work documents the continuity between home and school spaces. The use of these devices occurred in school-like social spaces, demonstrating how cultural practices frame communicative exchanges in diverse social contexts. Thus, teachers can leverage this finding, for example, by providing students with opportunities to create rap routines for memorizing parts of speech or geographic locations in the world. The creation and performance of comparative one-liners (cf. http://yomama.urbanhumor.com) in African American English and Standard American English could be used to distinguish lexical and grammatical differences. An interesting twist would be, after a lesson on *the Dozens*, assigning to students the creation of a monthly journal of one-liners collected from family and community members.

Another way to introduce discourse devices is through video and audio tapes. For example, video-taped sermons of a prominent African American minister such as Reverend Dr. Martin Luther King or Reverend Jesse Jackson can be used to demonstrate *Call and Response* and *Tonal Semantics*. A well known collection of traditional African American sermons is James Weldon Johnson's *God's Trombones*. Students can watch and listen to such performances, experiencing, for example, the impressive use of voice modulation, rhythmic speaker–audience participation, and vivid metaphor. As an assignment format, the performances could be used as models for oral reports on historical events. As an instructional tool, call and response could be use as a model for student and teacher comprehension during instruction. Mentioned previously was the DeKalb *Bidialectal Communication Program* (Cumming, 1997), which used the review of video tapes to instruct students in effective switching between home and school languages.

Importantly, the use of audio and video recordings demonstrates that African American discourse styles are living traditions (i.e., cultural practices) across time and space. Other useful and age-appropriate materials can be found at various websites (e.g., http://www.blackwebsites.com and California Newsreel at www.newsreel.org) dedicated to providing educators and interested others with relevant documentaries as well as interactive educational tools to carry African American culture into the classroom. By infusing age-appropriate cultural information about *Rapping* and *Rhyming, the Dozens,* and *Tonal Semantics* into lessons about factual information (e.g., Standard English grammar) and creative expression (e.g., poetry, personal narrative, and historical recounting), having students demonstrate an understanding of those devices, and providing opportunities to create and to use examples of those devices in teaching–learning exchanges, teachers support the transformation of the classroom that is both inclusive and affirming of students' experiences. Moreover, such actions expand both the cultural appreciation and knowledge of the discourse practices for students from other cultural backgrounds within the classroom. This is in line with Powell's (1999) notion of *literacy for a participatory democracy,* where the classroom promotes freedom of thought, enriches communicative competence, and nurtures a culture of respect and care.

Next Steps . . .

Many scholars and some teachers realize that African American and middle/upper class Anglo-American children differ in aspects of their behavior as well as participate in different everyday experiences. However, unlike Mica, these scholars and teachers tend to compare these differences in superficial ways (e.g., the number of books in the home, trips to the local library, the number of ungrammatical features in speech or writing, etc.). Reducing the number of differences between the two groups seems like a logical solution. But even at the tender age of seven, Mica intuitively realizes that this is a poor solution for her friends; the legitimate answer is to give African American students fair access to classroom learning opportunities. Teachers must offer African American students membership in a new learning experience that respects and includes their past learning.

To do so, we as teachers need to extend our own knowledge of the integral role that language plays in the transmission and maintenance of African American culture. We must become sensitive observers of African American students in recreational and learning activities. We must monitor the interplay between school setting, formal learning, language use, and cultural orientation and how this dynamic affects students' ability and motivation to learn. In addition, we must become teacher scholars and investigate African American students as speakers, learners, and participants within our classrooms so that we can construct a more pedagogically valid fit between our learning goals and their initial abilities. If we become more proactive in these ways, we will re-focus attention away from the perceived mainstream inadequacy of Ebonics as a means of expression toward the development of supportive curricular and instructional practices that facilitate formal learning for African American students.

Questions for Discussion

1. Have you ever interacted with individuals from a culture that was different from your own? Describe this experience.
2. In what ways do adolescents rebel against certain culturally defined linguistic standards? Why do you think this occurs?
3. Why are non-standard vernaculars, such as Ebonics, considered to be inferior to the standard vernacular in our society? How do historical relationships of power and domination relate to perceptions of appropriate language use?
4. The author suggests that schools tend to be oriented toward teaching "objective information" (e.g. facts) versus interpersonal information (e.g. judgments and opinions). Do you agree? How would this preferred orientation relate to African American students' responses to schooling and to teachers' perceptions of their competence?
5. Consider Howard Gardner's theory of multiple intelligences. How do these various intelligences relate to African American children's preferred styles of learning that have been suggested in this chapter?

Extension Activities

1. In this chapter, Blake emphasizes that language use is both *cultural* and *social.* Role play a situation that involves differences in power and authority. For instance, you might role play a parent–teacher conference with an upper-class and lower-class parent. Similarly, you might role play a job interview and a conversation with a friend at the local grill. Examine the discourse patterns.
2. Divide the class into two groups. Assign various cultural characteristics to each group that are reflected in their discourse patterns. For example, one group might favor interpersonal relations and might therefore tend to talk about personal matters, whereas the second group might feel awkward talking about such matters. Such cultural characteristics might also be reflected in their non-verbal patterns of communication (e.g., closeness, loudness, eye contact, overlapping patterns of speech, etc.). After practicing their particular role, have the two groups interact as if they are at a social function, and then discuss the experience.
3. Develop a Venn diagram that contrasts the African American belief system with the dominant European American belief system. Consider how these differences might be reflected in each group's communicative preferences or manner of using language.
4. Videotape groups of children from different cultural groups interacting in social situations. How do their manners of using language differ?

References

Abrahams, R. D. (1974). Black talk in the streets. In R. Bauman & J. Sherzer (Eds.), *Exploration in the ethnography of speaking*. London: Cambridge University Press.

Ball, A. F. (1995). Community-based learning in urban settings as a model for educational reform. *Applied Behavioral Science Reviews*, 3(2), 127–146.

Baratz, J.S., & Shuy, R.W. (1969). *Teaching Black children to read*. Washington, D.C.: Center for Applied Linguistics.

Bartolomé, L. I. (1998). *The misteaching of academic discourses: The politics of language in the classroom*. Boulder, CO: Westview Press.

Bereiter, C., & Engelmann, S. (1966). *Teaching disadvantaged children in preschool*. Englewood Cliffs, NJ: Prentice-Hall.

Black Web sites. (2003). Available from http://www.blackwebsites.com.

Blake, I. K. (1993). The socio-emotional orientation of mother-child communication in African American families. *International Journal of Behavioral Development*, 16(3), 443–463.

Blake, I.K. (1994). Language development and socialization in young African-American children. In P. Greenfield & R. Cocking (Eds.), *Cross-cultural roots of minority child development*. Hillsdale, NJ: Lawrence Erlbaum Associates, Publishers.

Blake, I. K. (1999). The significance of cognitive-linguistic orientation for academic well-being in African American children. In I. Okpewho, C. Davies, & A. Mazrui (Eds.), *The African Diaspora: African origins and new world self-fashioning* (pp. 139–151). Bloomington, IN: Indiana University Press.

Bloom, L. (1993). *The transition from infancy to language: Acquiring the power of expression*. Cambridge, UK: Cambridge University Press.

Boyd-Franklin, N. (2003). *Black families in therapy: A multisystem approach* (2nd ed.). New York, NY: Guilford.

Boykin, A. W. (1986). The triple quandary and the schooling of Afro-American children. In U. Neisser (Ed.), *The school achievement of minority children: New perspectives* (pp. 57–92). Hillsdale, NJ: Lawrence Erlbaum Associates.

California Newsreel (2003). Available from http://newsreel.org.

Cazden, C. C., & Dickinson, D. K. (1981). Language in education: Standardization versus cultural pluralism. In C. A. Ferguson & S. B. Heath (Eds.), *Language in the USA*. Cambridge, UK: Cambridge University Press.

Champion, T., & Bloome, D. (1995). Introduction to the special issues on Africanized English and education. *Linguistics and Education*, 7, 1–5.

Cole, M., Cole, S., & Lightfoot, C. (2005). *The development of children* (5th ed.). New York: Worth Publishers.

Confronting 'NOO-kyuh-luhr' proliferation a lost cause. (2002). *The Gazette*, October 13, p. A21.

Cumming, D. (1997). For the students who speak one way at home and another at school, DeKalb has a unique technique: A different approach to teaching language. *The Atlanta Constitution*. Retrieved July 19, 2005 from http://web.lexis-nexis.com/universe/printdoc.

Delpit, L., & Perry, T. (1998). The Oakland resolution. In T. Perry & L. Delpit (Eds.), *The real Ebonics debate: Power, language and the education of African-American children* (pp. 141–186). Boston, MA: Beacon Press.

Dillard, J. L. (1972). *Black English*. New York, New York: Random House.

Doucette-Gates, A. (1992). Concept of self as learner and temporal perspective: Associations with school failure among racial and ethnic minority male high school students. *Unpublished Doctoral Dissertation*. Columbia University.

Dunbar, P. (1999). *Jump back, honey: Poems by Paul Laurence Dunbar*. New York, NY: Hyperion Books for Children.

Fanon, F. (2007). *Peau noire, masques blancs/Black skins, white masks*. New York, NY: Grove Press Inc. (First published 1967.)

Feagans, L., & Farran, D. C. (1982). *The language of children reared in poverty: Implications for evaluation and intervention*. New York, NY: Academic Press.

Fields, C. D. (1997). Ebonics 101: What have we learned? *Black Issues in Higher Education*, 13(24), 18–21.

Gadsden, V. L., & Wagner, D. A. (Eds.) (1995). *Literacy among African-American youth: Issues in learning, teaching, and schooling*. Cresskill, NJ: Hampton Press, Inc.

Gee, J. P. (1989). Literacy, discourse, and linguistics: Introduction. *Journal of Education*, 171(1), 5–17.

Gee, J. P. (2001). Reading as situated language: A sociocognitive perspective. *Adolescent and Adult Literacy*, 44(8), 714.

Gilyard, K., & Stix, N. (1997). Q: Would Ebonics programs in public schools be a good idea? *Insight on the News*, 13(12), 24+.

Hale-Benson, J. (1986). *Black children: Their roots, culture and learning styles* (2nd ed.). Baltimore, MD: The Johns Hopkins University Press. (Original work published 1982.)

Harrison, A. O., Wilson, M. N., Pine, C. J., Chan, S. Q., & Buriel, R. (1990). Family ecologies of ethnic minority children. *Child Development*, 67, 347–362.

Heath, S. Brice (1983). *Ways with words: Language, life and work in communities and classrooms*. Cambridge, UK: Cambridge University Press.

Herskovits, M. J. (1948). *Man and his work: The science of cultural anthropology*. New York, NY: A.A. Knopf.

Hoover, M. R. (1998). Ebonics: Myths and realities. In T. Perry & L. Delpit (Eds.), *The real Ebonics debate: Power, language, and the education of African-American children* (pp. 71–76). Boston, MA: Beacon Press.

Hoover, M. R., Dabney, N., & Lewis, S. (1990). *Successful Black and minority schools*. San Francisco, CA: Julian Richardson.

Huber, T., Pewewardy, C., & Parscal, J. N. (1991). *An integrative review of the literature on cultural diversity synthesizing research on cognitive styles, learning modalities and family structure*. Paper presented at the meeting of the National Working Conference of the Administration for Children, Youth, and Families in collaboration with National Council of Jewish Women, Center for the Child, and The Society for Research in Child Development, Arlington, VA.

Jensen, A. (1969). How much can we boost I.Q. and scholastic achievement? *Harvard Educational Review*, 39, 1.

Jones, R. L. (Ed.) (2004). *Black psychology* (4th ed.). Hampton, VA: Cobb & Henry.

Kochman, T. (1981). *Black and white: Styles in conflict*. Chicago, IL: The University of Chicago Press.

Labov, W. (1973). *Language in the inner city: Studies in the Black English vernacular*. Philadelphia, PA: University of Pennsylvania Press.

Labov, W. (1995). Can reading failure be reversed? A linguistic approach to the question. In V. L. Gadsden & D. A. Wagner (Eds.), *Literacy among African-American youth: Issues in learning, teaching, and schooling* (pp. 39–68). Cresskill, NJ: Hampton Press, Inc.

Logan, J. R. (2001). *The new ethnic enclaves in America's suburbs*. Albany, NY: The Lewis Mumford Center for Comparative Urban and Regional Research.

McAdoo, H. P. (Ed.) (1999). *Family ethnicity: Strength in diversity* (2nd ed.). Thousand Oaks, CA: SAGE Publications.

Mitchell, J. (1982). Reflections of a black social scientist: Struggles, some doubts, some hopes. *Harvard Educational Review*, 52(1), 27–44.

Moore, E. G. (1982). Language behavior in the test situation and the intelligence test achievement of transracially and traditionally adopted black children. In L. Feagans & D. C. Farran (Eds.), *The language of children reared in poverty: Implications for evaluation and intervention* (pp. 141–162). New York, NY: Academic Press.

Morgan, M. (1994). Theories and politics in African American English. *Annual Review of Anthropology*, 23, 325–345.

Perry, T., & Delpit, L. (Eds.) (1998). *The real Ebonics debate: Power, language, and the education of African-American children*. Boston, MA: Beacon Press.

Potts, R. (1989). *West side stories: Children's conversational narratives in a Black low-income community*. Paper presented at the meeting of the Biennial Meeting of the Society for Research in Child Development, Kansas City, MO.

Powell, R. E. (1999). *Literacy as a moral imperative: Facing the challenges of a pluralistic society*. Lanham, MD: Rowman and Littlefield.

Pullum, G. K. (1999). African American Vernacular English is not Standard English with mistakes. In R. S. Wheeler (Ed.), *The workings of language: From prescriptions to perspectives* (pp. 39–58). Westport, CT: Praeger.

Rickford, J. R. (2005). *Using the vernacular to teach the standard.* Retrieved April 3, 2005, from http:///www.stanford.edu/~rickford/papers/VernacularToTeachStandard.html.

Rickford, J. R., & Rickford, A. E. (1995). Dialect readers revisited. *Linguistics and Education, 7*, 107–128.

Scott-Jones, D. (1984). Family influences on cognitive development and school achievement. *Review of Research in Education, 17*, 259–304.

Scott-Jones, D. (1995). Families, communities, and schools as contexts for literacy and learning. In V. L. Gadsden & D. A. Wagner (Eds.), *Literacy among African-American youth: Issues in learning, teaching, and schooling* (pp. 101–123). Cresskill, NJ: Hampton Press, Inc.

Shade, B. J. (1982). Afro-American cognitive style: A variable in school success? *Review of Educational Research, 52*(2), 219–244.

Shade, B. J. (1992). Is there an Afro-American cognitive style? An exploratory study. In A. K. Burlew, W. C. Banks, H. P. McAdoo, & D. A. Azibo (Eds.), *African American psychology: Theory, research, and practice* (pp. 260–278). Newbury Park, CA: SAGE Publications.

Sigel, I. E. (1990). Psychoeducational intervention: Future directions. *Merrill-Palmer Quarterly, 36*(1), 159–172.

Simpkins, G., & Simpkins, C. (1995). Cross-cultural approach to curriculum development. In V. Gadsden & E. Wagner (Eds.), *Literacy among African American youth* (pp. 212–240). Detroit, MI: Center for Black Studies, Wayne State University.

Smitherman, G. (1977). *Talkin' and testifyin': The language of Black America.* Boston: Houghton Mifflin. Reissued, with revisions (1986). Detroit: Wayne State University Press.

Smitherman, G. (1981). "What go round come round": King in perspective. *Harvard Educational Review, 51*(1), 40–56.

Smitherman, G. (2002). *Talkin' that talk: Language, culture, and education in African America.* New York: Routledge.

Spears-Bunton, L. (1993). Cultural consciousness and response to literature among African American and European American high school juniors. *Unpublished Doctoral Dissertation.* University of Kentucky, Lexington, KY.

Thomas, G. E. (1983). The deficit, difference, and bicultural theories of Black Dialect and nonstandard English. *Harvard Educational Review, 75*(2), 107–118.

Turner, L. D. (2002). *Africanisms in the Gullah dialect.* Columbia, SC: University of South Carolina Press. (Original work published 1949.)

Urbanhumor. Retrieved September 26, 2005 from http://yomama.urbanhumor.com.

Watson, D. J. (1993). Community meaning: Personal knowing within a social place. In Pierce and Giles (Eds.). *Cycles of meanings: Exploring the potential talk in learning communities.* Portsmith, NH: Heineman (3–15).

Willis, M. G. (1992). Learning styles of African American children: A review of the literature and interventions. In A. K. Burlew, W. C. Banks, H. P. McAdoo, & D. A. Azibo (Eds.), *African American psychology: Theory, research, and practice* (pp. 260–278). Newbury Park, CA: SAGE Publications.

Wolf, D., & Hicks, D. (1989). The voices within narratives: the development of intertextuality in young speakers, situations, and tasks. *Discourse Processes, 12*(3), 329–351.

Wolfram, W. (1998). Black children are verbally deprived. In L. Bauer & P. Trudgill (Eds.), *Language myths* (pp. 103–112). New York, NY: Penguin Books.

Wyatt, T. A. (1995). Language development in African American English child speech. *Linguistics and Education: An International Research Journal, 7*(1), 7–22.

8

The Potential of Oral Literacy for Empowerment

JESSICA S. BRYANT

Many challenges face educational institutions today, but none is more challenging than the task of eliminating racial, ethnic, and academic inequities in education. As educational reforms pervade our nation's schools, the formidable remnants of segregation still linger in classrooms. Research has focused on issues of segregation relative to marginalized populations of students such as tracking, high dropout rates, and test scores. This chapter, however, sheds light on a less researched form of segregation, that is, segregation as it relates to oral language. This chapter will examine oral language and its role as it relates to African American and other marginalized students and will discuss the following questions: What are some issues related to oral language that historically marginalized students face in schools? What have been the schools' responses to differences in students' language use? What can classroom teachers do to deal with students' language differences and to facilitate productive interaction in classrooms?

The Importance of Oral Language in Literacy

Oral language is the term used for classroom speaking. Known as the verbal form of literacy, oral language has traditionally shadowed its visual literacy counterparts, reading and writing. In fact, this language of speaking has merely been an assumed aspect of literacy that, in the wake of changing educational theory, has remained stagnant in terms of research and classroom practice.

Oral language is a particularly important function of literacy because its primary purpose is greatly served in "the real world." On the world scene, the importance of oral language is best conceptualized in its use to empower the masses and to bring about social reform. In spite of the elevated importance of reading and writing in schools, oral language has contributed as much, if not more, to social change and has been a major factor in creating great social movements. As an ally of reform, oral language was a positive social catalyst for the great orator, Frederick Douglass, who masterfully espoused rhetoric and evangelical Christianity to articulate his views of freedom during the time of slavery. Martin Luther King, Jr., arguably one of the greatest orators of all time, was a persuasive force in American history, as he advocated his views of freedom and equality through his call-and-response Black folk preaching style, rhythmic scheme of parallelism, and metaphorical analogies. Oral language was even a powerful negative tool in the hands of Adolf Hitler, as Hitler seductively swayed the masses through use of powerful repetitive speech and crafty oration advocating Nazi propaganda to the Germans. Whether used positively or negatively, oral language has been a powerful catalyst to implement change. With the significant historical importance of oration, it stands to reason that oral language would be a central element of literacy studied and evaluated in schools as a component for empowering students and bringing about social and educational reform. After all, if school is, indeed, a "microcosm of the world" as educators suggest, then literacy tasks in school should mirror literacy uses in society so that students can be equipped to function effectively in school and in the world. Therefore, oral language should have an authentic and important place in classroom instruction.

Use of Oral Language in Schools

Many educational reform efforts have attempted to increase use of oral language in the classroom. In fact, due to the emergence of diverse social, cultural and economic factors in our country, traditional notions of literacy have changed from the ability to read, write, listen and speak to the ability to communicate effectively, function socially and professionally, and access information. In essence, literacy means the ability to function in the world. With such a strong emphasis on speech and communication, the classroom should be the most conducive and inviting setting in which to encourage oral language. Among the general school population, however, the concept of oral language has advanced little as a major component of literacy in that students often do not speak for real purposes and audiences. Indeed, in some classrooms, students do not speak at all.

Classroom talk first gained attention in the 1930s. Educator T. H. Pear examined the phenomenon of classroom discourse, discovered its importance in literacy, and named this concept of classroom talk "euphasia." In the 1960s, however, the term was renamed "oracy" by Wilkinson, but skills and teaching methods involving oracy were not defined until later in that decade when the researcher Barnes observed, recorded and analyzed talk as it related to student learning. By analyzing students' speech, Barnes was able to determine if students comprehended instruction and to what extent, and how students learned and communicated in the classroom through talk (Watson, 1993).

Barnes discovered that students learned best when they were able to move from a performance form of talk which consists of memorization, to an active, free-flowing dialogue. He reasoned that "if sounding out words is not reading, and using correct grammar is not writing, then performance speech is not oracy" (Watson, 1993, p. 5). Oral language consisted of far more.

Today, talk among students is far from free-flowing. Researchers (Tharp & Gallimore, 1991) show that teachers still often dominate class discussion while students sit quietly, afraid or intimidated to speak for fear of sounding less than intelligent or getting the wrong answer. In addition, much classroom talk is centered on Bloome, Puro and Theodorou's (1989) idea of procedural display, the mainstream, rehearsed presentational style of talk which consists of students reading an assignment, memorizing facts, and feeding back the same information by giving the right answers based on assigned reading material. Much talk is also centered on Freire's (2000) idea of "banking education" where talk is only considered relevant when it relates to predetermined information and skills that students must know in order to demonstrate competency on a particular level. Instead of students feeling free to construct meaning, discover, synthesize, and form their own ideas, they become more concerned about memorizing facts, earning praise for having "the correct answer," and passing classroom, state, and national tests to reach the next level. Learning of this nature is without authentic purpose, and is less than engaging. Furthermore, this type of literacy use fails to function as a "literacy of promise" in that students do not speak for real purposes and with real audiences, and students are not taught about the power of the spoken word.

This is particularly true of marginalized populations of students. According to Ramirez, Yuen and Ramey (1991), in over half the interactions between teachers and students, students are silent because they are listening or responding with non-verbal gestures. In some classes, student silence is rewarded with a 'behavior' grade, and free talk is penalized. This teacher-domination/student-submission interaction limits a student's opportunity to create and manipulate language freely and limits students' ability to engage in more complex learning. Students become passive recipients of predetermined knowledge instead of active creators of knowledge. Thus, they never learn the ways in which spoken language can empower.

Oral Language: Literacy Segregation Among African American Students

Through oral histories, narratives, and language forms, oral language is akin to African American culture, which originated from strong oral traditions of indigenous African cultures and survived the Middle Passage; yet, present-day school oral language is often inconsistent and exclusive of African American discourse styles. This disparity can be attributed to current notions of literacy that often omit the component of culture. According to Powell (1999), literacy is based on certain ideological perspectives that ignore diverse social and cultural contexts of language and language acquisition. In fact, mainstream school structures and practices, pervasive in our nation's schools, devalue the literacy experiences of many marginalized students by excluding their cultural knowledge (Apple, 1996). Thus, schools still do not often consider African American students to be as literate as mainstream students. With such negative expectations from school, many African American students experience an education that segregates them in terms of equitable academic achievement and they often lag behind in the educational process.

Contrary to the notion that African American students enter school with lower levels of verbal abilities and skills, the oral language system of African Americans stems from strong, complex language forms which involve a shared knowledge and understanding within a social context of the group language structure (Banks, 2002). As Blake notes in Chapter 7, participants of this language structure learn and develop their skills of talk through extensive, sophisticated verbal skills from the home and the community. The conflict between these students' classroom performance and actual ability, however, is often the cause of lingering mainstream instructional practices that often contradict the cultural identity of these marginalized students. For example, Labov's (1973) study investigated the "academic underachievement" of inner-city African American students. Instead of observing their communication competency in the academic setting of school, he observed their verbal abilities in the context of their own communities. Labov found that these students possessed considerably advanced cognitive and linguistic skills, but these skills were not recognized or valued within the educational system or in mainstream society. Although Labov helped to refute the deficit notion associated with African American speech, educators still believe that "literacy learning as it relates to language is often obtained by following a single path to learning that stems from the power relations" between mainstream and marginalized cultures (Au, 1993, p. 124). However, according to Powell (1999), literacy is not a single, unified entity in which one discourse is more literate than another discourse; rather, literacy is socially constructed and can consist of many forms, depending on the context used.

Banks (2002) also attributes the lack of success of African American students in school to the resistance of society as a whole to recognize diversity. He asserts that Americans have always embraced the notion of the melting pot, and individuals who maintain their ethnic, racial and cultural characteristics are perceived to be different and are often prevented from full structural inclusion into American society. This is true of school; thus, students who perceive that literacy tasks affirm their cultural identities are most apt to become more involved in the learning process. Students who feel that tasks devalue their cultural identities, however, are more likely to show resistance or a dislike for the learning process (Delpit, 1996; Fordham, 1996). Since schools value standard forms of communication, students who become literate in non-standard ways are often students mistakenly identified as having literacy skill deficiencies.

Heath's (1983) classic study of literacy illustrates this point, particularly as it relates to the communities of Trackton and the Townspeople. Trackton is a working-class African American community entrenched in its own literacy traditions. Its members demonstrate their literacy skills through daily tasks such as reading food labels, reading the newspaper, giving and following directions, and reading the Bible. The Trackton residents do not read stories to their children or engage in extensive writing. Rather, talk is a particularly valued aspect of literacy evidenced by group talk, disseminating information, discussing the newspaper, and church and community activities. Since Trackton adults do not view children to be suitable partners for conversation, Trackton children learn by observing and listening to adults rather than interacting with them directly. Through emulating adult conversation, children learn language. In fact, children even learn to read before they attend school since reading is a necessary skill in picking up groceries, reading price changes and house numbers. These literacy skills are derived from participating in real world experiences and purposes. Because literacy in Trackton centers on strong oral communication skills, which are not highly recognized in schools, the literacy skills of the Trackton students are incongruent with the literacy skills students encounter in school.

The townspeople are mainstream Blacks and Whites who are advocates of school education because they define the type of literacy to be endorsed in schools. They believe that to be literate, people must conform to school notions of literacy. These parents talk to their babies and treat their babies and children as conversationalists. Adults supply children with an abundance of books and other written material that is used as a basis for talk. As adults read aloud to children, children are taught to respect readers by quietly listening. These literacy skills that the townspeople teach their children are consistent with dominant notions of literacy and are considered necessary for academic success in school. Thus, these students are more likely to obtain higher academic achievement than the Trackton students in spite of the lack of real world learning.

Attempts and Failures to Promote Effective Oral Language in the Classroom

Methods of encouraging or even evaluating oral language has still not become as widely refined in our nation's schools as reading and writing, where students receive grades based on their skill proficiency. Teachers who value oral language often award students with class participation grades based on the amount of classroom speaking in which they engage. The aim is to encourage class discussion, measure the comprehension of students, and encourage students to participate in an exchange of diverse ideas. This method of evaluating talk in classrooms, theoretically, points to a more inclusive definition of literacy, but in actuality, students are often so conscious of receiving a participation grade, they may restate a thought of another student instead of producing a creative, thoughtful response. Some students may even choose not to attempt to earn the points and simply remain silent when called upon to answer a question. Other students, however, may attempt to provide a thoughtful response but may "shut down" when their ideas are not valued. Such devaluing of students' ideas often stems from the failure of many teachers to respect students' cultural knowledge, and to teachers' beliefs that their "upper-class" knowledge is superior and, therefore, they have nothing to learn from their students. With the challenge of earning grades for classroom talk, students, particularly marginalized students such as African Americans, often feel inhibited from engaging in a true exchange of ideas and often feel hesitant to take risks in thinking, exploring, and speaking without penalty. In essence, efforts to use oral language in this manner often fail in purpose and further miss the mark in providing a link between students' home cultures and the classroom environment.

Failure to promote comfortable classroom talk also occurs when a mismatch exists between a traditional mainstream recitation structure and the cultural recitation structures of African American students. In the traditional school recitation structure, the teacher acts as the gatekeeper of talk. When the teacher calls on a student, that student is expected to respond. In fact, many teachers prefer not to be interrupted by students' questions and comments so they call for student responses only at the end of lectures. Many African American students, however, may deviate from this structure and may ask a question or comment on a relevant issue without the teacher first granting them permission to speak (Gay, 2000). In other cases, African American students may quickly and "out of turn," provide an answer for a struggling student who fails to respond when called upon, or they may provide an answer for a student who fails to provide the "correct" answer. Educators who ascribe to mainstream talk structures may mistakenly conclude that African American students defiantly disobey classroom protocol.

According to studies by Banks (2002) and Bennett (1999), students of marginalized groups receive more negative feedback from teachers than White students because of different verbal communication styles. In the classroom, these underrepresented students are less likely to raise their hands when responding to a question; instead, they may blurt out responses, which is often considered rude among teachers. To perpetuate this perception, these marginalized students often show greater emotion when responding to teachers and demonstrate quicker responses, greater animation, and higher energy. For this reason, their verbal communication may often be viewed as confrontational. The oral language structure between these students and the teacher then often becomes negative and counterproductive; thus, the traditional talk structure becomes a hindrance to student–teacher interaction and inhibits positive and productive student–teacher relationships.

The use of questioning techniques is another way teachers often unintentionally limit talk. By asking a number of questions, teachers try to evoke discussion and responses using various levels of questioning. Questioning techniques can often enhance the amount of talk in the classroom, but, depending on the type of questions asked, the resulting talk can be limiting. In many cases, students have the opportunity to fully explore their thoughts about an issue only when they are asked a higher order question. At the sound of a higher order question, students, on cue, are expected to move from the rehearsed presentation style of lower order questioning, into a reflective, exploratory talk that allows them and other members of the class to exchange ideas. This mechanical solicitation of responses, a "procedural display" form of question-response (Bloome, Puro & Theodorou, 1989), may not be effective in achieving the kind of talk needed to make all students in the class feel as though they are considered a part of a learning community. In essence, talk should not be solely controlled by various methods of questioning; rather, talk should primarily consist of unsolicited, free flowing dialogue within class sessions, and questioning prompts should be utilized thoughtfully and sparingly.

Another way classroom discourse styles limit African American students' opportunities to use oral language is when a mismatch exists between teachers' expectations of class discussion and students' delivery. For example, the discourse style characteristic of mainstream students is the topic-centered style of talk where explanations are focused on a single topic and follow a linear pattern through the beginning, middle, and ending. Characteristic of many African American students, however, is the topic-associating style of talk that involves a number of divergent plots and subplots. These events are not linearly aligned; rather, they are often organized according to their relevance to a subject or a theme and many key points are implicit in nature (Michaels, 1981). This talk style involves lengthy explanations, and although all the ideas emerge into place at the end, teachers are often so confused and impatient midway through the explanation with all the themes, plots and subplots, that they may halt the explanations before students finish making their points. In essence, conventional classroom recitation often fails to provide opportunities for oral language for African American students and other marginalized students whose talk structures differ from traditional dominant talk structures.

Educators who create an educational context involving critical literacy help students develop a sense of empowerment and identity by validating students' linguistic styles. For literacy learning to be effective, its members must be able to accept various ways of communication. This means that participants in different language communities must be willing to value each other's language. Thus, communities of learning must be characterized by genuine dialogue versus the traditional mainstream monologue.

Classroom Implications

Frequently, educators have neglected oral language in the classroom or have not understood the importance of linking oral language to culture and to real world uses, especially for African American students. In order for oral language to become a fully functional and beneficial form of literacy, educators need to consider the importance of talk in society and mirror the many uses in the classroom. In addition, educators need to become aware of mainstream oral language practices prevalent in classrooms and find more culturally conducive ways of incorporating talk into the teaching–learning process to improve classroom discourse.

Educators first need to become aware of mainstream recitation structures and the many ways teachers may act as gatekeepers over talk in the classroom. When talk is mechanically controlled in the classroom, students can become disempowered and may not become full participants in the learning process. Mandatory training sessions, workshops, and video-taped class sessions may help. These aids should not only contribute to building an awareness of these structures and practices used in classrooms, but should also teach teachers alternative methods of communicating, verbally and non-verbally, with students. Forums and training sessions can provide an opportunity for exchanging information and viewpoints on curriculum design, classroom climate, and various other ways to improve learning for all students.

Teachers should also learn the various ways students acquire literacy, and use students' home discourse patterns and language styles in teaching. Teachers can help students study various language structures and uses in literary works and teach students to incorporate discourse patterns into students' own works. Most importantly, teachers should also learn about, and teach to their students, the power of the Black vernacular. This way, teachers can help students make connections between their home and school literacy learning; students can see that their home literacy skills are valued, and their cultural identities are affirmed in the classroom.

By attending various community events and rallies, educators can capture a glimpse of talk and other literacy forms used by African Americans and other marginalized students. One of the best places teachers can learn African American talk structures is the traditional Black church, the historical rallying place for spiritual, political, and social reform. For a more diverse sense of literacy and for free-flowing, casual talk, however, teachers can visit restaurants, beauty parlors, barber shops and community centers in African American communities and other frequent gathering places of African Americans. Teachers can even capture African American discourse patterns by eating in the school cafeteria, attending school sporting events, and becoming involved with student life. Teachers must be open to acquiring knowledge of diverse discourse patterns and become researchers of culture so that they can adapt the linguistic patterns to accommodate students' language styles and facilitate learning.

Educators must also adopt a new paradigm for classroom talking, that is, a structure void of students rehashing stated facts and opinions of the teacher or the text. Rather, to promote students' linguistic development, teachers must provide more opportunities for students to respond freely and engage in purposeful talk. Teachers may consider organizing students into small discussion groups to encourage this type of oral language use. According to King (2001), children who are engaged in small group unstructured talk are able to articulate affective responses to their reading that will contribute to their understanding of the texts and of themselves.

Discussion guides, whereby students generate "pros" and "cons" in response to a particular question and then reach consensus, can also lead to productive exchange. For instance, teachers might have students provide evidence that both supports and opposes such questions as, "Do you think the Civil Rights Movement reduced racism in the United States?" and then reach consensus and justify their final response (Alvermann, 1991). In addition, as students are given reading assignments, they may keep journals in which they may provide questions, comments, and reflections relevant to the reading and use these as the basis of class discussion. This journal activity should minimize the trivial talk in which students may engage simply to gain participation grades in the classroom. At the same time, students will not feel "put on the spot" when teachers ask questions; rather, students will have had time to develop meaningful, thoughtful responses.

Teachers can also better utilize the literacy form of talk in the classroom by implementing literature circles. Engaging students in literature circles helps students to deepen their comprehension, develop skills in communication, generate ideas for writing, and make personal connections that leads to continued independent reading (Cullinan, 1993). According to Miller (2003), low socio-economic status African Americans are often viewed as lagging behind with literacy development. By using literature discussion groups, however, these students are able to blend their home literacy with their school literacy to critically analyze texts in ways that challenge the literacy responses of their middle-class counterparts.

Unlike early forms of literacy where reading and writing were presented in isolation, talk should be equally integrated with other forms of literacy. No form of literacy should be presented in isolation; rather, together, many forms of literacy should be utilized in the classroom and should reflect the cultural context of all students. Literacy learning should allow students to internalize materials in such a way that they make personal connections with the text because their form of literacy learning is acknowledged and valued in the classroom.

Real World Uses of Oral Language in the Classroom

In a contextual way, educators should teach various forms of oral language and its authentic uses as it applies to real world issues. Although numerous forms of oral language exist in society, this educator suggests that teachers focus on three areas: civic, aesthetic, and community. Since the focus of this chapter is on African American students, these oral language forms will be explained in such context; however, these language forms may include the experiences of all students, particularly the experiences of marginalized students, who in the past, have only been recognized as "add-ons" in curricula.

Civic Oral Language involves the political uses for talk. Students can learn about making arguments and speaking for various audiences as they read and listen to the speeches of their African American role models, past and present such as Frederick Douglass, Martin Luther King, Lani Guinier, Johnetta Cole, and other African American heroes and heroines. While analyzing this material, students can learn to critique oral texts to discover what makes effective oration. As students continue to build their knowledge base by reading books, articles, listening to the news and music, studying various periods, and learning about real world issues, students will form their opinions and synthesize their own ideas. The classroom can become the rallying place and the platform for civic activities of young political speech-writers and orators. The community will become the playground for debates, panel discussions, and addresses in which students share their learning. School personnel and government officials such as the mayor, the governor, and senators, may be invited to become participants in round table discussions as students give voice to their views regarding issues in their school, community, and in the world. In this way, the promise which literacy holds to empower individuals and to promote social change and social justice may become a living experience. Classroom talk in this sense is meaningful, purposeful and respectful.

Aesthetic Oral Language is the creative form of talk. This type of oral language centers on the spoken language as it relates to students creating poems, songs, drama and other artistic modes of expression. For example, students can dramatize historical events in a social studies class, or portions of novels in a language arts class. Students can even create spoken language for the visual language of art by attaching words to the way they interpret pictures, sculptures, and dance.

Aesthetic Oral Language is meaningful in that it may seek to preserve African American cultural traditions. Students can learn about the art of story-telling by reading African epic narratives in stories and studying these narratives in slave songs. As students interview other African American people in their communities and churches, they can research and learn the lost art of lining hymns and the long- and short-metered rhythms in which they evolve. In addition, students can study call-and-response literary traditions by studying the works of African American orators, preachers, and novelists such as Ralph Ellison and Jean Toomer. Honoring African American traditions supports the preservation of aesthetic talk forms despite mainstream gate-keeping and the devaluation of African American language forms in schools.

Community Oral Language is the kind of informal talk used in various communities. Studying various types of community language use helps students note differences between school talk and home talk, and between formal versus informal registers in talk. Importantly, students' ability to code switch in spoken language aids them in their understanding of register switches in written language forms. Students may learn to value home languages of other students by using their home oral language dialogue structures in drama, documentaries, or in poems. Critically important, students may learn to value school literacy as a means for communication at work, school, and other places.

By studying oral language in these three areas, students can become a part of many different language cultures and become literate for real purposes in real world situations. To do this, teachers need to diverge from the textbook, which typically promotes "procedural display" and move towards a more authentic form of literacy learning.

Student ownership in their learning requires finding an issue they feel passionate about—for example, violence in their community. Then they could decide how they want to structure their topic. If students use civic oral language, they could give presentations to schools, community groups, community leaders, or legislators emphasizing the need to reduce violence. Students who choose aesthetic oral language could use poetry or drama to emphasize their views on violence. If students focus on community oral language, they could incorporate their oral discourse styles in poetry, stories, and scripts. Using talk in this way helps students to understand and express themselves in compelling and meaningful ways. Such talk helps students to fulfill the promise that literacy holds: That is, to create, share and teach possibilities for individuals and communities.

The three forms of oral language can easily be incorporated in all classes—writing, reading, history, science, mathematics, and other classes. For example, aesthetic oral language could coincide easily with an art class. Civic oral language could easily be incorporated into a history class, and community oral language could be easily woven into an English class. This is not to say, however, that several forms of oral language cannot be used in a single class. Regardless of the form(s) used, oral language should be utilized as an important literacy component in the teaching and learning process.

Assessing Oral Language in the Classroom

Oral language should be taught and evaluated in conjunction with other aspects of literacy. Students are often required to demonstrate their knowledge of a particular subject matter using writing as the only mode of literacy expression. As with writing, teachers should give students opportunities to express themselves verbally and in other ways. Occasionally, teachers may even give students the option of responding in writing or verbally to demonstrate their knowledge.

Oral language can be evaluated in a number of ways. One method of evaluation is the use of scoring rubrics. For example, a scoring rubric for aesthetic oral language may include a category of evaluation on creativity or story plausibility. Categories for a scoring rubric on civic oral language may include persuasion and tone. Criteria for evaluation using rubrics would depend on the assignment given and the type of oral language used.

Another method of evaluating oral language is through videotaping. Depending on the assignment, students may be videotaped individually (e.g., speech, interview) and/or as a group (e.g., debates, panel discussions). Just as students select their best works for inclusion in writing portfolios, students could also select their best works in oral language and include them for evaluation, along with their writing portfolios. Teachers must note that, at first, videotaping may prohibit students from talking and interacting freely. After much practice, however, students will gain confidence in expressing themselves through their own creative work.

Conclusion

Historically, laws in this country failed to grant students freedom from various classroom practices that contribute to segregation in instruction. In fact, traditional instructional practices in which reading and writing are at the forefront have left out many students from the educational process, particularly those students from cultures with strong oral traditions (e.g., African American and other marginalized students). Educators' attempts to incorporate oral language into the learning process have often failed because of a lack of cultural translation between teacher and student and because educators failed to provide students with opportunities to speak for real purposes and audiences. Because of these issues, teachers must understand culture as it relates to literacy and value students' home literacy skills. Educators should also seek to teach oral language as a means of giving voice to students and become advocates of real world literacy.

As talk becomes one of many centerpieces of educational thought, it should be presented and utilized in such a way that students realize its importance in real world experiences. Talk should be presented in the classroom to the extent that when students read materials, they are aware of talk; as students write, they are aware of talk; as students participate in music and drama, students are aware of talk. Even as students become involved with technology, they become aware of talk. Teachers must teach students to appreciate various forms of talk and learn to use these forms confidently as students venture freely in and out of various language contexts. In this way, students become knowledgeable of talk, not talk typical of confining, mainstream arenas, but talk used to liberate, to empower, and to contribute to the world.

Questions for Discussion

1. In this chapter, Bryant argues that oral language ought to be a major component of the Language Arts program. Do you agree? Why or why not?

2. Why do you think oral language has become marginalized in schools? In what ways is this marginalization consistent with the ideology and practices of "schooled literacy"?

3. Relate Bryant's notions about oral language to a literacy of promise. In what ways are current oral language practices in classrooms consistent with a "banking" educational model (see Chapter 3)? How might the suggestions for teachers presented in this chapter support Paulo Freire's ideas of a "humanizing" education?

4. Share examples of times when differences in recitation structures and communication styles resulted in conflict in the classroom.

5. Brainstorm ways that you might incorporate the three forms of oral language—civic, aesthetic, community—in your classroom.

Extension Activities

1. Watch a video of Martin Luther King, Jr. as he delivers his famous "I Have a Dream" speech. As you view the video, write down words, phrases, and sentences that you find powerful. What are some delivery techniques that he uses to persuade the audience?

2. Attend an African American social gathering and make note of the discourse patterns and styles being used. Is there evidence of a "topic-associating" style? Compare your findings with the styles used in a social gathering of Whites. Is the discourse style there more "topic-centered"?

3. Develop questions, prompts, and/or discussion guides for a unit of study that would elicit creative thought and "free-flowing" dialogue.

4. Videotape and analyze a typical classroom session. In what ways is classroom talk controlled by the teacher? In what ways are students given the opportunity to contribute new ideas and to construct knowledge?

References

Alvermann, D. (1991). The discussion web: A graphic aid for learning across the curriculum. *The Reading Teacher, 45,* 92–99.

Apple, M. (1996). *Cultural politics and education.* New York: Teachers College Press.

Au, K. (1993). *Literacy instruction in multicultural settings.* Belmont, CA: Thomson Wadsworth.

Banks, J. (1993). Multicultural education. Characteristics and goals. In J. A. Banks and C. A. M. Banks (Eds.), *Multicultural education: Issues and perspectives.* Needham Heights, Mass: Allyn & Bacon (1–28).

Banks, J. (2002). *Teaching strategies for ethnic studies* (7th ed.). Boston: Allyn & Bacon.

Bennett, C. I. (1999). *Multicultural education: Theory and practice,* (4th ed.). Boston: Allyn & Bacon.

Bloome, D., Puro, P., & Theodorou, E. (1989). Procedural display and classroom lessons. *Curriculum Inquiry, 19*(3), 265–291.

Cullinan, B. E. (1993). *Children's voices: Talk in the classroom.* Newark: International Reading Association.

Delpit, L. (1996). The silenced dialogue: Power and pedagogy in educating other people's children. In T. Beauboeuf-Lafontant & D. S. Augustine (Eds.), *Facing racism in education* (pp. 127–148). Cambridge, MA: Harvard Education Publishing Group.

Fordham, S. (1996). *Blacked out: Dilemmas of race, identity, and success.* Chicago: University of Chicago Press.

Freire, P. (2000). *Pedagogy of the oppressed* (30th anniversary ed.). London: Continuum International.

Gay, G. (2000). *Culturally responsive teaching: Theory, research, and practice.* New York: Teachers College Press.

Heath, S. B. (1983). *Ways with words: Language, life and work in communities and classrooms.* Cambridge, UK: Cambridge University Press.

King, C. (2001). I like reading because we can share ideas: The role of talk with the literature circle. *Reading, 35*(1), 32–36.

Labov, W. (1973). *Language in the inner city: Studies in the Black English vernacular.* Philadelphia: University of Pennsylvania Press.

Michaels, S. (1981). Sharing time: Children's narrative styles and differential access to literacy. *Language in Society, 10,* 423–442.

Miller, T. D. (2003). Literature discussion groups respond to culturally relevant children's literature in the kindergarten classroom. Scholarly Commons @ Penn, AAI3084872.

Powell, R. (1999). *Literacy as a moral imperative: Facing the challenges of a pluralistic society.* Lanham, MD: Rowman and Littlefield Publishers, Inc.

Ramirez, J. D., Yuen, S. D., & Ramey, D. R. (1991). Executive summary: Final report: Longitudinal study of structured English immersion strategy, early exit and late exit transitional bilingual education programs for language-minority children. Contract No. 300–87–0156. Submitted to the U.S. Department of Education. San Mateo: Aguirre International.

Tharp, R., & Gallimore, R. (1991). *Rousing minds to life: Teaching, learning, and schooling in social contexts.* Cambridge, UK: Cambridge University Press.

Watson, D. J. (1993). Community meaning: Personal knowing within a social place. In Pierce and Gilles (Eds.), *Cycles of meaning: Exploring the potential talk in learning communities.* Portsmouth, NH: Heinemann.

9
Voices of Our Youth
Antiracist Social Justice Theater Arts
Makes a Difference in the Classroom

KAREN B. MCLEAN DONALDSON

A Preamble Introduction: The History Lesson

I can't erase what I know. I can't forget who I am. ***Centuries ago my people lived in rich villages, and none were dead.*** I can't erase what I know. I can't erase who I am. ***Europeans came and killed violently we put up a fight, we didn't go silently.*** I can't erase what I know. I can't erase who I am. ***Slave ships is what they were forced to board. We couldn't rebel without knives or swords.*** I can't erase what I know. I can't erase who I am. ***Being sold is what we faced. In the South is where we were placed.*** I can't erase what I know. I can't erase who I am. ***We went through segregation without a cash-in. Yet we survived in horrendous fashion.***

(A ninth grade, African American male's point of view of the Black experience in the United States titled, The History Lesson. His poem was taken from a 2003 English class assignment. Students were given the phrase "I can't erase what I know. I can't erase who I am" and told to add their poetic sentiments between the repetitive phrase.)

The Storyteller's Weave: Setting the Stage

This chapter section tells an abbreviated story of the makings of an antiracist "arts" educator. Giving an example of this process may support interested educators at whatever level they desire to integrate or transform curriculum to be culturally and creatively responsive. In this chapter section the voice of the storyteller is established, and the tone is set for the *storyteller's analysis* that is interjected throughout the following sections to assist the reader in synthesizing what was learned through the actions and voices of students.

All teachers have the potential to be creative and culturally responsive in various ways. Having had more than thirty years of crosscultural creative teaching and research experience, I have been among students who overwhelmingly revealed the joy of cultural creative learning and using real life situations to teach basic subject areas. As a teacher, I combined my own passion for reducing racism and other social injustices with my artistic talents to educate students, but one need not be an artist to teach creatively. Many times, students have expressed their appreciation for making education fun and real through creative processes.

I suppose I did not wholeheartedly think about all of these implications when at seventeen I started the Children's Theatrical Group of Boston in 1971. It was more a matter of having something constructive to do with my three younger siblings, and their friends. We were living in the projects, and I had just gotten accepted to Massachusetts College of Art. Theater for me as a youth and the creative teaching process technically started with a project in my drama class. I wrote a play titled "Who's Gonna Save the Children." It was about project life such as,

> Living in sub-standard housing, and
> Going to run down neighborhood schools,
> Parents having to work double-time, and
> Many children getting into crime,
> Our older brothers being drafted into the Vietnam War, and
> Drugs creeping into the back door,
> Babies having babies, babies dying, and
> The world not caring because,
> We were Black and poor.

The play toured many of the local universities in Massachusetts including Northeastern University, Wheelock College, Massachusetts College of Art, Mount Holyoke College, and so on. For three years, approximately twenty-five kids from the projects performed stories about project life. Their momentum was crushed when one member (fourteen-years-old) was shot and killed on the way home from a school party. The kids just seemed to grow up over night and had other, more important things to attend to. For the next decade I wrote and produced socially based theatrical productions, and worked diligently to become a social justice change agent through the use of my artistic talents.

I taught in schools and performed quite a bit for other theatre and dance companies. Having gained some recognition for my work, I was hired as a cultural artist-in-residence in 1981 by the Boston Public School system. I was assigned to a local high school in Roxbury, Massachusetts (1982–85), to help to address the racial crisis that arose with the desegregation order of Judge Garrity. It was the start of forced school integration and busing in the city of Boston.

On a daily basis students and staff alike were searched at the entrance of the school for weapons. We had a metal detector that went off frequently. Many students felt the "hype" came from the parents and the city, and that basically the youth were caught in the middle. For instance, if the South Boston parents and community bombarded the buses with rocks, food and paint, the Roxbury community would follow. I had White and Black students sitting in my drama class ready to fight at a moments' notice. However, before that happened we acted out how students in the school were feeling. We diverted the attention from class members, and role-played the general sentiments of "other students" at the school. This technique avoided direct confrontation between the students enrolled in class, and opened the class to critical dialogue and debate within the context of antiracist social justice theatre.

I can remember one White student refusing to participate because each day, he thought, would be his last. He thought that his parents would soon have him in a private school and end his forced schooling experience. By the time we hit midyear, and in the middle of an improvisation, a Black student remarked, "you're stuck here like the rest of us. All the White students that are still here aren't going anywhere. We are in the same boat; we are too poor to afford private schools. We should be standing together to get better school facilities and education." The White student laughed at himself, and everyone else began to laugh with him. We went on to perform antiracist social justice theatre for the remaining three years. With each year they became better artists and students of life and with that came greater respect for what they were doing. The students performed for other schools in the district, and for outside community agencies. Eventually, in 1985, I started Unity Through Creativity Productions, Inc. Many students from the school came to the afterschool theater production classes, and became a part of the youth company. We were able to employ them during the summer months. They performed for inner city day camps, hospitals, elderly homes, and community agencies. I wrote my masters thesis on the creation of an entrepreneurial endeavor and curriculum framework of Unity Through Creativity, Inc. As the youth grew up and moved on so did I. Every so often I receive letters or calls from the students. Many from this group have gone on to be successful in the arts field. Just as Maya Angelou found her *voice* through writing and poetry, the students found theirs through theater.

This storyteller's section connects my own youth activist interests and growth in critical antiracist arts education development with practical and anecdotal experiences working with youth. Entering a doctorate program added the dimensions of empirical research exploration. Furthermore, it fused together the practice, theory and research of antiracist arts curricula and the impact it had on student learning and development.

The research methodology used became action and applied research in the form of antiracist arts intervention projects and the storytelling of youth experiences with regard to racism in schools. Studies from these projects indicated that antiracist arts education made a difference for students such as improvement in school attitude and cultural appreciation. In many cases it assisted students in becoming more motivated to learn (Donaldson, 1996; 2001).

The exposure to antiracist-multicultural education assisted me in becoming more informed regarding the crosscultural needs of students, and gave me the skills to develop antiracist multicultural curriculum and assessment materials. Research has demonstrated that teachers who engage in multicultural education courses and professional development seminars are more prepared to teach in crosscultural environments, and to integrate multicultural concepts into basic curricula (Gillette & Boyle-Baise, 1996; Ladson-Billings, 1997; Nieto, 2003). The *Preamble Introduction: The History Lesson* highlighted in the opening of this chapter, reflects how students appreciate the crosscultural transformation of the curriculum. Having worked with this student one-on-one for some time and often hearing him say that he detested the Civil Rights films, plays and books presented at school, I assumed it was because he felt the times had changed as many students often state. Not until I read his poem did I finally ask *him* why the abomination? He remarked that he couldn't bear to watch the suffering that Black people had to go through, it made him physically sick. Yet, the poetry assignment allowed *him* to express himself rather than holding it in. Having teachers interview their students after an assignment like this is helpful in understanding the impact and learning acquired from this type of lesson. It can also take the lesson into a critical discourse session, enhancing appreciation for the literature, and continued self discovery in this area. Therefore this is what I did. I interviewed him about the lesson. His highlighted responses are as follows:

A: It was a book assignment. The book was called *House on Mango Street* [Cisneros, 1991], and it had Latino poetry in it. The poem in the book was about a Latina teenager, and we were assigned to use her style and theme for writing. We had to write about our culture. I wrote about how I feel about my culture. It was kind of easy because my parents instill strong cultural values at home. I didn't feel anything about getting the assignment, it was just an assignment.

Q: So, you had no reaction?

A: Well, I did find myself working on it more. I gave it more effort. I felt proud, and we had to read it in front of the class

Q: How did you like listening to your classmates' poems?

A: Pretty good. The poems were different as far as people having different experiences. Yeah, White, Latino, Black, and Asian kids all wrote about culture. Some of it was deep, and some not quite. But, I like listening to other students' creative thoughts.

Q: Do you get these kinds of creative assignments often?

A: Not as often as we should.

Q: Do you have any suggestions for teachers?

A: Yes, be competent teachers and teach from all aspects. This can bring out the best in every student. Also, students should try to learn from more than one aspect to get exposed. Young people need to step up to the plate and take the initiative. We know we have pressure, like it is not cool to go to school or to be smart. Actually, learning is so much easier than fighting this stupid battle of playing dumb. This assignment was good, it was different. It helped to shed a lot of light, and made me want to get a good grade because I am proud about my culture.

Opening Act

For centuries we have used theater arts to reflect what is going on within our societies, and as a modality for learning. It has often been a medium of socio-political advocacy, helping to change the way we think and encouraging social justice activism (Boal, 1985, 1996; Hill, 1987; Molette & Molette, 1992; Saldana, 1995). This chapter features several high schools over a twenty-year period that used the medium of theater arts to address racism in schools and society. The rationale for using this particular approach is to demonstrate the success of implementing a curriculum that is both academically creative and culturally responsive. Recent studies of implementing antiracist social justice art mediums, indicate that this universal language art form makes a difference in many young people's lives. This style of curriculum has a strong "liking" correlation to successful student learning and social development, self efficacy, and academic achievement (Donaldson, 2001; Donaldson, Garvin, and Tori, unpublished report 2004).

This chapter links to the overall theme of this book because critical literacy is practiced and voiced by (majority) African American secondary students using multiple intelligence techniques to learn successfully. The school projects highlighted in this chapter were administered within a variety of socio-economic and crosscultural school settings. However, African American students were often the largest ethnic group within these projects. In addition, they were frequently the most vocal, as it related to racist experiences that deterred learning interests in school.

Students of color are generally the targets of racism in schools, often experiencing a disproportionate amount of suspension, detention, ability grouping, lowered teaching expectation, biased curriculum and testing, less instruction time, and so on (Murray & Clark, 1990). In addition, White students also have many direct and indirect experiences that often lead to alienation from peers, guilt, shame, anxiety and embarrassment (Donaldson, 1996). Using the concept of antiracist social justice theater has helped to address racist experiences of high school youth as a whole. Students of all backgrounds are further motivated through antiracist and social justice education to become interdependent democratic world citizens.

Antiracist social justice theater helps students to have "voice" in their learning process and social concerns, and to realize that racism is a system of power and privilege that will likely exist for many years to come. This chapter presents a lived literacy of promise and is dedicated to reducing racial ignorance and discrimination, through the voices of students using varied art forms that can be integrated into basic curriculum structures. Much of the content of this chapter consists of excerpts from projects that the author-practitioner/researcher administered in various regions of the United States.

Defining Antiracist Education and Social Justice Theater Arts

In retrospect, the existence of racist experiences in many schools has not changed much for students (Donaldson, 2001; Kailin, 2002). Students still share many stories of discrimination, along with similar recommendations to eradicate racism. Students in the artistic projects presented have been empowered through social justice theater arts, a genre that includes (but is not limited to) antiracist creative writing, oration, poetry, song, dance, drama, and role-play discourse. This form of social literacy, antiracist theater arts, has the capability to address individual, institutional, and cultural aspects of racism. Culture and the arts are most often viewed as inseparable and a way of life for many cultures across the globe (Donaldson, 1996, 2001; Saldana, 1995; USSEA, 1992; Wasson, Stuhr & Petrovich-Mwaniki, 1990; 1992). In addition, the arts encompass an array of techniques that embrace multiple learning styles and intelligences (Gardner, 2006; Sternberg & Grigorenko, 2000), thereby making it an integral component to student success in education.

Theater arts, or as youth often refer to it today, the *spoken word*, is often used as a social education movement to bring attention to racial and other injustices. *Spoken word* is a term used to describe creative aesthetic and social justice languages stemming from various art forms, such as rap lyrics, poetry, plays, oration, and storytelling. *Spoken word* implemented in the classroom is a student input-based critical literacy technique that teachers can use to enhance overall academic and social achievement. Students who have been introduced to antiracist education frequently acknowledge it as a foundation for *spoken word* antiracist awareness, artistic development, and performance.

Antiracist education is critical pedagogy that seeks to take a stand against racial injustice and oppression (Donaldson & Verma, 1997). Social justice and social responsibility are seen as synonymous concepts. Justice requires equality and fairness, and social responsibility acknowledges that the human condition is above claims of a stratified system of role distribution in society. People and organizations that promote social justice generally exhibit courageous efforts and willpower in the pursuit of justice (Nieto, 2003).

The arts can address a variety of issues in unique ways, and can develop other important skills such as critical thinking, literacy and leadership ability (Donaldson, 1996). The combination of antiracist and social justice concepts with the arts produces a proactive teaching tool that reaches into the personalities and intellects of students, and motivates them to take action on social issues (Donaldson, 2001).

To best demonstrate student learning enrichment through creative teaching and an antiracist social justice theater arts curriculum, we'll begin with the *Baritone Section*. This section consisted of twenty students selected from a peer education program. At the time, their school was under great public scrutiny for the racist disparagement of Black and Latino students by a teacher employed by the school. This teacher wrote a letter to her hometown suburban school committee advising them not to participate in the volunteer exchange busing program due to the probability that "these" students will bring crime, promiscuity, and other hazards to such a wholesome community. This widespread letter sparked students, parents, community activists, the school district and others to hold an educational summit on racism in schools. Following the summit, over two thousand high school students in the community were surveyed on school race relations (88 percent of the students surveyed perceived there to be racism in their schools). In response to these findings, I was hired to develop an antiracist program that could be shared with other schools in the district. The students, most of whom were honor roll students, to my surprise had many racist school experiences to share. Many of their experiences were highlighted in the play, *Let's Stop Racism in Our Schools.*

Baritone Section: Let's Stop Racism in Our Schools

A NORTHEAST HIGH SCHOOL ANTIRACIST SOCIAL JUSTICE THEATRE PRODUCTION

At this high school, forty peer education program students of various ethnic backgrounds enrolled in a ten-week antiracist arts education course, and twenty of those students went on to perform on stage. The students were there to learn how to address some of the recent racist acts at school and within their community. Following many experiential lessons and academic lectures, students wrote the antiracist social justice production titled *Let's Stop Racism in Our Schools.* It was a forty-five-minute production showing how racism affects student learning and interest. The production begins with a student protest rally to stop racism in the schools. It then traces the roots of racism in the United States, and investigates in part, institutionalized racism as it affects U.S. school systems. The finale expresses the need for Americans to learn of one another's contributions to the United States, in order to appreciate them and to excel even further as a diverse nation.

The purpose of this production was to give students the opportunity to voice their concerns about racism in the schools and their nation. It further allowed the students to take leadership roles in developing an antiracism awareness model to be used by schools throughout the country. This group began the SARIS (Students Against Racism in Schools) Association. Through this group, students were able to practice the promise that literacy offers—to effect changes in their life circumstances and life choices. Students were able to read themselves as subjects of social action and agents of social change.

STORYTELLER'S ANALYSIS

What we see here are the students sharing tangible experiences with racism in schools. Frequently, racism is dismissed as an isolated incident or non-existent by educators and decision/policy makers in the field. This misconception that racism is non-existent in schools leads to the belief that antiracist multicultural education has no integral place within the school curriculum. The youth here help to dispel the myth that racism no longer exists in schools. They further acknowledge how painful it is to be discriminated against because of their race, and that in the long run racism hurts us all.

Students spoke of their racist experiences in class, and on stage. Performing such personal content for peer audiences took great courage. Behind the scene, in the classroom, students told numerous stories covering topics too sensitive to perform on stage, but that had harmful racial implications such as, *I'm nothing*. This is a low self-esteem internalized symptom that many students attribute more to the school environment than the home. Students discussed suicide attempts, depression, cutting the classes of perceived racist teachers, disinterest in school due to put downs and lack of multicultural curricula and so on. The concept of this scene was to script the stories that the students chose to share with the public, for the purpose of exposing racism in its many forms within schools. Students felt that by making others aware of its pervasiveness, the arts could help to sound the alarm and promote the necessity of social justice for all oppressed groups.

The students wanted their audiences to empathize with their experiences, to receive an education on the roots of racism, to offer suggestions, and open dialogue on reducing racism in schools. Using what students learned in the antiracist social justice classes, they wrote the script to that order.

Students in this course production who, as previously noted, had named themselves SARIS, met to discuss the creation of chapters throughout the United States. Unfortunately, when the furor surrounding the blatantly racist act of the teacher whose behavior prompted the initiation of SARIS died down, continued support for this group died also. This is the challenge with so many projects of this nature; that is, these programs are only supported when the wound can be seen. Once it receives a *band-aid*, the expectation is for the pain and anguish to completely disappear of its own accord.

The Baritone Section has given us a foundation for greater understanding of the existence of racism in schools, and the adverse affect it has on students. It further demonstrates how deeply youth are concerned about these issues, and their commitment to engage difficult topics and social action curriculum.

Alto Section: We Wear the Mask Production

MIDWESTERN SUBURBAN HIGH SCHOOL HUMAN RELATIONS: A FIFTEEN-WEEK (PILOT COURSE) FORUM

A similar case presented itself a few years later within a Midwestern School District. However, the students themselves negotiated having an ongoing human relations course taught at their high school. I was hired to develop the course, and was able to bring in a social justice theatre artistic director for creation of an antiracist production.

This antiracist social justice theater genre serves as a learning process for both students and teachers to gain self-awareness through personal and collective examination. Using this style of critical social justice curriculum helps students to explore their own identity and to understand how that identity influences what they do within the school environment. This next section highlights the challenges of mixed group identity interaction by sharing a more in-depth view of an antiracist human relations course and production. The teacher/artistic director is the facilitator of learning and must be open to student input; however, this can be difficult at times because it is a process of working through latent ignorance. This section reveals the conflict that goes on between White students understanding the degree of the ill effects of racism, and Black students who are the recipients of such discrimination. We also see the intra-group relationship challenged as some Black students choose to agree with their White counterparts to do a broad-based production on discrimination, as opposed to the assigned antiracist focus. The Black students who felt this production gave an opportunity to talk openly about the impact of racism at their school, expressed perceptions of betrayal to the other Black students who were seen as "sell outs." Educators must know that critical literacy and dialogue is not an easy task, and that there are many layers to address before coming to the core understanding of the problem.

The *We Wear the Mask* production represents an appropriate title for what went on during the whole process of this Midwestern suburban high school project. The school had many racial incidents reported to the district, such as teacher and administrator racial bias, and curriculum bias, and was reflective of the institutional racism nation-wide that includes but is not limited to ability grouping, suspensions, biased testing and lack of access to an equitable education. However, denial of racism was prevalent in the school, not only among many of the teachers, but also among students, as we'll witness in this section. How do students critically investigate racism and its impact on schools and society? I explored these questions with the following group of students in a pilot course.

The Midwestern suburban high school "Human Relations Forum" provided a series of multicultural topics for interested high school students. Although the principal investigator (myself) and research team presented three announced "Forum" seminars and provided newsletter advertisements to the larger student body (approximately 1600 student school enrollment), the main students to sign up for the course were the Human Relations Committee members and the Multicultural Support Group (formally the Students of Color Affinity Group). These students were of many ethnic backgrounds and mixed heritages, such as, East Indian, Arab, African, Korean, Columbian, Puerto Rican, Thai, Panamanian, African American, European American, Jamaican, Peruvian, Russian-Jewish, and included an exchange student from Germany. The sessions fluctuated in attendance due to a variety of student-school commitments. Yet, over the fifteen week period we had twenty-six students attend some portion of the course.

The forums included the use of several mediums, such as the arts and multimedia, to broaden student awareness of diverse groups and issues in the United States. The forums provided a basic introduction to multicultural education and examined from theoretical perspectives and through experiential exercises the nature of pluralism and intergroup relations in U.S. society. The intent was to expose the basic causes and complex dynamics of racism, sexism, and other forms of discrimination and intergroup conflict. Further, the forums explored the historical and contemporary experiences and contributions of people of color, white ethnic groups, and women in U.S. society and reexamined U.S. history, culture, and institutions from the perspective of these groups. This course description was adapted from Dr. Sonia Nieto's (University of Massachusetts-Amherst) Introduction to Multicultural Education course for college students.

The course began with a class oath of respect. It covered topics such as, *What is so Important About Developing Good Human Relations?*; *Oral Traditions: Telling Our Stories*; *Prejudice: Answering Children's Questions*; *Prejudice/Discrimination Based on Age, SES (socioeconomic status), Religion, Exceptionality, Race, Gender, Language, and Ethnicity*; *The Five Major Ethnic Groups in the United States*; *Defining Racism in the United States*; *Examining Sexism in the United States*; and *Understanding Classism in the United States*. The last two sessions focused on developing solutions to create better human relations at the school, within the community, and worldwide. The course was implemented in a lecture and experiential format. Originally, the expectation was to make the course very interactive regarding student–facilitator discussions, but because the material was in many instances new to the students, the lecture format was prevalent during the sessions.

Each session was videotaped for the purpose of review by teachers involved with a simultaneous antiracist curriculum and implementation study. Teachers made note of the techniques used and student dynamics in the session, to assist them in integrating antiracist curriculum into their own subject areas. Most of the teachers observed the dynamics of White privilege and its clash with the students of color expressing their experiences. The teachers felt the videotapes prepared them to better manage these dynamics in their own classrooms.

One observation made during the review of the videotaped sessions was that the European American students (specifically two) dominated the speaking time. They both appeared to be very eager to discuss the issues of their family histories and lineages with the group. In addition, they expressed that their respective [European] cultures are lost in America as well. This was a good start in hearing the perspectives of White students regarding race. However, the discussion also presented itself as a defense mechanism for stopping any blame for racism resting on them as White students, and on White society as a whole. White privilege became more noticeable as one European American female often monopolized the speaking time. Other students spoke [most often] after she had responded. When questions were asked, she usually responded first. This was a dynamic that may be noteworthy, especially with regard to what would happen later in the student input curriculum development and the antiracist projects that followed.

The course began February 21, 1996, and concluded May 29, 1996. Following the conclusion of the course, the students were invited to participate in the Midwest urban (study site) community's "Race Unity Day." Drama students from another school, a Midwestern urban school cohort, were also invited to participate in this event. During the preparation for this event, scheduled June 9, 1996, a renowned social change theater director was in the area working on another project associated with the principal investigator. The investigator invited the director to visit both suburban and urban sites and work with the students to generate ideas for the event. This director had the students begin with writing (as an independent assignment) a fictitious letter to a racist. The letters that were produced were very thought provoking. In almost every letter the students asked the racist to please try to understand the pain and divide that racism generated and to make the time to speak with them to find solutions to the problem. One White student wrote that the racist person's views caused problems with him becoming friends with people of color because most people of color were convinced that all Whites are racist. The students invited the racist to open his or her mind and assured the individual that he or she did not have to be racist. Some said that the racist was putting the world in a bad situation. In essence, the students told the racist that if the door was opened for positive discussion, he or she would never regret it.

Following the return of the letters, students discussed what they had written and why. These discussions helped the students to develop short vignettes for the "Race Unity Day" event. Some of the presentations dealt with institutional racism, i.e., applying for a bank loan and being denied; shopping at the mall and being followed and forced to show an I.D.; visiting a clinic and being encouraged to take birth control pills because of ethnicity; and a case of mistaken identity and arrest. The other components of the performance focused on racial prejudice, i.e., a White girl accused of trying to be Black, and the Black "sell-out." Both groups were well-received during these performances. It was apparent that they felt a sense of pride and achievement. I decided at that point to invite the students to participate in two upcoming events taking place in the fall of 1996. Those included a panel discussion for the state (teachers) social studies conference and a national multicultural education conference. The students were very excited by the invitations and looked forward to the fall events.

As the events approached, both schools contributed to bringing the social change theater director to the Midwest to work on the preparation for the panel discussion and national production on antiracist education. The artistic director worked with each student in preparing remarks for the panel discussion. The students discussed diversity issues and experiences in schools. Each had a particular area of emphasis, such as gender, class, race, and language issues. The teacher-audience asked numerous questions such as, "Does racism really exist that strongly in schools?" "Do they feel multicultural education is a key to addressing social justice issues?" "How do you as students think teachers can incorporate diversity more into their curriculum?" The teachers wanted to know what students would like to see by way of social studies curriculum development and what suggestions they might have for more sensitive approaches for the classroom. The students were very articulate, and received very high ratings in the conference evaluations.

The idea that students were being listened to by teachers empowered the students greatly. Yet, along with that confidence came challenges to the artistic director. The artistic director attempted to prepare the students for the national multicultural education conference in which the primary objective was to deliver a presentation dealing with antiracist education. The students were told on several occasions that this presentation would deal with racism issues because it was being slotted into an antiracist education seminar and presentation. The suburban students agreed to the focus initially, but later resisted the artistic director's ideas for the presentation because they preferred to do a presentation that would be inclusive of many other social justice issues. Although this was not an option given to the students, this preference came especially from a few of the White students who took on leadership roles, and who had convinced a number of the students of color to fight for this change in focus.

The argument was that there was no racism in their school. Therefore, they could not share stories or experiences about racism in school. At this point some of the students made some disrespectful comments to the artistic director, and she refused to return to coach the group. When it appeared that the students' participation would be canceled, the students involved came to apologize. Furthermore, parents had a part to play in this learning experience, because most advised their children that this was a unique opportunity to learn about themselves and institutional racism that has an impact on all human beings. In addition, they encouraged their children to apologize to the artistic director, and to ask for a second chance. The apology was accepted, but the director felt it best not to return. Instead, she focused on the urban drama group. This event is fascinating and has potential for great discussion. Some readers may argue the kids were empowered, but not so empowered that they could not say racism was an issue. Other people might say that the dynamics of White privilege served to shift the locus of control from one "space" to another. The parent dynamic is likewise fascinating. One may easily have suspected just the opposite from suburban parents and would have been quite wrong. As principal investigator and producer of the presentation, I took over the last rehearsals, which combined both the suburban and urban groups. Despite the challenges, lessons in respect were learned. Students created less argument over the way the production had to be done, and focused on issues of racism. They performed their stories to full audiences, and in both the workshop and evening performances the students received standing ovations. In addition, during the all-day workshop the students received the opportunity to participate in and work along side the antiracist teacher cohort group (Antiracist Teacher Study 1995–98: Donaldson, 2001) as they presented their sections.

The suburban overall production was titled, *We Wear the Mask*. It consisted of a number of vignettes featuring actual "racist" experiences of the students. How could this be if there was no racism in their school? The point is made once again that denial runs deep even at the student level. This group used a bell/timer to go from one presentation to the other. Some of the subtitles were, "I Colored Myself Brown"; "Advised to Take Less Complicated Classes"; "Making Jokes about Jews"; "Stereotyped as a Gang Member"; "Fed Up with Racial Epithets Between Friends in the Lunch Room"; "A National Achievement Finalist Not Recognized"; and "Malcolm X Shirt Offensive." As demonstrated with many prior projects with students, using art mediums greatly assisted students and their audiences in opening the door for discussing deeply ingrained issues of racism.

STORYTELLER'S ANALYSIS

Mask making was used as a social justice technique during the project. During the making of the mask students discussed how things are masked within society, and how they themselves have masked their pain and experiences with racism. In addition, they talked about the uncomfortable process of using plaster mold to get the impression of their faces. They equated this process metaphorically. Reflecting on the making of the mask and being frightened as it is pressed to your face, students took it upon themselves to hold the hands of those who were afraid of this process. We discussed the symbolism of this process, and that this is what we must do to see each other through the tough struggle of being change agents for social justice. One student remarked that it feels like you cannot breathe and have to have complete control of not moving your facial muscles in any way, but after a while you get used to it and can somewhat forget that it is there. We also spoke about the symbolism of this statement as a socialization process and how we give in and accept injustice in our society. Students spoke about their choices of how they painted and designed their masks, and felt they could pretend to be anything they wanted to be with the mask. However, most of the students painted their mask in a solemn fashion in response to the antiracist social justice theme. Importantly, these discussions were carried over to the critical dialogue about the poem *We Wear the Mask*. Most students were deeply saddened by the message of the poem, and agreed that we bear the mask of silence in times that we should give voice to what is unjust within our society.

At the national multicultural conference the students began the performance reciting the poem and wearing their masks. The audience somehow knew the mask represented hidden pain and silenced voices. As the mimed recitation drew to a close the first school bell rang for a change for the first vignette. The mask was removed by the student leading the particular vignette, and each following vignette was done in this same manner. Each mask was placed back on the student's face, and the masks were not removed in their entirety until the end of the production.

It is important to understand that the use of this critical genre is always left open-ended, because it is part and parcel of a lifelong learning process. Moreover, it was important that parents understood the importance of this experience for their children. A holistic approach to education is key, and in all of the antiracist education social justice theater projects we keep parents, teachers, and the community informed of the project and process. As a community of educators we must also be aware that all students process differently, and because the topic of racism can be explosive we must learn the different dynamics that can arise. We should use those dynamics as a teaching tool to gain an even deeper understanding of the complexities of racism rather than an excuse for avoiding meaningful engagement. We must also seek to educate ourselves about those complexities if we are to be able to help others intelligently through the process, and to have a good understanding of the theory and practice of antiracist education.

Some of the pervasive issues around using antiracist education techniques became evident within the suburban group. Black students especially, were angry with other Black students they described as "sell outs" for going along with the White students whose argument was that racism didn't really exist "that much" in their school. In addition, some of the White students struggled or missed the opportunity to recognize the reality of White privilege and how it acts in schools and society to oppress people of color. "Teachable moments," being prepared to address these common issues, helped to facilitate student discussions of White privilege, such as silencing Black students' voices and their experiences of racism. The students of color, especially those who had been members of the Students of Color Association at the school, in general made comments about their White peers still not getting it, and that was why they needed to have a student of color affinity group. They felt that in a student of color group they understand the issues better and could work them out themselves. However, it is important to note that both cultural affinity groups and mixed group projects and clubs are important because we live in a pluralistic society (Brown, 1995).

This group had many experiences to share regarding racism. Learning in this context is richly layered, multifocal and necessarily respectful. In honoring the promise of literacy, White students must learn to listen and support the struggles and experiences of their peers, and students of color must understand the denial impact that racism has had on White students regarding the notion of White privilege. Clearly, critical discourse is spoken, heard and felt from written and oral assignments intentionally designed with a view toward social justice. This discourse can assist students in working through limited understanding, and direct them toward the ideal goal of reducing racism in schools and society.

Students continue to have strong feelings about racial prejudice; the eradication of prejudice, defined by Du Bois as ignorance in 1953, remains the challenge of the new century if America's children are to receive an equitable and enriched multicultural-centered education. The following section leads us to the voices of Black students enrolled in the Black Student Union at their school. The Black Student Union is designed to give Black students the opportunity to affirm and support each other through their high school years. The students in the group take on leadership projects such as putting up messages, signs and posters about Black history, and arranging Black speakers to come in and do lectures and workshops. This is how I came to be invited to do a lecture with parents, teachers and students about issues of racism in schools, and following that up with a workshop for the BSU students, invited teachers and administrators. The section is a demonstration of conducting an antiracist theater arts workshop, and how it can be used as an introductory lesson for students. Linking multiple school subjects, units and activities is also a technique demonstrated in this final section.

Soprano Section: New Millennium Voices

A WESTERN REGION HIGH SCHOOL: ANTIRACIST SOCIAL JUSTICE THEATRE WORKSHOP
WITH THE BLACK STUDENT UNION (BSU)

This participatory antiracist social justice workshop, titled *From Africa to America*, is a workshop that I had developed and taught for over twenty years.

In many school textbooks the first exposure to African American culture is slavery. It is imperative that we begin our starting point at a more positive juncture to eliminate the misconception that Blacks were descendants of slaves, and therefore are a lowly cultural group. African Americans are descendants of Africa. Many of their ancestors were kings, queens and people who were architects, mathematicians, philosophers, herbalists, surgeons, warriors, artisans, griots/historians, traders, explorers, classical musicians, linguists, educators, etc. African Americans are the second largest minority group in the United States (U.S. Census Bureau, 2000), and have made major contributions to this nation and world civilizations.

The style of the workshop is student participation through enactment and improvisational drama, dance and storytelling. The objective is for students to receive an overview of African American culture with highlights of the forced migration and the roots of racism in the United States from the perspective of African Americans. The BSU students, teachers and administrators participated with great enthusiasm. They became a West African village, and through the enactment were able to empathize with all aspects of the workshop.

The reaction is always pretty much the same. Students generally respond by sharing their reactions brought on by their participation such as, (1) they have never been taught in regular classroom settings in this way; (2) textbooks do not bring to life the experience the way the dramatization does; (3) their anger about slavery and racism; and (4) their feeling of empowerment by human agency to make a difference in the world.

During the deconstruction role-play that followed the workshop, BSU students shared that getting over slavery was not easy. Some students reported feeling left out because slavery robbed them of knowledge of their heritage. Other students reasoned that as a Black Student Union they made available more opportunities to explore their culture, educate others, advocate for inclusion within basic curriculum, and to address discrimination such as racist jokes. The students said they refused to ignore racist comments, and instead interrupted or made it obvious that they didn't buy into it. In addition, they commented that it made them feel good when other cultures learned about their struggle as Blacks in America. They thought the workshop enabled them to participate actively, therefore to be highly engaged in learning the lesson. They also expressed disappointment that most of their teachers do not provide these types of lessons in the classroom.

STORYTELLER'S ANALYSIS

African American students have been pioneers, willing to step out of their comfort and/or discomfort zones to share with others their pain, strength, endurance, resilience and human legacy. Antiracist social justice theater often opens the door more delicately for all who want to watch, listen, learn, and become active in social justice transformation. The voices of our youth are dynamic, intellectual, socio-political and powerful. Students throughout American classrooms and beyond are asking us to provide "real life" education, to address social ills such as racism in schools, and to use our creativity in the process. Are we up for the challenge?

Students had critical discourse throughout these three vocal sections, and their thoughts blended into a tearful symphony of the problems manifested by racism. The melodies carried by a song of caring, thoughtfulness and pur-posefulness presents us with a living literacy of promise realized. Importantly, the students went beyond problems to solutions and made creative recom-mendations for educators. Students used scripts, poetry, and critical oral analysis for sharing issues of racism. Whether within a classroom or on stage, discourse that stimulates student critical thinking, social action and achievement should be taught more broadly across the curriculum. Students featured in this chapter have said that their learning has been enriched by social justice arts integrated curriculum.

The benefit of using antiracist social justice theatre, *the spoken word*, makes a positive difference in the classroom, and with student learning and development. Literacy is taught in its many forms, and students are motivated to engage more in the learning process. There are many exciting learning situations that this genre can bring about, especially hearing the voices of our youth on social issues. Students appear to come alive when the curriculum is real life. They become encouraged to read more and to take greater pride in their assignments, as demonstrated through the interview with the ninth-grade poet. Bringing students together for a common cause or goal helps to provide a means through which students can make a difference in the world. Hopefully, these examples of creative approaches to addressing social issues, developing the *voices* and artistic literacy of our students, has contributed favorably to the goal of this book, *to explore the notion of critical literacy and include ways that secondary teachers might use various texts—both oral and written—to address racial oppression, thereby providing what we are calling a "literacy of promise"* (Spears-Bunton & Powell, 2009).

Questions for Discussion

1. In what ways is social justice theater representative of a literacy of promise?
2. What are the benefits of using the arts in schools to promote social justice?
3. Donaldson talks about wearing the "mask of silence." What masks do we each wear on a daily basis? How might we use the arts to break out of our masks?

Extension Activities

1. Write reflections on times that you have experienced discrimination. Develop vignettes from these reflections and perform them in class.
2. In small groups (preferably with members from different ethnic groups), make a list of events which might be considered racist in your school or community. Write a script or editorial to be shared with the class. Utilize the discussion which emerges for further learning.
3. Study the work of Augusto Boal and others who have been involved in social justice theater.
4. Write letters to a fictitious racist. Read and discuss.
5. Design masks that represent the various faces of racism and create vignettes that can accompany the masks.
6. Write your own "I can't erase what I know . . . I can't forget who I am" poem.
7. Perform and discuss the various vignettes included in this chapter.

References

Boal, A. (1985). *Theatre of the oppressed*. New York: Theatre Communication Group.

Boal, A. (1996). *The rainbow of desire: The Boal method of theatre and therapy*. New York: Routledge.

Brown, P. (1995). Cultural identity groups overview and framework. Unpublished document, Fort River School, Amherst, MA.

Cisneros, S. (2000). *House on Mango street*. Burr Ridge, IL: McGraw-Hill Higher Education.

Donaldson, K. (1996). *Through students' eyes: Combating racism in United States schools*. Westport, CT: Greenwood Publishing Group.

Donaldson, K. (2001). *Shattering the denial: Protocols for the classroom and beyond*. Westport, CT: Greenwood Publishing Group.

Donaldson, K., & Verma, G. (1997). Antiracist education definition. In C. Grant and G. Ladson-Billings (Eds.), *Dictionary of Multicultural Education*. Phoenix, AZ: Oryx Press.

Donaldson, K., Garvin, L., & Tori, C. (work-in-progress). Measuring creative and crosscultural learning: The kuumba learning model.

Gardner, H. (2006). *Frames of mind: The theory in practice* (2nd ed.). Moorpark, CA: Academic Internet Publishers Group.

Gillette, M., & Boyle-Baise, M. (1996). Multicultural education at the graduate level: Assisting teachers in gaining multicultural understandings. *Theory and Research in Social Education, 24*(3), 273–293.

Hill, E. (Ed.) (1987). *Theatre of Black Americans: A collection of critical essays*. New York: Applause: Theatre Book Publishers.

Kailin, J. (2002). *Antiracist education: From theory to practice*. New York: Rowman & Littlefield Publishers, Inc.

Ladson-Billings, G. (1997). *The dreamkeepers: Successful teachers of African American children*. Hoboken, NJ: John Wiley & Sons, Inc.

Molette, C.W., & Molette, B.J. (1992). *Black theatre: Premise and presentation* (2nd ed.). Lima, OH: Wyndham Hall Press.

Murray, C.B.C., & Clark, R.M. (1990). Targets of racism. *American School Board Journal, 17*(6), 22–24.

Nieto, S. (2003). *What keeps teachers going?* New York: Teachers College Press.

Saldana, J. (1995). *Drama of color: Improvisation with multiethnic folklore*. Portsmouth, NH: Heinemann Publishers.

Spears-Bunton, L. A., & Powell, R. (2009). *Toward a literacy of promise: Joining the African American struggle*. Oxon: Routledge.

Sternberg, R., & Grigorenko, E. (2007). *Teaching for successful intelligence: To increase student learning and achievement* (2nd ed.). Thousand Oaks, CA: Corwin Press.

United States Society for Education Through Art (USSEA) (1992). *Newsletter, 16*(2).

Wasson, R.F., Stuhr, P.L., & Petrovich-Mwaniki, L. (1990). Teaching art in the multicultural classroom: Six position statements. *Studies in Art Education: A Journal of Issues and Research, 31*(4), 234–46.

Wasson, R.F., Stuhr, P.L., & Petrovich-Mwaniki, L. (1992). Curriculum guidelines for the multicultural art classroom. *Art Education, 45*(1), 16–24.

10
The Promise of Critical Media Literacy
REBECCA POWELL

In her book titled *Why Are All the Black Kids Sitting Together in the Cafeteria?* (1997), Beverly Daniel Tatum recounts an incident with three- and four-year-olds at a local day care center. When the children were asked to draw a picture of a Native American, they were stumped. But when their teacher rephrased the question and asked them to draw a picture of an Indian, they immediately responded. Their pictures all contained feathers, and several contained weapons such as knives and tomahawks. When they were asked where they acquired such images of native people, the children cited cartoons, and most notably the Disney movie *Peter Pan*, as their primary source of information. By the age of three, largely as a result of popular media, these children had internalized an essentially aggressive and negative image of Native Americans.

Recently, scholars have begun to view popular culture as an area worthy of academic pursuit (e.g., Cortés, 2000; Spring, 2003; Tobin, 2000). Sholle and Denski (1993) argue that the expansion of popular texts in the postmodern era has "ushered in forms of domination and control that appear to thwart rather than extend the possibilities of human emancipation" (p. 307). Acknowledging the profound ideological influence of the media on the general populace, "critical media literacy" has emerged as a distinct discipline within the field of critical pedagogy. Building upon a critical theoretical perspective, critical media literacy seeks to challenge and disrupt the messages inherent in various popular texts.

In this chapter, I argue that to realize a literacy of promise, we need to expand what counts as "literacy." A literacy that is consistent with the notion of promise and emancipation does not confine reading to words on the page, but rather acknowledges that a variety of signifiers can be read and deconstructed for their inherent ideological messages: t-shirts, billboards, children's toys, bumper stickers, advertisements, television programming, commercials, films, and so on. Various popular texts represent "codifications" (Freire, 1998) that encode cultural information, and that subsequently can be decoded and critiqued. In this sense, "texts" are viewed as representations that can be used as "pedagogical resources to rewrite the possibilities for new narratives, identities, and cultural spaces" (Giroux, 2003, p. 84).

This chapter builds upon previous chapters by exploring how visual literacy can be used to realize a literacy of promise. I intend to show how popular media can be used in critical ways in classrooms to help students and teachers recognize—and thereby disrupt—its power to define what social behaviors are considered "normative," and what are considered "exotic" or "deviant."[1] I begin by exploring the notion of popular culture and its relationship to academia. I then provide several examples of critical analyses from the literature, to illustrate how such analyses can be used in secondary classrooms to stimulate counter-hegemonic discourse and debate.

Making Room: Popular Culture and the Academy

In their chapter entitled "Promises to Keep, Finally? Academic Culture and the Dismissal of Popular Culture" (2003), John Weaver and Toby Daspit argue that since the age of Socrates, popular culture has been viewed with suspicion and dismissed as an area worthy of serious study. They write that:

> For most academics, popular culture is an imitative art form that panders to the lowest human desires. It is seen as a worthless endeavor that symbolizes the hedonism of our postmodern world. Critics do not interpret the work of popular artists as serious but fun; nor do they view these artists as having the capabilities to grasp the important intellectual ideas of our age.
>
> (p. 141)

For Weaver and Daspit, such paternalistic omissions in the world of academia pose a threat to democracy. For democracy to flourish, they argue, the will of the people must be respected. When popular culture is diminished or even ignored in the education arena, then academic work becomes increasingly irrelevant to the lives of most citizens.

> We see no problem with raising doubts . . . about the tastes of people or warning against the possible consequences of popular decisions . . . Where we think academics have failed democratic ideals is in not giving popular cultures and tastes serious and sustained attention. For a democracy to develop, intellectuals have to treat popular culture with the utmost respect and seriousness. Without this respect, the wills of people will be ignored and erased, thereby assuring that academics will fail, again, to keep their promise of nurturing a democratic nation.
>
> (p. 138)

The authors make an important point when they suggest that as critical researchers and educators, we ought to become connected to people's lives, so that we can understand why people value what they do. That is, part of our role as critical literacy theorists is to acknowledge the possibility that an individual's response to popular texts is not necessarily always unconscious or uncritical.

Rather, people negotiate meaning and are discerning in their responses to popular media. Our job, then, becomes one of determining how people interact with popular texts and what they do with that information.

Acknowledging a discerning stance enables us as educators to build upon students' inherent interest in popular culture. Steven Goodman writes, and I concur, that the mass media culture "has grown to challenge and supersede the role of school as a powerful socializing influence on our nation's children, shaping their values, beliefs, and habits of mind" (2003, p. 10). Given the profound impact of the media culture, it's essential that educators begin to challenge the traditional factory model of schooling—with its concurrent notions about what "counts" as literacy and literacy instruction—and consider alternative models. Such models, I would argue, ought to consider the ways in which popular media works in society to define our culture, that is, to create notions in the popular mind about what is normative, and what is not. Such models also ought to consider the ways in which popular media works to create divisiveness in society, for instance by shaping our perspectives about normal versus deviant behaviors; about primitive versus cultured peoples; about acceptable versus unacceptable images of beauty, and so on. It is to this topic that I now turn.

Creating the Exotic: Reading *National Geographic*

In examining human difference and the ways in which we categorize and define various groups, it's important to recognize that systems of oppression—racism, classism, homophobia, and the like—are all embedded in inequitable relations of power. That is, systems of oppression go beyond individual prejudice in that they also involve power. For instance, being White or light-skinned in our society affords certain privileges, such as never having to think about skin color, or knowing that race will not be a factor in procuring housing, a job, or an education (Goodman, 2000; McIntosh, 1988; Powell, 2001). Peggy McIntosh describes these benefits as an "invisible knapsack" that act in insidious and powerful ways to maintain a system of White supremacy.

Racism was socially created in order to rationalize slavery and imperialism in this nation. To justify the taking of land and to maintain a brutal system of bondage, Whites had to be convinced of their own superiority and of the relative inferiority of those being subjugated. Thus began the systematic and sustained effort to "prove" that persons of African descent, along with Native Americans, Filipinos, and anyone else the White race desired to enslave or conquer or dominate, were inferior in intelligence—even barbaric and sub-human. Despite scientific evidence that shows that genetic variations among all humans is exceedingly small and tend to be greater within races than between them, such essentialist positions remain popular. (Consider, for instance, the popularity of the genetic theory put forth in Hernstein and Murray's book *The Bell Curve.*)

In what ways is racism shaped and reinforced in the popular imagination? Racism is generally not overtly acquired; rather, it is learned through messages that are embedded in our daily lives. For instance, Debra Van Ausdale and Joe Feagin (2002) write about a young preschooler who displayed prejudice toward African American males. His parents were puzzled until they began to examine where he might have acquired these negative images. It seems that he and his mother often walked down a street frequented by panhandlers, most of whom were men of color. When they neared the spot where these individuals normally hung out, they crossed to the other side of the street. The youngster soon began to perceive persons of color as individuals one should avoid.

Like the children described by Beverly Tatum who viewed Indians as savages with feathers, such perceptions form early. Unfortunately, they are also continuously reinforced by media images that tend to glorify whiteness and portray "white" as "right." Authors Catherine Lutz and Jane Collins (1993) ask us to consider, for example, the images portrayed in the third most popular magazine in the U.S., *National Geographic*. Most of us can probably recall reading this publication as young children, or perhaps more accurately, "reading the pictures." When I asked my students to describe the images they remember from this magazine, they listed traits such as "dark-skinned," "little clothing," "elongated necks," "nose rings," "lip plates," and so on. The perception was generally one of "the exotic"—that is, these people were not like us, but rather, were part of the uncivilized world. Importantly, their images were also those of dark-skinned people.

Lutz and Collins suggest that it is through images like these that we learn to divide the world, that is, how to categorize it along the lines of "us" and "them," "self" and "the Other." "They" are not like "us." "They" are not civilized or enlightened; "we" are. Such thinking gives rise to the elevation of certain bodies of knowledge over others, such as Western Civilization, rationalized scientific reasoning, and a European literary canon. Other forms of knowledge are deemed to be those of "the Other" and hence are of lesser value and little consequence.

Thus, media images do far more than merely reinforce racism and other forms of human oppression. They also help to shape our images of difference and mask our common humanity. In so doing, media images and other popular texts can reinforce a system of patriarchy that denies the value of anything that is non-western or non-White, thereby severely restricting our ability to view the world through multiple lenses. In effect, such divisive thinking distorts reality and leads to what might be termed "cultural blindness"—it inhibits our ability to see.

Just as importantly, such images reinforce our collective identity by demarcating what constitutes "us" and "them." Traditionally, our dominant national identity has been one of "civilized," "White," and "western," effectively ignoring our multiracial history from our country's very inception. Such identity politics continue to this day and in fact are continually refueled by efforts to deny a multicultural and multiracial heritage.

In recent years, critical multiculturalism has challenged traditional notions of difference and the texts that reinforce them. Henry Giroux suggests that texts can be used to produce a "multicultural politics" that encourages teachers and students to engage in critical dialogue about how "racialized meanings in cultural texts gain the force of commonsense" (2003, p. 90). He writes that:

> Texts in this instance would be analyzed as part of a social vocabulary of culture that points to how power names, shapes, defines, and constrains relationships between the self and the other, constructs and disseminates what counts as knowledge, and produces representations that provide the context for identity formation.
>
> (p. 90)

To realize a critical agenda, texts should be viewed as representations of broader social and political contexts, rather than as isolated icons. The texts of rap artists such as 50 Cent, for instance, must be viewed as part of a larger discourse that defines masculinity—and in particular, Black male masculinity—in a market-driven and racialized society. What societal forces have led to the creation of the popularized Black male image reflected in contemporary rap? In what ways has our society failed the Black male? In what ways do popular rap artists reflect dominant ideologies? Framing popular media within a larger social and historical context is vital if we along with our students are to understand fully the meanings associated with such texts.

Deconstructing a Colonial Discourse: "Reading" Barbie

What would a "multicultural politics of difference" look like in classrooms? In this section, I borrow from the writing of Hannah Tavares, whose chapter entitled "Reading Polynesian Barbie: Iterations of Race, Nation, and State" (2003) has inspired thoughts on how we might help students to deconstruct articulations of race, class and gender using "Barbie" as a cultural text. Through viewing Mattel's Polynesian Barbie as a symbolic cultural icon, Tavares shows how dominant notions of Pacific cultures as infantile and idyllic are encoded and reinforced.

Polynesian Barbie codifies the popular "hula girl" image, which emerged during the period of colonization and commercialization of Hawaii. This image consists of a beautiful, dark-haired girl clad in a grass skirt and wearing a lei. Such images have been popularized through postcards, photographs, and even Hollywood films, which offer "the romantic myth of the noble savage in which the tropics were a pagan paradise where Anglo-Saxon customs and inhibitions could be shed along with Western clothes" (Man, 1991, p. 17, cited in Tavares, 2003, p. 58). Through popular media, the "hula girl" has come to personify a popular stereotypical version of Hawaii, with its idyllic beaches and "primitive but happy" (p. 58) people.

Tavares also analyzes the narrative included in the packaging of Polynesian Barbie. The customs of Polynesians are written in first person: "I live with my family in a thatched hut made from bamboo and woven palm branches . . . To preserve peace and happiness among our people, it is our custom to speak only kind words to each other" (p. 63). The narrative continues with a description of a *luau*, and information on the warm beaches and gentle waters. Tavares writes that such texts reinforce our notions of the "exotic other" which serve to create hierarchical social divisions between the civilized (those who don't live in bamboo huts) and the uncivilized (those who do). The notion of an entire family living together in a single dwelling invites hegemonic perceptions of the "moral progress" of typical western dwelling practices. And certainly, the image of the placid native ignores the colonization of Hawaii and the resistance of many of its citizens who are engaged in a continuous struggle for the right to their own sovereignty. Tavares writes that through such texts,

> Polynesians are located outside historical time and are consequently inscribed with an unchanging essence. Insofar as contemporary urban life no longer involves "building huts" or requires "gathering food". . . these descriptions of Polynesian life are codes for a past time, not a now-time. In effect, Mattel's narrative reinscribes colonialist discourse by rearticulating some of the most insidious tropes in European observations and writings that textualized Polynesians as infantile and idyllic and in allochronic time-space.
>
> (p. 68)

I wish now to turn to an analysis of Black Barbie, and examine the ways in which this particular cultural icon "reinscribes colonialist discourse."

In recent years, Mattel has marketed a new line of Barbies called the Birthstone Collection. In this collection, there are Black and White Rapunzel dolls, Black and White Nutcracker dolls, and Black and White Swan Lake dolls. All have shimmering gowns, birthstone necklaces, and long straight hair that reaches beyond their waist. In deconstructing these Black Barbies, we might ask: In what ways does Black Rapunzel (or Nutcracker, or Swan Lake) reflect a colonial discourse? How might students "read" Black Rapunzel? In what ways is Black Rapunzel representative of a culturally racist ideology?

Surely, we might suggest, the manufacturer's intentions must have been noble, for now we have dolls that represent the diversity of the human experience. Further, some might argue that producing a beautiful Black doll could potentially have a positive effect on young African American girls, who might embrace Black Barbie as a role model. Yet it's important that we look beyond the matter of inclusion and consider the real messages that are embedded in the Barbie "text."

Perhaps what is most revealing is that Mattel chose to use traditional European narratives to market their Birthstone Collection. "Rapunzel," "Swan

Lake," and so on all carry meanings that are distinctively "White" and that are a part of a European collective memory. It might be argued that Africa has a rich heritage of folk narratives; yet rather than situate her within an African context, Black Barbie becomes yet another representation of White goodness and beauty as portrayed in European fairy tales. Hence, the opportunity to provide a venue for young children to examine and celebrate Black royalty is missed, and like much of the information contained in the "official" knowledge of the school (Apple, 1993), Black Rapunzel and her cohorts merely reinforce White narrative discourse. (Consider, for instance, that Mattel might have chosen instead to market an Ashanti Barbie.)

To further reinforce the notion of whiteness, Black Rapunzel and the other Black Barbies in this collection have characteristically Anglo features. The text that accompanies Rapunzel reads, in part: "Long, long ago, in a time of magic dragons, there lived a young maiden named Rapunzel who had beautiful, long flowing hair . . ." The underlying message of such "texts" is that persons of color—if their skin is light enough, if their hair is straight enough, if they have the "right" facial features, and of course, if they have enough money—can, in fact, become "White princesses." Of course, their experiences must also be consistent with those of White suburbia: riding in a convertible with Ken, shopping for "just the right dress," attending a fancy party. Thus, Black Barbie as cultural "text" is far from innocent, but rather reflects and reconstructs a dominant ideology that celebrates whiteness and reinforces consumer values.

In her book *Black and White Identity Theory*, Janet Helms (1993) defines cultural racism as "societal beliefs and customs that promote the assumption that the products of White culture (e.g., language, traditions, appearance) are superior to those of non-White cultures" (p. 49). Mapping "blackness" onto White templates of appearance and traditions, therefore, are more than just exercises of omission. Rather, such practices create culturally racist texts in that they ascribe beauty and goodness to a particular race—the White race—while simultaneously denying the inherent beauty and rich heritage of persons of color. Further, they deny the identity of many of our African American children, as everything from their names to how they spend their leisure time is cloaked in whiteness. In fact, nothing remains to indicate that Black Barbie is actually Black, except for the shade of her skin.

Reading Popular Film: Reinforcing a Discourse of Resentment

Thus far I have argued that popular texts portray notions of the exotic and hence tend to demarcate humanity along lines of race and "otherness." I have also argued that such texts reflect a cultural racist ideology that celebrates certain cultural knowledge and ways of being in the world, e.g., language, beauty, social behavior and so on, while simultaneously denigrating other cultural forms. In this section, I discuss how popular media, such as films and television programming, tend to reinforce what Cameron McCarthy et al. (1997) refer to as a "discourse of resentment"—the practice of defining one's identity through the negation of the other.

White supremacy was fortified in the post World War II era with governmental policies designed to create a new, surburban identity that was almost exclusively White and middle-class. In the popular mind, "America" became synonymous with suburbia; suburbia became "mainstream," while the increasingly segregated urban centers were viewed as aberrations. America's problem became its cities, as "white flight" led to centers of urban decay that were becoming increasingly ghettoized and impoverished. McCarthy et al. write that:

> As tax-based revenues, resources, and services followed America's fleeing middle classes out of the city, a great gulf opened up between the suburban dweller and America's inner-city resident. Into this void contemporary television, film, and popular culture entered creating the most poignantly sordid fantasies of inner-city degeneracy and moral decrepitude.
>
> (p. 230)

The suburban-urban divide was demarcated along racial lines, with suburbia conceptualized as "White" and the urban ghetto as "Black." Reflecting an individualistic ideology, urban dwellers were increasingly viewed as "problem people" who were poor because of their own moral ineptitude. In writing about contemporary urban society, Cornel West (1993) suggests that the greatest threat to Black America is what he terms the "nihilistic threat"—the sense of valuelessness and lovelessness that emerges within a racist environment. Thus, as "blackness" (and "brown-ness") became associated with urban decay, White America came increasingly to blame—and hence, to resent and perhaps even despise—"the other."

McCarthy et al. (1997) term White America's perception of the urban ghetto a "discourse of resentment" whereby mainstream sentiment is one of fear and distrust. They write that popular discussion of violence and crime:

> follows [a] logic of closed narrative where the greatest fear is that the enemy will be let into our neighborhoods. And the greatest stress on public policy may be how to keep the unwanted off the tax payer-dependent welfare rolls and out of our town, safely in prisons, and so forth.
>
> (p. 231)

Contemporary media portrayals of urban life tend to feed such paranoia in that they reinforce suburban fear. Historically, the response has been one of further divisiveness through the need to keep "those people" out of "our" communities. Commenting on the effects of television and the news media, McCarthy et al. write that "The dangerous inner city and the world 'outside' are brought into the suburban home through television and film releasing new energies of desire mixed with fear" (p. 232). Suburbanites come to know the world of the inner city through media portrayals that do little to incite social commentary about the historical and political complexity of racism and poverty. Rather, such portrayals tend to reinforce an individualistic pathology that separates "us" from "them" and blames the victims for their own failures.

Media images of urban violence, crime, and drug infestation perpetuate stereotypes of urban youth and families as non-caring and indolent. Yet teachers and schools can do much to deconstruct such stereotypes through critiquing media images and examining the social, political and historical contexts that created them. Henry Giroux (2003), for example, uses the film *Baby Boy* to address issues relating to race and representation. In this film, Jody, the main protagonist, grows up in a harsh urban environment that is defined by violence. The plot is riddled with images of Black male power defined by "excessive machismo, lurid sexuality, exoticized athleticism, and patriarchical masculinity" (p. 101). Rather than providing pedagogical sites for hope and possibility, for collective struggle and resistance, Giroux argues that films such as *Baby Boy* merely reinforce narrow conceptualizations of what it means to be simultaneously Black and male in American society. He writes:

> In the end, *Baby Boy* falls prey, regardless of how it attempts to complicate masculinity, to constructing black men through the performance of violence, and in doing so it both infantilizes them and numbs them to the plight of others. Similarly, by decontextualizing the violence in their lives, it mystifies the sources and real nature of violence that assaults the minds and bodies of black men throughout the United States in the form of poverty-ridden schools, low teacher expectations, racist profiling, housing discrimination, employment block outs and police brutality.
>
> (p. 101)

Thus, such films perpetuate a discourse of resentment by reinforcing the notion of the violent Black male. Just as important, however, they perpetuate the image of a negative black/brown pathology by placing blame for urban violence in the hands of the victims themselves, rather than examining the role of a society severely divided along lines of race and class. In so doing, they fail to provide alternative responses to violence—responses that require collective agency and commitment versus individual action. Absent is any discussion of civic engagement or social responsibility for addressing what ought to be viewed as *our* problem, one that has been created through our common history of racism and that concerns our national community.

How might teachers use films such as *Baby Boy* to help to realize a literacy of promise? Giroux suggests that teachers ought to practice what he calls a "pedagogy of disruption"—a pedagogy that raises critical questions about how certain meanings become part of our commonsense, taken-for-granted assumptions that remain largely unchallenged. A pedagogy of disruption requires that we examine the social, political and historical contexts within which such meanings are formed. For instance, we might pose questions such as "why this Hollywood film received such popular praise in a largely White-owned, dominant press," or "how it functions as a public text that rationalizes both the demonization of minority youth and the defunding of public and higher education at a time when Black youth are in desperate need of jobs, education, and resources" (p. 105). Teachers might also raise issues on social policies and the criminal justice system:

> For example, the depictions of youth in *Baby Boy* resonate powerfully with the growth of social policies and highly visible criminal justice system whose get-tough policies fall disproportionately on poor black and brown youth. Students might be asked to weigh what the potential effect of a film such as *Baby Boy* might be in addressing the political, racial, and economic conditions that threaten to wipe out a whole generation of young black males . . .
>
> (p. 103)

Acknowledging the power of films such as *Baby Boy* to define Black male masculinity in the popular mind requires that we as literacy teachers use such texts to help students redefine that image. It also requires that we embrace a pedagogy of disruption that helps students to contextualize black-on-black and brown-on-brown violence within a larger social framework of racism, classism, sexism, and other forms of oppression.

Conclusion

In this chapter, I have argued that popular texts serve as cultural icons that can perpetuate divisiveness in society by reinforcing culturally racist assumptions of normalcy and deviation. By expanding our notion of what counts as "text," literacy teachers can help students to deconstruct hegemony by implementing a pedagogy of disruption—one that renders problematic our commonsense beliefs and assumptions that are encoded in popular culture. It is important to acknowledge that texts are not neutral, but rather are cultural commodities that are produced within particular social and political contexts. Thus, texts endorse and reinforce dominant cultural knowledge and ways of perceiving the world while simultaneously negating others. What appears "normal" or "natural" (our notions of beauty, for example, or popular conceptions of the black male) are in actuality culturally constructed beliefs and perceptions that can, in turn, be deconstructed and critiqued. Critical media literacy, therefore, is one way that a literacy of promise can be realized, by encouraging teachers and students to engage in discussions of identity and difference as portrayed in popular media.

Critical media literacy affords the opportunity to examine how individuals internalize dominant meanings and how those meanings might be reconstituted to mobilize us toward social action. Critical analyses of contemporary film and television programming, for instance, can reveal how such programs often reinforce commonsense notions about what it means to be "black" or "brown" in urban societies. Similarly, a critical examination of other texts, such as toys and toy packages, t-shirts, billboards, magazines, cartoons, video games, and so forth, can make visible how the messages embedded in such texts can re-create a culturally racist, classist, and sexist ideology.

As English language arts teachers, we have important choices to make. We can continue to endorse the traditional literary canon, thereby perpetuating the myth that texts are neutral; or, we can begin to include non-traditional texts— including popular texts—in our instructional programs. In this chapter, I have suggested that academics ought to make room for popular texts, for they provide an important opportunity for examining our commonsense notions about society. Grounding our instruction in the everyday lives of our students not only makes what they are learning personally relevant, but helps them to recognize how power works and meaning is reproduced. Such a literacy is one that truly educates, and as such, can be potentially transformative.

Questions for Discussion

1. Consider some of the questions posed in this chapter. What societal forces have led to the creation of the popularized Black male image reflected in contemporary rap? In what ways has our society failed the Black male? In what ways do popular rap artists reflect dominant ideologies?

2. In what ways do we tend to "divide the world"? How do popular texts mitigate or reinforce these divisions?

3. In this chapter, the author argues that media portrayals of inner city life "do little to incite social commentary about the historical and political complexity of racism and poverty." Discuss this statement. Should the popular media take on this role? Or is the role of popular media merely to provide entertainment?

Extension Activities

1. Keep a media journal for a specified period of time. Use this journal to record images from popular texts (e.g., magazine images, billboards, TV commercials). Discuss entries with your peers.

2. Analyze the images found in popular cartoons, and the toys that represent them. Who plays the role of "hero"? Who plays the role of "buffoon"? Who plays the lead? Who plays the servant? What would children learn about particular "people groups" from watching this cartoon? What are the physical characteristics of toys that represent heroic characters? What are the physical characteristics of toys that represent evil characters?

3. Create a collage using pictures that are designed to reflect a particular stereotype (e.g., beauty, manliness). Using a combination of words and images, display your creation, using it to educate others about the impact of popular texts.

4. Create a multimedia presentation using a combination of popular images and music to show how popular texts reinforce negative stereotypes.

Notes

1. In this chapter, I have chosen to define "media" broadly, using the following definition: "Channels of communication that serve many diverse functions, such as offering a variety of entertainment with either mass or specialized appeal, communicating news and information, or displaying advertising messages" ("Media", n.d.). While we typically tend to confine definitions of media to its electronic and print forms, I argue that popular texts such as video games and children's toys can also be considered "media" in that they communicate messages concerning what is normative and desirable in our society.

References

Apple, M. (1993). *Official knowledge: Democratic education in a conservative age.* New York: Routledge.

Cortés, C. E. (2000). *The children are watching: How the media teach about diversity.* New York: Teachers College.

Freire, P. (1998). *Education for critical consciousness.* New York: Continuum.

Giroux, H. A. (2003). Pedagogies of difference, race, and representation: Film as a site of translation and politics. In P. P. Trifonas (Ed.), *Pedagogies of difference: Rethinking education for social change* (pp. 83–109). New York: RoutledgeFalmer.

Goodman, D. J. (2000). *Promoting diversity and social justice: Educating people from privileged groups.* Thousand Oaks, CA: Sage Publications.

Goodman, S. (2003). *Teaching youth media: A critical guide to literacy, video production, and social change.* New York: Teachers College.

Helms, J. A. (1993). *Black and white racial identity: Theory, research, and practice.* Westport, CT: Praeger.

Lutz, C. A., & Collins, J. L. (1993). *Reading* National Geographic. Chicago: University of Chicago Press.

McCarthy, C., Rodriguez, A., Meecham, S., David, S., Wilson-Brown, C., Godina, H., Supryia, K. E., & Buendia, E. (1997). Race, suburban resentment, and the representation of the inner city in contemporary film and television. In M. Fine, L. Weis, L. C. Powell, & L. M. Wong (Eds.), *Off white: Readings on race, power, and society* (pp. 229–241). New York: Routledge.

McIntosh, P. (1988). *White privilege and male privilege: A personal account of coming to see correspondences through work in women's studies* (Working Paper Series no. 189). Wellesley, MA: Center for Research on Women.

Media (n.d.). *Dictionary of marketing terms.* Retrieved January 10, 2007, from Answers.com Web site: http://www.answers.com/topic/media

Powell, R. (2001). *Straight talk: Growing as multicultural educators.* New York: Peter Lang.

Sholle, D., & Denski, S. (1993). Reading and writing the media: Critical media literacy and postmodernism. In C. Lankshear & P. L. McLaren (Eds.), *Critical literacy: Politics, praxis, and the postmodern* (pp. 297–321). Albany, NY: State University of New York Press.

Spring, J. (2003). *Educating the consumer-citizen: A history of the marriage of schools, advertising, and media.* Mahwah, NJ: Lawrence Erlbaum Associates.

Tatum, B. D. (1997). *"Why are all the Black kids sitting together in the cafeteria?" and other conversations about race.* New York: Basic Books.

Tavares, H. (2003). Reading Polynesian Barbie: Iterations of race, nation, and state. In M. W. Apple (Ed.), *The state and the politics of knowledge* (pp. 51–80). New York: RoutledgeFalmer.

Tobin, J. (2000). *"Good guys don't wear hats": Children's talk about the media.* New York: Teachers College Press.

Van Ausdale, D., & Feagin, J. R. (2002). *The first R: How children learn race and racism.* Lanham, MD: Rowman & Littlefield.

Weaver, J. A., & Daspit, T. (2003). Promises to keep, finally? Academic culture and the dismissal of popular culture. In G. Dimitriadis & D. Carlson (Eds.), *Promises to keep: Cultural studies, democratic education, and public life* (pp. 137–151). New York: RoutledgeFalmer.

West, C. (1993). *Race matters.* New York: Vintage Books.

Contributors

Ira Kincade Blake is Assistant Vice Chancellor for Academic and Student Affairs for the Pennsylvania State System of Higher Education. She has published several articles and chapters on the relationship between culture, language and school achievement. She is currently on leave serving as Executive Intern in the Office of the Chancellor for the Pennsylvania State System of Higher Education.

Jessica S. Bryant is an Associate Professor of English and the Coordinator of Academic Integrity at Eastern Kentucky University. During her twelve years at the University, she has taught literacy theory, academic literacy and learning, various reading and writing courses, and composition studies for future teachers. Dr. Bryant received her doctoral degree in Curriculum and Administration with an emphasis in multicultural studies and literacy. Her research focuses on literacy and culture as it relates to African American and Asian students. She has published articles and textbooks in the United States and China.

Kimberly L. Bunton is the Director of Family Services for Louisville Metro Government overseeing metro Louisville's housing, community development and anti-poverty strategies. Prior to her recent appointment, Kimberly served as the first Director of Policy and Strategic Planning for Louisville's recently merged Metro Government. In addition, she is founder and member of Egghead Educational Services LLC, an education provider specializing in academic services for gifted and talented children. An attorney by trade, prior to joining Louisville Metro Government, she practiced commercial litigation in Louisville's largest large firm, Frost Brown Todd LLC.

Julia Johnson Connor is the assistant director of the Center on Democracy in a Multiracial Society at the University of Illinois at Urbana-Champaign. She has taught undergraduate methods courses in secondary literacy. Her research interests include children's literature depicting biracial characters and teaching and learning with multiethnic adolescent literature. She worked as an editorial associate for a children's literature journal, *The New Advocate*. Her research has been featured in *The Journal of Adolescent and Adult Literacy, Research in the Teaching of English, Reading Online*, and *The Journal of Curriculum Studies*. She received her Ph.D. in curriculum and instruction from the University of Illinois at Urbana-Champaign.

Lisa Delpit is the Executive Director/Eminent Scholar for the Center for Urban Education and Innovation at Florida International University. Her work has focused on the education of children of color and the perspectives, aspirations, and pedagogical knowledge of teachers of color. Her book *Other People's Children* received the American Educational Studies Association's Book Critic Award, *Choice Magazine's* Eighth Annual Outstanding Academic Book Award, and has been named a "Great Book" by *Teacher Magazine*. Some of her other publications include: *The Real Ebonics Debate: Power, Language, and the Education of African-American Children*, and *The Skin That We Speak: Thoughts on Language and Culture in the Classroom*.

Karen B. McLean Donaldson holds the post of Professor at Spelman College, and is the Chairperson of the Education Department. She has published several books, invited chapters, and articles, among them being *Through Students' Eyes: Combating Racism in United States Schools* (1996); *Shattering the Denial: Protocols for the Classroom and Beyond* (2001); "Antiracist Education and Curriculum Transformation for Equity and Justice in the New Millennium: United States and South Africa Challenges" (*International Journal for Education Reform*, 1999); "Antiracist Education: A Few Courageous Teachers" (*Journal of Equity and Excellence in Education*, 1997); and *The Psychology of Prejudice and Discrimination* (Praeger Press Book Series; chapter contribution, 2004).

Letitia Hochstrasser Fickel is an Associate Professor of Education at the University of Alaska Anchorage, where she is involved in a school–university collaborative partnership to enhance K-12 student learning through innovative practices in pre-service teacher education and high-quality professional development for in-service teachers. She is an experienced public school teacher, having taught social studies and Spanish in an ethnically, linguistically, and economically diverse urban middle school. Her current research interests include issues related to school–university collaboration, and quality teacher professional development, especially that which supports equity and the development of culturally responsive practices.

Sherman G. Helenese works as a lawyer for the Microsoft Corporation. He is an active member of the Washington State Bar Association and has earned an M.A. degree in Public Policy and Management from the University of Southern Maine, a J.D. from the University of Utah, College of Law, and a M.B.A. from Seattle Pacific University.

Rebecca Powell holds the Marjorie Bauer Stafford Endowed Chair in Education at Georgetown College in Georgetown, Kentucky, where she serves as Dean of Education. She has authored two previous books, *Literacy As a Moral Imperative: Facing the Challenges of a Pluralistic Society*, and *Straight Talk: Growing As Multicultural Educators*. She has also published articles in numerous journals, including *Multicultural Education, Multicultural Perspectives, The Reading Teacher, Language Arts,* and *The Journal of Early Childhood Literacy.*

Linda A. Spears-Bunton is Associate Professor of English Education and an affiliated faculty member of African New World Studies at Florida International University. Her work is focused on the intersections among literature, literacy, culture and social justice. Some of her publications include chapters in *Reader Response in Secondary and College Classrooms* and *Transforming Curriculum for a Culturally Diverse Society.* She has made numerous scholarly presentations at home and abroad and is the creator and director of an annual Teachers' Summer Institute in Grenada, West Indies. In addition to her work at the university, she has taught in elementary, middle, and high schools and at community and four-year colleges.

Arlette Ingram Willis is a Professor at the University of Illinois at Urbana Champaign. Her research and teaching interests include the examination of the socio-historical foundations of literacy, teaching and learning in a multicultural society, and multicultural/multiethnic literature for grades 6–12. Dr. Willis has been a frequent contributor to professional journals, including *Harvard Educational Review, Language Arts,* and *Reading Research Quarterly.* She has also edited and co-edited several books: *Multicultural Issues in Literacy Research and Practice, Multiple and Intersecting Identities in Qualitative Research,* and *Teaching and Using Multicultural Literature in Grades 9–12.*

Index